See the WIDER picture

The Mosaic Tile House, Venice, California, USA

Gonzalo Duran and Cheri Pann are both artists and this is their very unusual house. When they bought the house it looked very boring, so they put pieces of colourful tiles on a few walls to make them more attractive. Over many years they covered the whole house and garden in their colourful mosaic tiles. Cheri and Gonzalo now welcome visitors into their extraordinary home.

Do you want to live in a house like this?

Course Map

Your Student's Book comes with access to:

▶ The Student's eBook

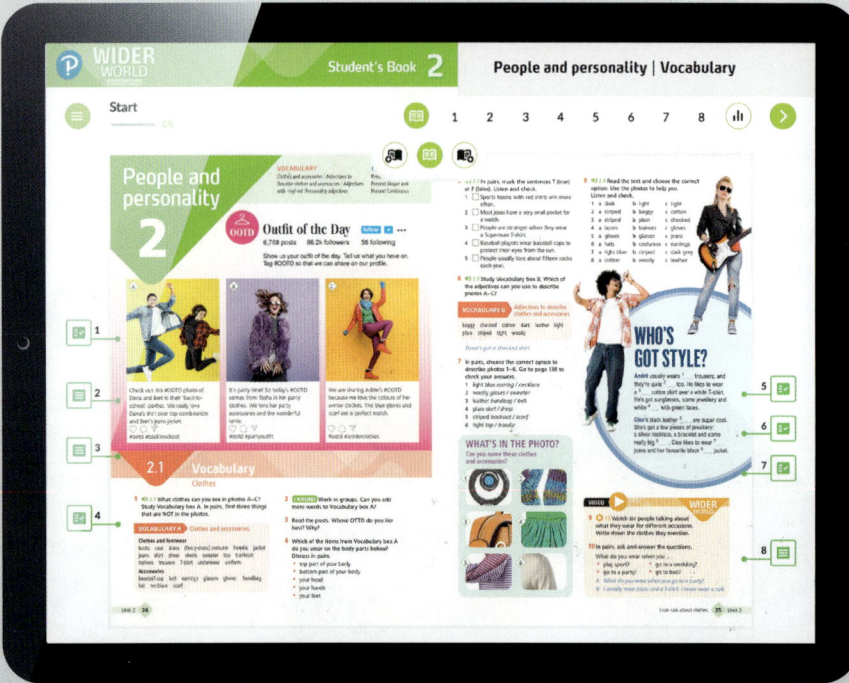

Audio, video and interactive activities with instant marking bring the content of the Student's Book to life in the eBook. It includes everything you need to participate in online lessons.

> *Wider World Second Edition* is fully accessible on your computer, tablet and mobile phone. You can enjoy the full functionality of your course wherever you are.

You can access your digital components through the Pearson English Portal.
See the inside front cover for access details.

Classroom Lessons

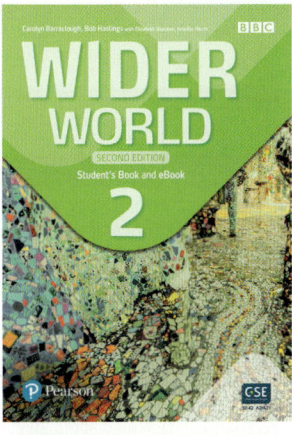
Student's Book

Workbook

Online Lessons

eBook

Homework

Workbook

Contents

Unit	Vocabulary	Grammar	Reading and Vocabulary	Grammar
Welcome to West Green 0	**0.1 Introducing Lena** — Family members | Possessive adjectives | Possessive 's | Have got — pp. 6–7		**0.2 Introducing Noah** — Possessions | There is/are with some and any | Articles — p. 8	
Creating culture 1	Culture: • People in the arts • Cultural activities • Creative hobbies pp. 12–13	• Present Simple: affirmative and negative • Adverbs of frequency BBC VIDEO Wider World p. 14	Crazy for culture? A blog about cultural hobbies p. 15	• Present Simple: questions and answers VIDEO Do you go to West Green? p. 16
	BBC CULTURE Let's dance!	VIDEO Get dancing!	Visible Thinking: Think, Puzzle, Explore	
People and personality 2	Clothes: • Clothes and accessories • Adjectives to describe clothes and accessories BBC VIDEO Wider World pp. 24–25	• Present Continuous VIDEO What are you wearing? SET FOR LIFE Self-management p. 26	Family Day: how are Canadians celebrating? An article about a family holiday BBC VIDEO Wider World p. 27	• Present Simple and Present Continuous p. 28
	SET FOR LIFE Communication	Understand other people's emotions	Is everything OK? pp. 34–35	
Animal life 3	Animals: • Animals • Animal body parts BBC VIDEO Wider World pp. 36–37	• Past Simple: was/were BBC VIDEO Wider World p. 38	Animal adventures A blog about an animal rescue centre p. 39	• Past Simple: regular and irregular verbs VIDEO A weekend with a dragon BBC VIDEO Wider World p. 40
	BBC CULTURE Perfect pets	VIDEO Wild at heart	Visible Thinking: Why do you say that?	
Cool tech! 4	Technology: • Digital devices • Using technology • Computer equipment pp. 50–51	• Used to VIDEO We didn't use to have phones p. 52	My day in the future at the MWC A report about new technologies p. 53	• Verb patterns p. 54
	SET FOR LIFE Social responsibility	Behave well on social media	My digital life pp. 60–61	
My place, my space 5	Things in the home: • Things in the home • Prepositions of place • Housework pp. 62–63	• Defining relative clauses p. 64	A campfire story A story about a personal experience p. 65	• Modal verbs: can, have to and must VIDEO Rules to follow BBC VIDEO Wider World p. 66
	BBC CULTURE Home sweet home	VIDEO I want my own room!	Visible Thinking: See, Think, Wonder	
Look after yourself 6	The body: • Parts of the body • Sports and fitness • Accidents and injuries pp. 74–75	• Countable and uncountable nouns • Quantifiers VIDEO Good for you p. 76	An open letter An open letter about sleep BBC VIDEO Wider World p. 77	• Past Continuous and Past Simple BBC VIDEO Wider World p. 78
	SET FOR LIFE Collaboration	Resolve arguments with other people	Let's sort this out! pp. 84–85	
Spending and saving 7	Shopping: • Types of shops • Containers • Shopping centres BBC VIDEO Wider World pp. 88–89	• Comparatives and superlatives of adjectives BBC VIDEO Wider World p. 90	Planet-friendly shopping An article about shopping habits p. 91	• Going to and Present Continuous for the future VIDEO What are you going to buy? SET FOR LIFE Social responsibility p. 92
	BBC CULTURE Shopping experiences	VIDEO Fashion for all	Visible Thinking: Take a different view	
Learning for the future 8	Jobs and work: • Jobs • Work collocations pp. 100–101	• Will for future predictions p. 102	Mikaila and Mateusz: our role models An article about a teenage ambitions p. 103	• First Conditional VIDEO If you don't study … BBC VIDEO Wider World p. 104
	SET FOR LIFE Critical thinking	Support your opinions with arguments	You've got a point! pp. 110–111	
It's only natural 9	Landscapes: • Geographical features • In, on, by • Talking about countries BBC VIDEO Wider World pp. 112–113	• Present Perfect p. 114	Young heroes: Jade Hameister An article about a teenage explorer BBC VIDEO Wider World p. 115	• Present Perfect with just, already and yet VIDEO The hiking trip p. 116
	BBC CULTURE Save our seas!	VIDEO Coral islands	Visible Thinking: See, Think, Wonder	

GRAMMAR TIME pp. 126–136   **IRREGULAR VERBS** p. 137   **STUDENT ACTIVITIES** pp. 138–139, 144

0.3 Introducing Mia Months and dates | Free time activities | Sports p. 9	**0.4 Introducing Mateo** School subjects | *Can/Can't* for ability | Skills and abilities p. 10	**0.5 Revision** p. 11

Listening and Vocabulary	Speaking	Writing	Revision	Progress Check
Five people talk about different types of media **BBC VIDEO** Wider World p. 17	**VIDEO** *Love and Laugh* Asking for and giving opinions SET FOR LIFE Collaboration p. 18	A personal introduction • Capital letters p. 19	Vocabulary Activator p. 20 Revision p. 21	**1-3** pp. 48–49 • Vocabulary and Grammar: transformations, open cloze, word formation • Speaking: describe a picture • Listening: matching • Reading: multiple choice • Writing: a blog entry
Project: a video podcast about a dance pp. 22–23				
Five people talk about their friends p. 29	**VIDEO** *The street dance lesson* Giving and responding to news p. 30	A semi-formal email • Prepositions of time p. 31	Vocabulary Activator p. 32 Revision p. 33	
A conversation about pets p. 41	**VIDEO** *Working with animals* Apologising and responding to apologies SET FOR LIFE Social responsibility p. 42	A blog entry • Linking words p. 43	Vocabulary Activator p. 44 Revision p. 45	
Project: a digital presentation about a pet pp. 46–47				
A radio interview about a popular website **BBC VIDEO** Wider World p. 55	**VIDEO** *The computer crashed* Talking about technology problems SET FOR LIFE Creativity p. 56	A review of a gadget • Expressions of purpose p. 57	Vocabulary Activator p. 58 Revision p. 59	**1-6** pp. 86–87 • Vocabulary and Grammar: multiple choice cloze, open cloze, transformations • Speaking: discussion task with visual stimulus • Listening: multiple choice • Reading: sentence completion • Writing: a narrative
A conversation about a town **BBC VIDEO** Wider World p. 67	**VIDEO** *Noah's new room* Asking for, giving and receiving advice SET FOR LIFE Self-management p. 68	An informal email • Adjectives to describe places p. 69	Vocabulary Activator p. 70 Revision p. 71	
Project: a mood board pp. 72–73				
A conversation about health problems p. 79	**VIDEO** *What's the matter?* Talking about health problems p. 80	A narrative • Narrative linkers p. 81	Vocabulary Activator p. 82 Revision p. 83	
A radio interview about money p. 93	**VIDEO** *Shopping is hard* Shopping for clothes p. 94	A message • Polite phrases p. 95	Vocabulary Activator p. 96 Revision p. 97	**1-9** pp. 124–125 • Vocabulary and Grammar: multiple choice cloze, open cloze, transformations • Speaking: role play • Listening: note completion, matching • Reading: matching • Writing: an informal email
Project: a website for a new shop pp. 98–99				
A podcast about a school p. 105	**VIDEO** *You'll probably do well* Expressing probability SET FOR LIFE Self-management p. 106	A personal statement • Adjectives + prepositions p. 107	Vocabulary Activator p. 108 Revision p. 109	
A conversation about outdoor activities p. 117	**VIDEO** *Can I see the map?* Asking for, giving and refusing permission SET FOR LIFE Leadership p. 118	An informal email about a holiday • Adjective synonyms to avoid repetition p. 119	Vocabulary Activator p. 120 Revision p. 121	
Project: a digital poster about an endangered animal pp. 122–123				

CLIL LITERATURE p. 140 HISTORY p. 141 SCIENCE p. 142 GEOGRAPHY p. 143

Welcome to West Green

0

VOCABULARY
Family members | Possessions | Months and dates | Free time activities | Sports | School subjects | Skills and abilities

GRAMMAR
Possessive adjectives | Possessive *'s* | *Have got* | *There is/are* with *some* and *any* | Articles | *Can/Can't* for ability

This is Lena Taylor. She's fifteen and she's from West Green, a small town near London, England.

Lena's mum, Marie, is a nurse. Lena's dad's a photographer. His name is Alex. Lena hasn't got a sister, but she's got a brother, Adam. He's eleven and he's nice (for a little brother). Lena's gran, Kathy, is Lena's mum's mother.

Lena has got a guitar, and her favourite hobby is music. She's friendly and kind and she loves animals.

Lena's in Year 10 at West Green High School. She's got three good friends in her class at school. Their names are Noah, Mia and Mateo. They have a lot of fun together.

0.1 Introducing Lena

Family members | Possessive adjectives | Possessive *'s* | *Have got*

1 ▶ 1 🔊 0.1 Watch or listen. Find these people in the photos.

Adam   Alex   Kathy   Lena   Marie

2 Read the text again. Mark the sentences T (true) or F (false). In pairs, correct the false sentences.
1. ☐ Lena's surname is Green.
2. ☐ Her home town is West Green.
3. ☐ Lena's mum is a photographer.
4. ☐ Alex is Lena's brother.
5. ☐ Noah, Mia and Mateo are Lena's classmates.

3 🔊 0.2 Listen and write the names you hear. Then, in pairs, spell more names from Exercise 1.

4 🔊 0.3 **I KNOW!** Study the Vocabulary box. Work in pairs. How many words can you add in two minutes?

VOCABULARY Family members

aunt   cousin   dad   gran   mum   parents
sister   son   wife

Kathy

Jack

Alex

Marie

Kate

Trevor

Lena

Adam

Ella

5 Study Grammar box A. Then look at Lena's family tree and complete the sentences with the correct possessive adjectives.

GRAMMAR A	Possessive adjectives						
I	you	he	she	it	we	they	
my	your	his	her	its	our	their	

1 'This is <u>my</u> husband. _____ name is Jack.'
2 'I've got a sister. _____ name is Kate.'
3 'I've got a brother. _____ brother's name is Adam.'
4 'We've got two children. _____ names are Marie and Kate.'
5 'We've got a baby cousin. _____ cousin's name is Ella.'
6 'Ella's our child. _____ cousins are Lena and Adam.'

6 Look again at Lena's family tree and write who is speaking in sentences 1–6 in Exercise 5.
1 <u>Kathy</u>   3 _____   5 _____
2 _____   4 _____   6 _____

7 Study Grammar box B. Add the apostrophes (') or possessive 's to the sentences about Lena's family.

GRAMMAR B	Possessive 's
Singular	my brother's laptop / Lena's brother
Regular plural	my parents' car
Irregular plural	the children's parents
Two words	Lena's mum's mother / Alex and Marie's house

1 Lena brother is Adam. *Lena's brother is Adam.*
2 Her dads name is Alex.
3 Jack is Adam grandad.
4 Kate is the childrens aunt.
5 Ella is Kate and Trevor daughter.
6 Lenas parents names are Alex and Marie.

8 Study Grammar box C. Complete the dialogues with the correct form of *have got*.

GRAMMAR C	Have got	
+	I've got (have got) a sister. She's got (has got) a guitar. They've got (have got) a cat.	
–	I haven't got a brother. She hasn't got a sister. They haven't got a dog.	
?	Have you got a sister?	Yes, I have. No, I haven't.
	Has she got a brother?	Yes, she has. No, she hasn't.
	Have they got a pet?	Yes, they have. No, they haven't.

1 A: <u>Has</u> Lena <u>got</u> a sister?
   B: No, she _____ . But she _____ a brother.
2 A: _____ Jack and Kathy _____ any children?
   B: Yes, they _____ . They _____ two daughters.
3 A: _____ Marie _____ any brothers or sisters?
   B: Yes, she _____ . She _____ a sister, Kate.
4 A: _____ Kate and Trevor _____ a son?
   B: No, they _____ .
5 A: _____ Adam _____ a sister?
   B: Yes, he _____ .

YOUR WORLD

9 In pairs, use these questions to talk about your family.
- Have you got any brothers or sisters? How old are they?
- What's your cousin's name?
- Where are your parents from?
- Have you got a pet? What's its name?

10 Tell the class about your partner's family.

Frank has got one brother and two sisters. His brother's name is Tony.

0.2 Introducing Noah

Possessions | *There is/are* with *some* and *any* | Articles

This is Lena's friend, Noah Lewis. He's fifteen, he's in Lena's class at West Green High School, and his house is near Lena's house.

Noah's favourite hobby is drawing. He's a good artist. Today, he's in the park with his friends. He's got a bag with him. In the bag there's a notebook, and in the notebook there are some drawings of animals. They're very good. But Noah isn't very tidy. There are lots of things in his bag: keys, headphones, a phone, sunglasses, socks and an old sandwich, but there aren't any schoolbooks because it's Saturday.

Noah's other hobbies are playing video games and dancing. His new hobby is street dance. It's fun, but he's only a beginner, so he isn't very good at it.

1 ▶ 2 ◀ 0.4 Watch or listen. Mark the sentences T (true) or F (false). In pairs, correct the false sentences.
1 ☐ Noah is Lena's cousin.
2 ☐ Noah and his friends are in the park after school.
3 ☐ Noah can't draw very well.
4 ☐ Noah's bag is full of things.
5 ☐ Noah's favourite hobby is playing video games.
6 ☐ Noah is an excellent street dancer.

2 ◀ 0.5 Study the Vocabulary box. Which of the possessions are in Noah's bag? Read the text again and check.

VOCABULARY ▸ Possessions

biscuit   book   bus ticket   drawing   headphones   key
notebook   notes   pen   pencil   phone   sunglasses

3 Study Grammar box A. Complete the sentences about Noah's bag.

GRAMMAR A ▸ *There is/are* with *some* and *any*

	Singular	Plural
+	There's (There is) a notebook.	There are some drawings.
−	There isn't a pen.	There aren't any books.
?	Is there a ball? Yes, there is./No, there isn't.	Are there any notes? Yes, there are./No, there aren't.

1 *There is* a notebook in the bag.
2 _____ some headphones.
3 _____ a laptop.
4 _____ a phone in the bag? Yes, _____ .
5 _____ any video games? No, _____ any video games.

4 In pairs, use the Vocabulary box to ask and answer questions about Noah's bag.
A: Are there any biscuits in Noah's bag?
B: No, there aren't.

5 ◀ 0.6 Study Grammar box B. Complete the text with *a* or *the*. Listen and check.

GRAMMAR B ▸ Articles

- The first time we talk about a person/thing we use *a/an*, but the second time we use *the*.
  He's got *a* bag. There are a lot of things in *the* bag.
- If it's clear what person/thing we mean, we use *the*.
  Noah's in *the* park with his friends.

I've got ¹*a* new bag. ²_____ bag isn't very big, but I like it. In my bag there's ³_____ phone. On ⁴_____ phone there's ⁵_____ photo of me and my friends. In ⁶_____ photo we're at ⁷_____ London Aquarium.

6 Write sentences about the things in your bag. Use *a/an* and *the*.
There is a key in my bag. The key opens the front door of my house.

YOUR WORLD

7 In pairs, ask and answer questions about the things in your partner's bag.
A: Are there any video games in your bag?
B: No, there aren't, but there's a phone.

0.3 Introducing Mia

Months and dates | Free time activities | Sports

Mia Robinson from West Green is fifteen years old. Her birthday's on 26 September. She hasn't got any brothers or sisters, but she's got three great friends: Lena, Mateo and Noah. Mia is sometimes bossy, but she's a good friend and very kind.

One of Mia's favourite hobbies is listening to music. She's also interested in cooking and eating healthy food.

Mia's other hobbies are sports and outdoor activities, especially walking and hiking with friends in the countryside. Mia has a very busy life!

1 ▶ 3 🔊 0.7 Watch or listen and answer the questions.
1. Has Mia got lots of brothers and sisters?
2. Is she a good friend?
3. Has Mia got a busy life?

WATCH OUT!
We write: 1 March, 22 April, 3 June, 26 September
We say: **the 1st of** March, **the 22nd of** April, **the 3rd of** June, **the 26th of** September

2 🔊 0.8 Write the dates in words. Listen and check. When is your birthday? Tell the class.
1. 21/01 = <u>the twenty-first of January</u>
2. 12/10 = _____
3. 15/02 = _____
4. 22/07 = _____
5. 04/05 = _____
6. 30/08 = _____

3 Read the text about Mia again. What are her hobbies and her favourite outdoor activities?

4 🔊 0.9 **I KNOW!** Study Vocabulary box A. Can you add more activities?

VOCABULARY A ▸ Free time activities

doing nothing   going to the cinema   listening to music
playing video games   reading books/magazines
seeing friends   spending time online   taking photos
tidying your bedroom   visiting relatives
watching films/videos on YouTube

5 🔊 0.10 Listen and write down the free time activities you hear.

6 Say which two free time activities in Vocabulary box A are your favourite.
My favourite free time activities are …

7 🔊 0.11 Study the Speaking box. Listen and repeat.

SPEAKING ▸ Giving opinions

I **think** reading is ⎰ OK.
⎱ exciting/fun/great/interesting.
⎱ boring/terrible.

8 In pairs, say what you think about the activities in Vocabulary box A. Use the Speaking box to help you.
A: *I think spending time online is fun.*
B: *I think listening to music is great.*

9 🔊 0.12 **I KNOW!** Study Vocabulary box B. Work in pairs. How many sports can you add in two minutes?

VOCABULARY B ▸ Sports

basketball   cycling   football   hiking   running
swimming   tennis   volleyball

10 Work in pairs. In your opinion, which sports in Exercise 9 are fun and which are boring?

11 Tell the class about your partner's favourite sports and free time activities.
Marta's hobbies are taking photos and …

YOUR WORLD

0.4 Introducing Mateo

School subjects | Can/Can't for ability | Skills and abilities

Fifteen-year-old Mateo Garcia is from the USA. Lena, Mia and Noah are his new friends at West Green High. Mateo is happy at school because he has the same sense of humour as his friends.

Mateo's favourite subjects are Spanish and Music. His dad's Mexican, so Mateo can speak Spanish. His dad is a musician, and Mateo can read music, but he can't sing very well!

Science isn't Mateo's favourite subject, but it's important because his dream is to be a vet. Mateo's mum, Tina, is a vet. She and Mateo are both interested in animals, and Mateo is very excited about his new pet!

1 ▶ 4 ◀) 0.13 Watch or listen. Why is Mateo happy at school?

2 ◀) 0.14 **I KNOW!** In pairs, match the school subjects in Vocabulary box A with pictures A–F. Listen and check. Can you add more subjects?

VOCABULARY A ▸ School subjects

☐ Art ☐ Geography ☐ History
☐ Information Technology ☐ Music ☐ Science

3 Read the text again. What are Mateo's favourite subjects? What are yours?

4 Study the Grammar box. Complete the sentences with *can* or *can't*.

GRAMMAR ▸ *Can/Can't* for ability

+	I can cook. He can speak Spanish.	
–	We can't (cannot) dance. He can't (cannot) sing.	
?	Can you sing? Can he speak English?	Yes, I can./No, I can't. Yes, he can./No, he can't.

1 I can speak French, but I _can't_ speak German.
2 I'm afraid of water because I _____ swim.
3 Zoe can sing, but she _____ play the piano.
4 I _____ make a cake, but I can't cook a meal.
5 What a terrible group! The singer _____ sing!

5 ◀) 0.15 Study Vocabulary box B. Which of these things can Mateo do?

VOCABULARY B ▸ Skills and abilities

act   cook   dance   drive a car   play the guitar/piano
repair a computer   speak English/Spanish   swim

6 ◀) 0.16 Listen to Mateo's dad and write down the things he can do.

7 In pairs, ask and answer the questions.

Can you ...

1 say 'hello' in French or German?
2 read music?
3 swim 400 metres?
4 act in a school play?
5 draw people's faces?
6 play basketball?
7 cook a meal for your family?
8 do street dance?
9 take fantastic photos?
10 run one kilometre?
11 study to music?

A: Can you say 'hello' in French or German?
B: Yes, I can./No, I can't.

YOUR WORLD

8 Tell the class about five things your partner can do and two things he/she can't do. Use Exercise 7 to help you.

0.5 Revision

1 In groups, do the quiz. Use the texts in Lessons 0.1–0.4 to help you.

How much can you remember?

01 How old is Adam?
02 Are both of Lena's parents nurses?
03 Who is Kathy?
04 What's Noah's favourite hobby?
05 Is Noah in Lena's class?
06 Has Mia got any brothers or sisters?
07 When is Mia's birthday?
08 Where is Mateo from?
09 What are Mateo's favourite subjects?
10 Can Mateo sing?

2 Complete the questions with the words below. Then ask and answer the questions in pairs.

> How old   What   When   Where   Who

1 _Where_ are you from?
2 _____ is your birthday?
3 _____ are you?
4 _____ is your favourite hobby?
5 _____ is your school?
6 _____ is next to you in class?
7 _____ is your favourite possession?
8 _____ is your favourite song ever?

3 Complete the questions with *is*, *are*, *can*, *have* or *has*. Then ask and answer the questions in pairs.

Questionnaire

1 _Is_ there a phone in your bag?
2 _____ there any photos on your phone?
3 _____ you got any brothers or sisters?
4 _____ your family got any pets?
5 _____ your birthday in January?
6 _____ you sing?
7 _____ you sporty?
8 _____ you a good student?
9 _____ you play a musical instrument?
10 _____ English your favourite subject?
11 _____ football and basketball exciting sports?

YOUR WORLD

4 In pairs, change the highlighted words in Exercise 3 to make new questions. Ask and answer your new questions.

Creating culture

1

VOCABULARY
People in the arts | Cultural activities | Creative hobbies | News and entertainment

GRAMMAR
Present Simple: affirmative and negative | Adverbs of frequency | Present Simple: questions and answers

WHAT'S ON?

FREE EVENTS | RESTAURANTS | PLACES TO STAY | THE CITY

Here are some free things you can do in the summer holidays.

Beach Festival
This year we've got great live music with fantastic artists from all over the world. Join us on the beach and enjoy two days of music, food and dancing.
Where: The Amphitheatre
When: July

Outdoor Movies
Enjoy free movie shows under the stars! Bring your friends, snacks, a chair and some warm clothes!
Where: Fresh Air Cinemas
When: July–August

Comic Book Day
Come to one of the city's comic bookshops to meet famous comic creators and get a FREE copy of a comic book. It's a family fun day out for all!
Where: Comic shops across the city
When: July–September

Street Art Walking Tour
Join us for a walking tour of street art through the city. Admire the amazing wall paintings and learn about the artists too. Are you artistic? Get a chance to paint your own graffiti.
Where: Main square
When: July–August

1.1 Vocabulary

Culture

1 Read the posts on the website above. Which event A–D would you like to visit? Why?

2 🔊 1.1 Complete Vocabulary box A with the categories below. Listen and check.

> art and photography   cinema and theatre   ~~dance~~   music   writing

VOCABULARY A	People in the arts
¹*dance*	dancer
2 _____	actor director
3 _____	guitarist musician singer
4 _____	artist painter photographer
5 _____	poet writer

Unit 1

3 Look at Vocabulary box A again. Which of the people can you meet or see at events A–D?

You can see musicians at the beach festival.

4 🔊 1.2 Listen to four recordings. Match them with events A–D in Exercise 1.

1 ☐ 2 ☐ 3 ☐ 4 ☐

5 🔊 1.2 Listen again. Mark the sentences T (true) or F (false).
1 ☐ The piece of art is small.
2 ☐ *Mission X* isn't a romantic comedy.
3 ☐ The two friends like the same kind of music.
4 ☐ Phil James writes comic books.

6 What can you do for free in the place where you live? Discuss in pairs.

7 🔊 1.3 **I KNOW!** Complete Vocabulary box B with the words below. Listen and check. Can you add more words?

| ~~action film~~   animated film   ballet   classical music |
| rock   short story   street art   street dance   techno |

VOCABULARY B — Cultural activities

Types of films
¹*action film*   ²_____ fantasy film
romantic comedy   science fiction (sci-fi) film

Things to read
comic   novel   poem   ³_____

Types of dance
⁴_____   ballroom dancing   rumba   salsa
⁵_____

Types of music
⁶_____   hip hop   pop   rap   ⁷_____
⁸_____

Types of art
painting   photo   picture   ⁹_____

WATCH OUT!
After these verbs and phrases you can use a verb + *-ing* or a noun.
I'm into art.
Tia's interested in painting.
We like/love/enjoy watching comedies.
They hate singing. They prefer listening to music.

8 Choose three cultural activities from Exercise 7. Use the phrases from the Watch Out! box to say what you think about these things.

I enjoy watching fantasy films.
I'm into dance, but I don't like street dance.

9 🔊 1.4 **WORD FRIENDS** Complete the sentences with the correct form of the verbs below. Listen and check.

| act   dance   draw   ~~listen~~   play   read   take   watch |

1 I really like *listening* to rock music.
2 I hate _____ fantasy films.
3 I'm interested in _____ in a play or a short film.
4 I don't really like _____ selfies.
5 I'm not really into _____ the guitar.
6 I enjoy _____ pictures with coloured pencils.
7 I don't like _____ salsa much.
8 I love _____ poetry.

10 Change the sentences in Exercise 9 to make them true for you.

I don't like listening to rock music much. I prefer hip hop.

11 🔊 1.5 Complete the words in the text. Listen and check.

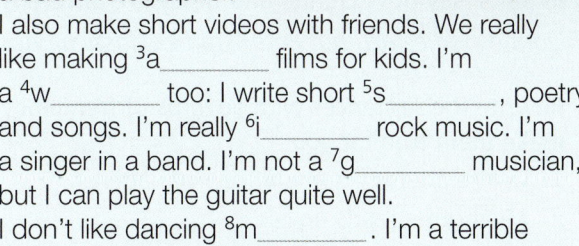

KIERAN'S HOME PAGE

I'm an artist. I love painting and drawing ¹p*ictures* of beautiful places in the country. I enjoy ²t_____ photos when I'm in the country too. I'm not a bad photographer. I also make short videos with friends. We really like making ³a_____ films for kids. I'm a ⁴w_____ too: I write short ⁵s_____, poetry and songs. I'm really ⁶i_____ rock music. I'm a singer in a band. I'm not a ⁷g_____ musician, but I can play the guitar quite well. I don't like dancing ⁸m_____. I'm a terrible ⁹d_____. My friends say I've got two left feet!

YOUR WORLD

12 Work in pairs. Tell your partner about yourself using the language from this lesson. Say if your partner's sentences are true or false.

A: *I'm a good singer.*
B: *True.*

I can talk about people in the arts, cultural activities, likes and dislikes.

1.2 Grammar

Present Simple: affirmative and negative | Adverbs of frequency

10 February, 4.56

The same but different

We look the same, but we don't like the same things. Betsy studies classical music, but I study art. She reads novels and poems, but I don't read much. And she often watches TV, but I never watch TV – it doesn't interest me. Betsy writes poems. I write texts on my phone. I paint pictures. Betsy tries to paint, but she never finishes her paintings. She doesn't understand art! I love hip hop. She says that hip hop annoys her. Our friends don't understand us. 'You don't like the same things!' they say. 'But we always see you together! Why?' 'We have some fantastic arguments!' I say.

1 🔊 **1.6** Read Lianne's blog. Has Lianne got the same interests as her sister Betsy?

2 Study the Grammar box. Find more examples of the Present Simple in Lianne's blog.

GRAMMAR | **Present Simple: affirmative and negative | Adverbs of frequency**

+ | I <u>love</u> hip hop.
She <u>writes</u> poems/<u>watches</u> TV/<u>studies</u> classical music.
We <u>look</u> the same.

– | I <u>don't read</u> much.
She <u>doesn't understand</u> art.
We <u>don't like</u> the same things.

Adverbs of frequency (*always, usually, often, sometimes, never*) go after *to be* but before all the other verbs.

GRAMMAR TIME ▸ PAGE 126

---

3 In pairs, say how Lianne and Betsy are different.
Lianne studies art, but Betsy studies classical music.

4 Rewrite the sentences with adverbs of frequency to make them true for you.
1 I write poems. *I sometimes write poems.*
2 My mother reads novels.
3 My teacher gives us homework.
4 We (my friends and I) go dancing.
5 My classmates listen to classical music.

5 🔊 **1.7** Complete the text with the correct form of the verbs in brackets. Listen and check.

I ¹*live* (live) in a small town, so I ²_____ (not go) to the theatre very often. My brother often ³_____ (watch) films on TV, but I ⁴_____ (prefer) playing games with my friend, Dylan. He usually ⁵_____ (win), but he ⁶_____ (not win) every game.

6 Correct the sentences. Use the words in brackets to help you.
1 Lewis Capaldi plays the drums. (sing)
 Lewis Capaldi doesn't play the drums. He sings.
2 Billie Eilish plays classical music. (pop)
3 Director John Woo makes sci-fi films. (action films)
4 J.K. Rowling acts in films. (write books)
5 Daniel Radcliffe and Emma Watson paint pictures. (act in films)

7 🔊 **1.8** Complete the text with the words below. There is one extra word. Listen and check.

~~dancing~~   doesn't   don't   go   loves   sometimes

I love ¹*dancing*! I ²_____ to dance classes with my friend Kay. We do hip hop – it's great! We ³_____ practise salsa too, but not very often. I ⁴_____ like salsa much, but Kay ⁵_____ it.

VIDEO ▶ **WIDER WORLD**

8 ▶ **5** Watch four people talking about how they spend their free time. Write down the free time activities they mention.

9 What do you do at weekends? Discuss in pairs. Then form new pairs and talk about your previous partners.

I sometimes go to the cinema at weekends. Adam sometimes goes to the cinema at weekends.

1.3 Reading and Vocabulary

Cultural activities

1 How often do you do these things? Discuss in groups.
- play music with friends or go to a concert
- paint a picture or draw on a computer
- read poems or write poems
- go dancing or dance in your bedroom

I sometimes play music with friends.

2 Read the introduction to the blog. Mark the sentences T (true) or F (false).
1. ☐ Colleen mentions a study about young people in the world.
2. ☐ The study says that nearly half of young people take part in cultural activities.

3 🔊 1.9 Read the whole blog. Match posts A–D with questions 1–5. One post can match with two questions.
1. ☐ Who learns a skill online?
2. ☐ Who performs with other people?
3. ☐ Who uses a computer to change real things?
4. ☐ Who shares their work online but not in public?
5. ☐ Who is not sure what job he/she would like to have?

4 🔊 1.10 **WORD FRIENDS** Find these phrases in the blog and write the missing verbs. Listen and check.
1. *create* art
2. _____ short films
3. _____ on stage
4. _____ video games
5. _____ something on social media
6. _____ concerts/videos

5 Complete the questions with the verbs in Exercise 4. Then ask and answer the questions in pairs.
1. Do you enjoy *creating* art? Why?/Why not?
2. How hard is it for you to _____ on stage?
3. How often do you _____ music videos on your phone?
4. Who do you _____ video games with?
5. Would you like to _____ a short film or an animation? Why?
6. What kind of things do you _____ on social media?

YOUR WORLD

6 Which three cultural activities in this lesson do you like doing the most? Discuss in groups.

I love dancing, watching concerts and sharing my films on social media.

A blog from Ireland for the world

COLLEEN'S CORNER

CRAZY for culture?
Are young people into art?

Some people say that young people don't care about culture. But a recent study shows that almost fifty percent of young people in the UK love watching online videos, playing video games and reading. They enjoy creating and performing too. And thirty five percent of them share their cultural interests on social media.

What about you? Do you enjoy watching films, reading books or listening to music? Do you perform or create art? Send me your posts and let me know.

A Bitmap17
I love art, but I never get paint on my fingers. I draw on my computer and I make pictures and animations with real world objects and computer images. It's amazing!

B LadyNote
I watch music videos every day, usually on my phone. I love going to concerts and watching them online too. At weekends I watch videos of piano lessons and copy what I see. It's not easy, but I love it.

C NaomiX
I want to be an actor. Or maybe a director. Every year I act in the school play and in my free time, I make short films with my friends. We film them on our phones and share them on our video channel.

D JCC77
I love reading, especially poetry. I write poems on my phone or my computer and put them on my blog. I also write rap songs, but I'm too shy to perform on stage.

I can understand a blog about cultural hobbies.

1.4 Grammar

Present Simple: questions and answers

VIDEO **DO YOU GO TO WEST GREEN?**

Mia: First day back at school after the summer holidays. What a pain! ... Bye, Mum!
Rachel: Sorry! Oh, do you go to West Green High?
Mia: Yes, I do.
Rachel: Me too. It's my first day. I'm the ...
Mia: I love your accent. Where do you come from?
Rachel: I come from Paris.
Mia: Really? Where do you live?
Rachel: I live in South Street. My name's Rachel.
Mia: I'm Mia.
Rachel: What are you listening to?
Mia: K-pop. I love it. What kind of music do you like?
Rachel: I like classical music. My dad's a musician.
Mia: Oh! What instrument does he play?
Rachel: He plays the violin.
Mia: Does he work in London?
Rachel: No, he doesn't. He plays for an orchestra in Paris.
Mia: Oh! So how often do you and your mum see him?
Rachel: Eh … my mum sees him every day. They live together.
Mia: Do they live in Paris?

Rachel: Yes, they do.
Mia: So who do you live with?
Rachel: I live on my own.
Mia: You live alone? How old are you?
Rachel: Twenty-one. I'm the new French assistant.
Mia: Oh!

1 ▶ 6 🔊 1.11 Watch or listen. Who is Rachel? What nationality is she?

2 Study the Grammar box. Find more Present Simple questions and answers in the dialogue.

GRAMMAR	Present Simple: questions and answers	
?	**Do** you **go** to West Green High?	Yes, I **do**./No, I **don't**.
	Does he **work** in London?	Yes, he **does**./No, he **doesn't**.
	Do they **live** in Paris?	Yes, they **do**./No, they **don't**.
	Where **do** you **come** from?	I **come** from Paris.
	What instrument **does** he **play**?	He **plays** the violin.
	How often **does** she **see** him?	She **sees** him every day.

Time expressions (*once/twice/three times a week/month*) go at the end of a sentence.

GRAMMAR TIME > PAGE 126

3 Complete the questions with one word in each gap. Then answer the questions in full sentences.
1 Where *does* Rachel come from?
2 _____ does she live?
3 _____ kind of music does she like?
4 What _____ her father do?
5 How _____ does her mother see her father?

4 🔊 1.12 Make questions in the Present Simple. Listen and check.
1 how often / you / go to the cinema / ?
   How often do you go to the cinema?
2 what kind of films / you / like watching / ?
3 where / your parents / live / ?
4 how many / languages / you / speak / ?
5 you / play / a musical instrument / ?
6 you / go / to dance classes / ?

5 🔊 1.13 Rewrite the questions in Exercise 4 in the third person (*he*). Then listen and write down the answers.
How often does he go to the cinema?
He goes to the cinema a lot.

YOUR WORLD

6 In pairs, ask and answer the questions in Exercise 4.
A: How often do you go to the cinema?
B: I go to the cinema once a month. I like watching films at home.

I can use the Present Simple to ask and answer questions about facts and routines.

1.5 Listening and Vocabulary
Types of media

1 In groups, do The Media Survey. What are the three most popular types of media in the class? Which is the least popular?
- the radio
- the internet
- newspapers
- the TV

2 🔊 **1.14** Listen and match speakers A–E with questions 1–8 in the survey. There are three extra questions.

A ☐ B ☐ C ☐ D ☐ E ☐

3 🔊 **1.15** Study the Vocabulary box. Match these things with the correct types of media.

> **VOCABULARY** ▸ News and entertainment
>
> blog   current affairs   documentary   film/game review
> game show   message board   news headline   phone-in
> reality show   soap opera   sports page   talent show
> talk show   video clip   vlog   weather forecast

4 Complete the sentences with the correct form of words from the Vocabulary box.
1. My dad loves watching *game shows*. He usually shouts out the answers at the TV!
2. The group's _____ is a place on the internet for fans to meet and write about the group.
3. My favourite _____ is on Channel 4 on Mondays. I think the actors are fantastic!
4. I don't often read _____ because my friends tell me which games to buy.
5. My sister often sends me links to funny _____ with cats on the internet.

5 In pairs, take turns to name a programme for your partner to say which category from the Vocabulary box it belongs to.

A: *'Lego Masters.'*
B: *That's a reality show.*

6 🔊 **1.16** Listen and match speakers 1–4 with types of radio programmes they like a–e. There is one extra answer.

1 ☐ Cara	a	current affairs
2 ☐ Cara's dad	b	Pop Top 20
3 ☐ Cara's brother	c	sports
4 ☐ Cara's mum	d	phone-ins
	e	rock music

The Media Survey

What type of media do you use …

1. to listen to new music?
2. to watch pop videos?
3. to check news about your favourite celebrity?
4. to check sports results?
5. to see what's on at the cinema?
6. to find information for school projects?
7. to check the news headlines?
8. to check the weather forecast?

VIDEO ▶ **WIDER WORLD**

7 ▶ 7 Watch four people and write down the types of media they use.

8 In pairs, ask and answer the questions below.
- What magazines or newspapers do you read?
- What are your favourite websites?
- What programmes do you watch?

A: *What magazines or newspapers do you read?*
B: *I often read …*

I can understand people talking about different types of media.

1.6 Speaking
Asking for and giving opinions

VIDEO LOVE AND LAUGH

Noah: I love drawing.
Lena: Hmm, I don't like it much. I'm into music and photography and I really enjoy watching TV series. What do you think of that new show?
Noah: Which new show?
Lena: This one … *Love and Laugh*.
Noah: You mean that new comedy series?
Lena: Yeah, I think it's brilliant.
Noah: No, it's no good.
Lena: What's wrong with it?
Noah: Honestly? Everything. If you ask me, it's boring. It's not funny. The actors are terrible.
Lena: Well, I don't agree with you. I think it's funny. How do you feel about that, Mateo?
Mateo: I agree with you, Lena. I think it's cool. And in my opinion, the actors are great, especially … my aunt Miriam!

Noah: Oh no! Is your aunt in *Love and Laugh*?
Mateo: Yes, she's the star!
Noah: Oh, I'm so sorry.
Mateo: It's OK.

SOUNDS GOOD!   You mean …?   •   Honestly?

1 ▶ 8 🔊 1.17 Describe the photo. Watch or listen and answer the questions.
1 What kind of show is *Love and Laugh*?
2 What do Lena and Noah think about the show?
3 Why is Lena smiling in the photo?

SET FOR LIFE

2 Discuss in pairs. What do you do when you disagree with someone? Which of these things is the most difficult for you to do?
- say you agree even if you don't
- say politely what you think and why
- explain why the other person is wrong

4 🔊 1.18 Use the Speaking box to complete the dialogue with one word in each gap. Listen and check.

A: So, how do you feel ¹*about* pop music?
B: I don't think ²_____ of it.
A: What's ³_____ with it?
B: If you ⁴_____ me, it's always the same – easy listening.
A: What's the problem ⁵_____ easy listening?
B: It's all right, but I prefer hip hop. I ⁶_____ pop music's boring.
A: No, it isn't. It's ⁷_____ ! Here, listen to this … So, what do you think ⁸_____ that?

3 Study the Speaking box. Find examples of the phrases in the dialogue.

SPEAKING   Asking for and giving opinions

Asking for opinions	Giving opinions
What do you think of …?	In my opinion, …
How do you feel about …?	If you ask me, …
What's wrong/ the problem with …?	I think it's great/brilliant/ all right.
	I think it's terrible/awful/boring.
	I don't think much of it.
	It's no good.
	I agree/don't agree (with …).

YOUR WORLD

5 In groups, ask for and give opinions about your favourite and least favourite TV shows, actors and singers. Use the Speaking box to help you.

A: What do you think of Ed Sheeran?
B: I think he's brilliant.

I can ask for and give opinions.

1.7 Writing
A personal introduction

About me
My name is Olivia James, and I'm fifteen years old. I'm English. I live with my parents and my brother Archie in Pudsey, a market town in Northern England between Bradford and Leeds. I'm in Year 10 at Pudsey High School. My favourite subjects are Music, Art and English.

I like books and movies and I love music. My favourite band is Twin Peaks – they're from Chicago in the USA and they're awesome. In my free time I sing and play the guitar.

I make music on my laptop every day and I sometimes write songs. Click <u>here</u> to listen to them and tell me what you think!

Olivia James
Pudsey, Yorkshire, England
Friends

1 Have you got a personal blog or social media page? What is it about?

2 In pairs, quickly look at Olivia's introduction. Which sentence is not true?
1 There is a photo of Olivia.
2 You can listen to some of Olivia's songs.
3 You can look at Olivia's photo gallery.
4 There is some personal information about Olivia.
5 You can see some of Olivia's friends on this page.

3 Read Olivia's introduction. In pairs, tick (✔) the things she writes about.
☐ school   ☐ nationality   ☐ hobbies
☐ best friend   ☐ name and age   ☐ family/home town
☐ personality   ☐ interests

4 Compare yourself with Olivia. Use *and* and *but*.
She's English, but I come from Turkey.
She's got a brother and I've got a brother too.

5 Study the Writing box. Find examples of the phrases in Olivia's introduction.

WRITING 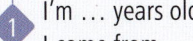 A personal introduction

Personal details
My name is …
I'm … years old.
I come from …   I'm …
I live with my family in …   My home town is …
I'm in Year … at …

Interests/Hobbies
I like/love …   I'm into/interested in …
My favourite … is …
In my free time I …   Outside school I …

Routines
I often/sometimes/usually …
I … once a week/every day.

6 Study the Language box. Find an example for each use of capital letters in Olivia's introduction.

LANGUAGE   Capital letters

Use capital letters:
- for the personal pronoun
- at the beginning of a sentence
- for names of people and places
- for countries and nationalities
- for school subjects

Music, Art and English – school subjects

WRITING TIME

7 Write a personal introduction for a social media page or website.

 Find ideas
Make notes about your:
- personal details.
- favourite school subjects.
- interests and hobbies.

 Plan
Organise your ideas into paragraphs. Use Olivia's text to help you.

 Write and share
- Write a draft personal introduction. Use the Language box and the Writing box to help you.
- Share your text with another student for feedback.
- Write the final version of your introduction.

 Check
- Check language: is the spelling (capital letters) correct?
- Check grammar: is the Present Simple in your text correct?

I can write a personal introduction.

Vocabulary Activator

WORDLIST 🔊 1.19

People in the arts
actor (n)
artist (n)
dancer (n)
director (n)
guitarist (n)
musician (n)
painter (n)
photographer (n)
poet (n)
singer (n)
writer (n)

Cultural activities
action film (n)
animated film (n)
ballet (n)
ballroom dancing (n)
classical music (n)
comic (n)
fantasy film (n)
hip hop (n)
novel (n)
painting (n)
photo (n)
picture (n)
poem (n)
pop (n)
rap (n)
rock (n)
romantic comedy (n)
rumba (n)
salsa (n)
science fiction (sci-fi) film (n)
short story (n)
street art (n)
street dance (n)
techno (n)

Word friends (creative hobbies)
act in a play
act in a (short) film
dance salsa
draw pictures
listen to (rock) music
play the guitar
read poetry
take selfies
watch (fantasy) films

Word friends (cultural activities)
create art
make short films
perform on stage
play video games
share something on social media
watch concerts
watch videos

News and entertainment
blog (n)
current affairs (n)
documentary (n)
film review (n)
game review (n)
game show (n)
message board (n)
news headline (n)
phone-in (n)
reality show (n)
soap opera (n)
sports page (n)
talent show (n)
talk show (n)
video clip (n)
vlog (n)
weather forecast (n)

Extra words
awful (adj)
be afraid of
be interested in
be into
be mad about
brilliant (adj)
cinema (n)
cool (adj)
creative work (n)
culture (n)
drums (n)
enjoy (v)
famous (adj)
go dancing
great (adj)
hate (v)
like (v)
love (v)
make animations
news (n)
newspaper (n)
opinion (n)
orchestra (n)
paint (v, n)
photography (n)
programme (n)
routine (n)
share interests
sing (v)
(social) media (n)
song (n)
take part in
take photos
terrible (adj)
theatre (n)

1 Use words from the wordlist to find these things.
1 two words that have a similar meaning and one letter different *blog, ...*
2 a word that stays the same when you read it backwards
3 two things that are funny
4 five things you can find in a newspaper or magazine
5 four types of programme where you or your family can be on TV

2 In pairs, ask and answer the questions.
1 Who can perform on stage? *actor, ...*
2 Can you name a Latin American dance?
3 What kind of films have no real actors?
4 What classical music piece do you know?
5 What can you share on social media?

3 In pairs, say what jobs are represented in the pictures. What do these people make or do?

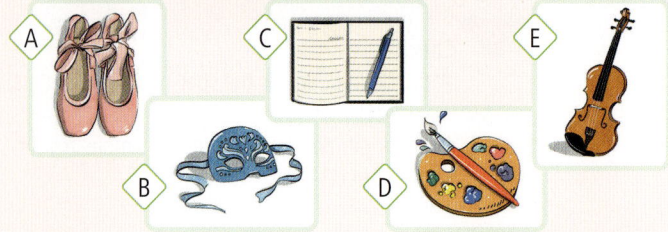

4 Complete the sentences with one word in each gap. In pairs, say if the sentences are true for you.
1 I listen *to* rock music every day.
2 I want to _____ in a play.
3 I often play _____ games with friends.
4 I sometimes _____ things on social media.
5 I never _____ short films. I prefer to watch them.

I don't listen to rock music every day.

5 🔊 1.20 **PRONUNCIATION** Listen to the underlined vowel(s) in each word and decide which sound you hear. Write the word in the correct column.

art<u>i</u>st   b<u>e</u>   com<u>i</u>c   compl<u>e</u>te   f<u>i</u>lm   gu<u>i</u>tar
m<u>e</u>dia   mus<u>i</u>c   r<u>e</u>ad   str<u>ee</u>t

/iː/	/ɪ/
	artist

6 🔊 1.21 **PRONUNCIATION** Listen, check your answers to Exercise 5 and repeat.

Unit 1 20

Revision

Vocabulary

1 Write the correct word for each definition.
1 This type of writing is an online diary. b *l o g*
2 This person makes films and tells actors what to do. d_____
3 You can read these. They're longer than short stories. n_____
4 This programme gives you lots of information about one topic. d_____
5 These pieces of writing give opinions about books, films or games. r_____
6 This information tells you about things in the news. c_____ a_____

2 Complete the text with the words below.

> films make media music performing
> pictures play shares ~~taking~~

Modern dancers

Street dancers Hasan and Elsa like ¹*taking* selfies. Sharing things on social ² _____ is very important to them. They often ³ _____ short films of dance moves, then Hasan ⁴ _____ video clips online. 'We don't ⁵ _____ an instrument, but we listen to lots of ⁶ _____ at the weekend and we often watch dance ⁷ _____ on TV or at the cinema,' says Hasan. 'Our families help too. Elsa's brother often draws ⁸ _____ of dance costumes. And my cousin is a photographer, so she loves taking photos of us ⁹ _____ on stage.'

3 Choose the correct option. In pairs, ask and answer the questions.
1 What's your favourite reality *show / opera*?
2 Do you sometimes *read / act* poetry?
3 Do you enjoy watching soap *operas / films*?
4 Have you got a favourite game *film / show*?
5 Can you *play / perform* the guitar?

Grammar

4 Complete the sentences with the Present Simple form of the words in brackets.
1 The singer *lives* (live) in the USA. She _____ (not live) in England.
2 Adam _____ (go) to dance classes on Saturdays.
3 No, I _____ (never/watch) reality shows.
4 My friends _____ (enjoy) science fiction films. They _____ (not like) romantic comedies.
5 Yes, I _____ (do). I _____ (listen) to it every day.

5 Make questions for the answers in Exercise 4.
1 Where *does the singer live* ?
2 When _____ ?
3 _____ reality shows?
4 What kind of _____ ?
5 _____ to hip hop?

6 In pairs, match words from box A with words from box B to write five sentences about a classmate. Then ask your classmate to correct the false information.

> **A** always often once/twice/three times a …
> never sometimes usually

> **B** act go listen paint play read watch

A: *Lucas always listens to rap music. He goes to dance classes once a week.*
B: *I sometimes listen to rap music.*

Speaking

7 In pairs, role play the situation. Student A, look below. Student B, go to page 138.
Student A
- Tell Student B you want to watch a film. Ask him/her for ideas.
- Give your opinion of Student B's film.
- Suggest a film you want to watch. Ask your partner for his/her opinion.
- Decide together on a film to watch.

Dictation

8 🔊 1.22 Listen. Then listen again and write down what you hear during each pause.

BBC CULTURE
Let's dance!

WHY DANCE?

Dance is very popular today. Millions of people around the world regularly dance or watch dance performances. There are many different types of dance, but why do people do them?

STREET DANCE is popular with young people. It's got many different types, including breakdance and hip hop. Street dance moves are all about showing people how strong and skilful the dancers are.

ZUMBA® is a fitness class and a dance party at the same time! People do Zumba to energetic South American music. They want to have a fun physical workout.

BALLET tells stories and shows emotion. There are many difficult positions and moves, and you need a lot of training to be good at it.

SALSA is from Cuba. In Spanish, the word 'salsa' is a hot and spicy sauce. Salsa dancers dance because they want to express their passion and energy.

So there are different reasons why people love dancing. But maybe the best reason is that moving to music just feels really good!

skilful (adj) good at doing something
spicy (adj) a strong, hot taste

1 **VISIBLE THINKING** In pairs, follow these steps.
THINK
1 Write down the names of all the dance styles that you know.
PUZZLE
2 What would you like to learn about dance? Choose one of the questions below or write your own question.
   a Why do people enjoy dancing?
   b What are the most popular dance styles?
EXPLORE
3 🔊 1.23 Read the text. Which questions in the Puzzle section does it answer? How could you find out more about dance? Use the ideas below to help you.

> go to a dance lesson
> go to a dance performance
> talk to a dancer
> watch dance videos

2 Read the text again. Mark the sentences T (true) or F (false).
1 ☐ There's only one type of street dance.
2 ☐ Zumba is a type of exercise.
3 ☐ Ballet is easy to learn.
4 ☐ Salsa is also a type of food in Spanish.

3 In pairs, discuss the questions.
1 Do you like dancing? Are you a good dancer?
2 Are any of your friends or family good at dancing?

BBC ▶ Get dancing!

4 Look at the photos of dancers. Match parts of the body 1–6 with the words below.

☐ back   ☐ feet   ☐ head
☐ leg   ☐ shoulders   ☐ toes

5 ▶ 9 Watch a video about dancing. Number the dance styles in the order that you see them.

☐ ballet
☐ breakdance
☐ street dance

6 ▶ 9 Answer the questions. Then watch again and check.
In which of the dances does the dancer …
1 stand on her toes?
2 turn around fast?
3 lie on the floor?
4 move one leg around?
5 point her feet?

7 In pairs, discuss the questions.
1 Which one of the dance types in the video do you prefer?
2 Which of the dance moves look easy? Which look difficult?
3 Which moves would you like to try?

PROJECT TIME

8 In groups of four, prepare a video podcast about a type of dance. Follow these steps.

1 In groups, choose a dance style and a title for your video podcast. Decide who in your group can find the answers to these questions.
- Where in the world is the dance popular? Who is it popular with?
- Is it modern or traditional? What type of music do they dance to?
- What clothes or shoes do people wear for this dance?
- How do you dance it?

2 Individually, create your part of the video podcast.
- Find the information and write the script for your section.
- Find photos, music or videos for each piece of information.

3 In your group, create your video podcast. You can use a video app.
- Put all the parts of the script together and decide who can read it.
- Record the script and add photos or videos.
- Watch and edit the video podcast.

4 Show your video podcast to the class.
- Answer other students' questions.
- Watch your classmates' video podcasts. Ask questions.

People and personality

2

VOCABULARY
Clothes and accessories | Adjectives to describe clothes and accessories | Adjectives with -ing/-ed | Personality adjectives

GRAMMAR
Present Continuous | Present Simple and Present Continuous

Outfit of the Day   follow ▼ ...

6,768 posts   86.2k followers   56 following

Show us your outfit of the day. Tell us what you have on. Tag #OOTD so that we can share on our profile.

A

Check out this #OOTD photo of Dana and Bret in their 'back-to-school' clothes. We really love Dana's shirt over top combination and Bret's jeans jacket.
♡ ◯ ◁

#ootd #backtoschool

B

It's party time! So today's #OOTD comes from Tasha in her party clothes. We love her party accessories and the wonderful smile.
♡ ◯ ◁

#ootd #partyoutfit

C

We are sharing Addie's #OOTD because we love the colours of her winter clothes. The blue gloves and scarf are a perfect match.
♡ ◯ ◁

#ootd #winterclothes

2.1 Vocabulary

Clothes

1 🔊 2.1 What clothes can you see in photos A–C? Study Vocabulary box A. In pairs, find three things that are NOT in the photos.

> **VOCABULARY A** Clothes and accessories
>
> **Clothes and footwear**
> boots coat dress (fancy-dress) costume hoodie jacket jeans shirt shoes shorts sweater top tracksuit trainers trousers T-shirt underwear uniform
>
> **Accessories**
> baseball cap belt earrings glasses gloves handbag hat necklace scarf

2 **I KNOW!** Work in groups. Can you add more words to Vocabulary box A?

3 Read the posts. Whose OOTD do you like best? Why?

4 Which of the items from Vocabulary box A do you wear on the body parts below? Discuss in pairs.
- top part of your body
- bottom part of your body
- your head
- your hands
- your feet

Unit 2 24

5 🔊 2.2 In pairs, mark the sentences T (true) or F (false). Listen and check.
1. ☐ Sports teams with red shirts win more often.
2. ☐ Most jeans have a very small pocket for a watch.
3. ☐ People are stronger when they wear a Superman T-shirt.
4. ☐ Baseball players wear baseball caps to protect their eyes from the sun.
5. ☐ People usually lose about fifty socks each year.

6 🔊 2.3 Study Vocabulary box B. Which of the adjectives can you use to describe photos A–C?

| VOCABULARY B | Adjectives to describe clothes and accessories |

baggy   checked   cotton   dark   leather   light
plain   striped   tight   woolly

Dana's got a checked shirt.

7 In pairs, choose the correct option to describe photos 1–6. Go to page 138 to check your answers.
1. light blue *earring / necklace*
2. woolly *gloves / sweater*
3. leather *handbag / belt*
4. plain *skirt / dress*
5. striped *tracksuit / scarf*
6. tight *top / hoodie*

WHAT'S IN THE PHOTO?
Can you name these clothes and accessories?

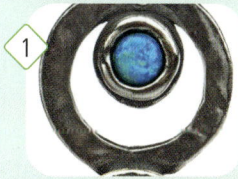

8 🔊 2.4 Read the text and choose the correct option. Use the photos to help you. Listen and check.

	a	b	c
1	dark	light	tight
2	striped	baggy	cotton
3	striped	plain	checked
4	boots	trainers	gloves
5	gloves	glasses	jeans
6	hats	costumes	earrings
7	light blue	striped	dark grey
8	cotton	woolly	leather

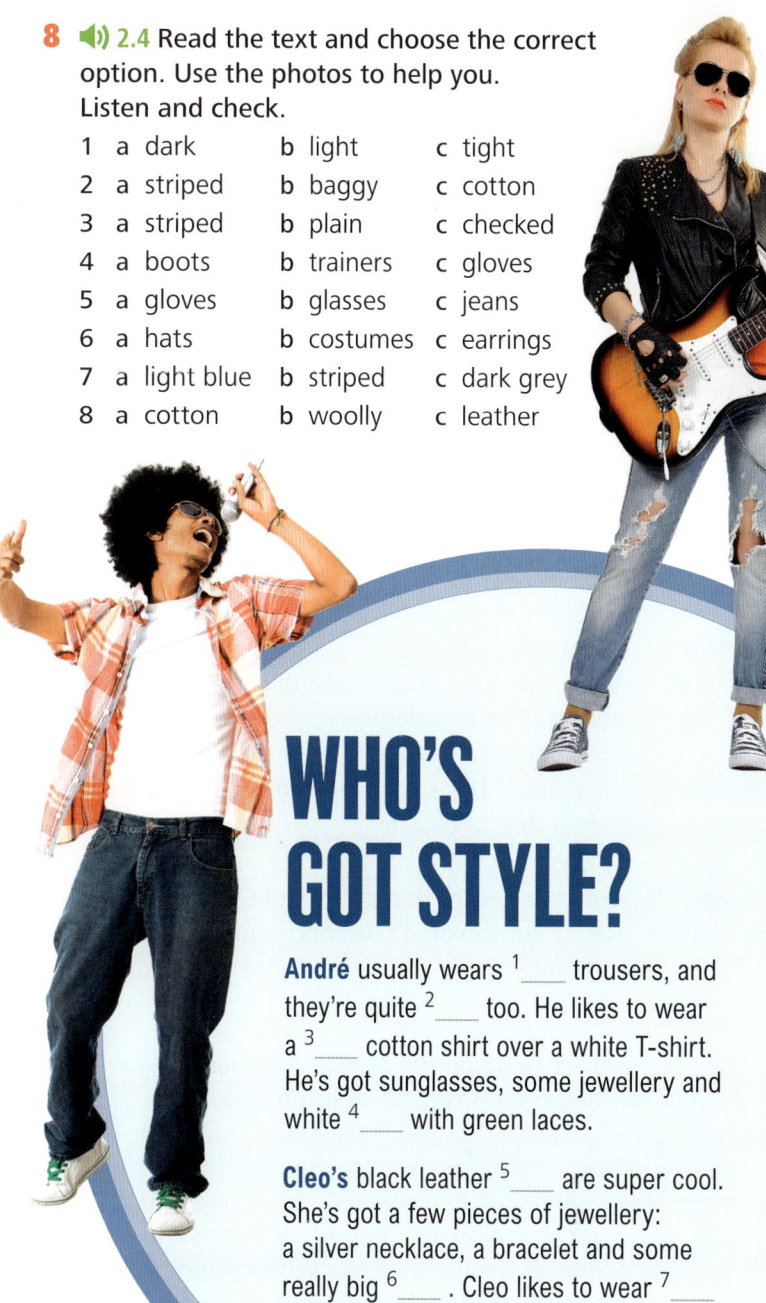

WHO'S GOT STYLE?

André usually wears ¹___ trousers, and they're quite ²___ too. He likes to wear a ³___ cotton shirt over a white T-shirt. He's got sunglasses, some jewellery and white ⁴___ with green laces.

Cleo's black leather ⁵___ are super cool. She's got a few pieces of jewellery: a silver necklace, a bracelet and some really big ⁶___ . Cleo likes to wear ⁷___ jeans and her favourite black ⁸___ jacket.

VIDEO   WIDER WORLD

9 ▶ 10 Watch six people talking about what they wear for different occasions. Write down the clothes they mention.

10 In pairs, ask and answer the questions.
What do you wear when you …
- play sport?
- go to a wedding?
- go to a party?
- go to bed?

A: *What do you wear when you go to a party?*
B: *I usually wear jeans and a T-shirt. I never wear a suit.*

I can talk about clothes.

2.2 Grammar
Present Continuous

VIDEO **WHAT ARE YOU WEARING?**

Mum: Mia? Are you getting ready? Dad's making some toast. Do you want some?
Mia: Yes, I'm nearly ready. Don't worry. I'm having some fruit and yoghurt.
Phone ringing
Noah: Mia? Are you coming? I'm at the bus stop.
Mia: Er, yes, I am. I'm leaving now. Hey, what are you wearing?
Noah: Huh? I'm wearing my uniform, of course. See you in a minute.
One minute later
Mia: Ta-Da!
Noah: What? Mia, you've got a beard! People are looking at you. And why are you wearing a scarf on your head?
Mia: I'm a pirate! This is my fancy-dress costume for Charity Day, of course.
Noah: It's cool, but …
Mia: Yeah. I've got my dad's shirt and Gran's old belt … But you aren't wearing your fancy-dress costume.
Noah: Is it really Charity Day today? I'm going home to change.
Mia: Noah! There isn't time. The bus is coming.
Noah: You're right. I'm just checking something …
Mia: Why are you laughing?
Noah: Guess what? It isn't Charity Day today. It's next week!

1 11  2.5 Describe the photo. Why hasn't Mia got her uniform on? Watch or listen and check.

SET FOR LIFE

2 How can you remember important events? In pairs, discuss the ideas below. Which things do you normally do? What would you like to try?
- have a noticeboard at home with sticky notes
- use app/phone notifications
- make a note in your diary or on a calendar

3 Study the Grammar box. Find more examples of the Present Continuous in the dialogue.

GRAMMAR | **Present Continuous**

+	−
I'm leaving now.	I'm not laughing.
He's making some toast.	He isn't wearing a costume.
They're looking at you.	They aren't talking.

?	
Are you coming?	Yes, I am./No, I'm not.
Is he going home?	Yes, he is./No, he isn't.
Are they eating?	Yes, they are./No, they aren't.
Why are you laughing?	

GRAMMAR TIME > PAGE 127

4 Make affirmative (✓) and negative (✗) sentences in the Present Continuous.
1 Mia: sleep ✗   get ready for school ✓
 Mia isn't sleeping. She's getting ready for school.
2 Noah: pack his bag ✗   wait for Mia ✓
3 Mia's parents: eat lunch ✗   have breakfast ✓
4 Mia: leave early ✗   talk on the phone ✓

5 Make questions in the Present Continuous. In pairs, use the dialogue in Exercise 1 to answer the questions.
1 Mia / have / breakfast / ?
2 Mia's parents / eat eggs / ?
3 Mia / wear / her school uniform / ?
4 Why / Noah / laugh / ?
A: *Is Mia having breakfast?*   B: *Yes, she is.*

6 2.6 Complete the dialogue with the Present Continuous form of the verbs in brackets. Listen and check.
1 Dad: *Are* you *having* (have) breakfast, Katie?
 Katie: Yes, I _____ (eat) a sandwich.
2 Mum: Why _____ you _____ (put on) your trainers?
 Sam: I _____ (go) for a run.

YOUR WORLD

7 In pairs, ask and answer questions about what your friends and family are doing at the moment.
A: *What's your mum doing?*   B: *She's …*

Unit 2 | I can use the Present Continuous to talk about things that are happening now.

2.3 Reading and Vocabulary
Family Day

1 🔊 **2.7** Which of these activities do you and your family often do together? Read the article and tick (✓) the activities which are mentioned.

- ☐ doing a sport
- ☐ having a meal or a snack
- ☐ playing board games
- ☐ shopping
- ☐ watching films
- ☐ taking part in outdoor activities

Family Day: how are Canadians celebrating?

Research shows that many families are only together for about thirty minutes each weekday and ninety minutes on weekend days. Canada's answer to this problem is Family Day in February. Special activities are free for families, so they can spend time together. Do families enjoy it? Here's our mini survey from the Winter Festival.

Justin: It's really cold in Ottawa today – about minus ten degrees – so we're all wearing thick jackets and snow boots. We're spending Family Day at the Winter Festival. Dad's got his penguin hat on and is singing songs from *Frozen*. It's embarrassing, but he's very funny. The Winter Festival is definitely better than boring family shopping trips!

Fleur: At home, I sometimes argue with my brother as he can be annoying. But right now, we're enjoying Family Day together. The music's relaxing, and we're looking at interesting ice sculptures of animals and birds.

Natasha: The giant ice slides are really exciting! My little sister's frightened of big slides, but there are small slides for kids. I'm tired because there's a long queue for the slide, but it's OK because we're drinking hot chocolate and we're eating marshmallows.

What about you? Are you celebrating Family Day? Is it a good idea? We want to hear your opinions.

2 Read the article again and answer the questions.
1. How long do families normally spend together each weekday?
2. When do Canadian families celebrate Family Day?
3. What is the temperature in Ottawa today?
4. What types of frozen statues are at the festival?
5. What food and drink can you find at the festival?

3 🔊 **2.8** Study the Vocabulary box. Which of the words can you find in the article?

> **VOCABULARY** — Adjectives with *-ed/-ing*
>
> A person, thing or situation is …
> annoy**ing**   bor**ing**   embarrass**ing**   excit**ing**
> frighten**ing**   interest**ing**   relax**ing**   tir**ing**
>
> You are/get/feel …
> annoy**ed**   bor**ed**   embarrass**ed**   excit**ed**
> frighten**ed**   interest**ed**   relax**ed**   tir**ed**

4 Complete the words in the sentences with *-ing* or *-ed*.
1. Ella loves ice-skating, but I'm not interest*ed*.
2. I hate high slides. They're frighten_____ .
3. Do you feel tir_____ on Fridays?
4. I feel embarrass_____ in this costume.
5. The music at this festival is annoy_____ .

5 In pairs, use words from the Vocabulary box to give your opinions about the activities in Exercise 1.

A: *I think playing board games is interesting.*
B: *I don't agree. I think it's boring.*

VIDEO **WIDER WORLD**

6 ▶ **12** Watch three people talking about how they feel on different occasions. Write down as many adjectives to describe feelings as you can.

7 In pairs, use words from the Vocabulary box to say how you feel in these situations.
- Your team is losing 5–0.
- You make a silly mistake.
- It's the last day of school.

I feel annoyed/It's annoying when …

I can understand an article about a family holiday.

2.4 Grammar

Present Simple and Present Continuous

Time for a change?

It's good to get outside and try new activities. Share your photos and ideas with us.

Dylan, Glasgow

I always get up late on Saturdays. I usually have breakfast at lunchtime! But this week my parents are doing some work on the house. They're changing the windows and they're putting in a new kitchen. The noise is terrible. So today I'm breaking my usual Saturday routine. It's only 9 a.m., but I'm not lying in my bed. I'm with my friend Gareth, and we're walking up a mountain. The sun is shining on my back. It's great! Gareth does this every week. Now I understand why.

1 🔊 2.9 Read Dylan's text and answer the questions.
1. When does Dylan usually have breakfast on Saturdays?
2. What is he doing today? Why?

2 Study the Grammar box. Find more examples for each rule in Dylan's text.

> **GRAMMAR** — **Present Simple and Present Continuous**
>
> - **Present Simple**
>   Facts, habits and routines
>   I *usually have* breakfast at lunchtime.
> - **Present Continuous**
>   Things happening at the moment of speaking
>   We *are walking* up a mountain.
>   Things happening around now but maybe not at the moment of speaking.
>   This week my parents *are doing* some work on the house.

GRAMMAR TIME > PAGE 127

3 Choose the correct option.
1. We *study / are studying* algebra this semester.
2. Leo *saves / is saving* his money to buy trainers.
3. Sam's two, so he *doesn't go / isn't going* to school.
4. How often *do you play / are you playing* video games?
5. You *don't watch / aren't watching* this. Can I change the channel?

4 Make sentences with *but* to compare what usually happens and what is happening now.

	Usually	Now
Jenny	go to bed late	tonight/early
Mike	get the bus	today/ride a bike
Abel	not read novels	a great book/at the moment
Anna	wear jeans	this morning/a skirt
We	eat meals inside	this week/sit outside

Jenny usually goes to bed late, but tonight she's going to bed early.

5 Look at Exercise 4 and make sentences about you.

6 🔊 2.10 Complete the text with the Present Simple or the Present Continuous form of the words in brackets. Listen and check.

Poppy, Norwich

I ¹*usually go* (usually/go) straight home after school. I ²_____ (do) my homework and then I ³_____ (play) games online. But today I ⁴_____ (not sit) at home. I ⁵_____ (walk) our dog because I want to be outdoors and get fit. Dottie ⁶_____ (never/listen) to me, so she ⁷_____ (not walk), she ⁸_____ (run)!

YOUR WORLD

7 In groups, ask and answer questions to complete the sentences. Compare answers with another group.
1. *Adam* doesn't like dancing.
2. _____ always arrives on time.
3. _____ laughs a lot.
4. _____ is learning to play an instrument.
5. _____ is working hard these days.

A: *Adam, do you like dancing?*
B: *No, I don't.*

I can talk about what usually happens and what is happening now.

2.5 Listening and Vocabulary
Describing a friend's personality

1 🔊 2.11 Study the Vocabulary box. Are these adjectives positive (+), negative (–) or neutral (0)? In pairs, compare your answers.

VOCABULARY ▶ Personality adjectives

☐ bossy ☐ chatty ☐ cheerful ☐ clever
☐ confident ☐ friendly ☐ funny ☐ helpful
☐ kind ☐ lazy ☐ polite ☐ quiet ☐ rude
☐ selfish ☐ shy ☐ tidy

2 🔊 2.12 Complete the texts with words from the Vocabulary box. Listen and check.

> My friend Jamie's nice, but he can be ¹*selfish* because he often thinks of himself first. Also, he never listens to the teacher at school. I think that's very ² _____ ! Jamie's still a good friend because he's very ³ _____ – he's always smiling.

> My friend Zanna gets good grades because she's ⁴ _____ and she studies a lot too. She leaves clothes all over her room, but her older sister is ⁵ _____ and puts things away. Zanna's sister is ⁶ _____ . She often tells Zanna what to do!

3 Tell your partner about the personality of a person in your family.

My sister is always happy. She's also kind.

4 Look at the photos. What are the people doing? Think of some adjectives to describe their personalities.

5 🔊 2.13 Listen to five people talking about their best friends. Which speakers (1–5) are talking about photos A and B?

6 🔊 2.13 Listen again and choose the correct answer.
1 What does the speaker say about Zanna?
  a She's a good student at school.
  b She likes to wear her sister's clothes.
  c They share the same hobbies.
2 What is the speaker doing to help his grandfather?
  a cooking
  b telling stories
  c making tea
3 How is Kim helping her friend?
  a She's teaching her skateboarding.
  b She's helping her make friends.
  c She's practising a new language with her.
4 When do the two friends have football training?
  a On Tuesdays.
  b On Thursdays.
  c On Saturdays.
5 What does the speaker say about her friend Jordan?
  a He's older than her.
  b He makes her laugh.
  c He sees her every day.

YOUR WORLD

7 In pairs, choose three adjectives from the Vocabulary box to describe:
- your personality.
- your best friend's personality.
- the personality of a perfect friend.

I'm chatty, Tom is quiet …

I can understand people talking about their friends.

2.6 Speaking
Giving and responding to news

VIDEO **THE STREET DANCE LESSON**

Noah: Hiya Lena! What's up? You don't look very happy.
Lena: I'm having a bad day. My phone isn't working. It's really annoying.
Noah: That's terrible! So what are you doing here?
Lena: I'm waiting for Mia. We're working on an art project together this week.
Noah: Good for you!
Lena: What about you? How's life?
Noah: Fine … Er, I'm learning street dance. The class usually starts at seven.
Lena: Street dance? No way! How's it going?
Noah: I'm enjoying the lessons. They're fun and relaxing! Hang on, I've got a message. Oh no, I don't believe it!
Lena: What's the matter? What does it say?
Noah: There's no lesson today. The teacher isn't coming. He's ill.
Lena: What a shame! Do you want to practise some dance moves?
Noah: Cool! Let's warm up first. Copy me.
Lena: Um. It isn't easy in skinny jeans. This is interesting, but it isn't relaxing!

SOUNDS GOOD! What's up? • How's life? • How's it going?

1 ▶ 13 🔊 2.14 Watch or listen. What are Lena and Noah doing? Why?

2 Study the Speaking box. Find examples of the phrases in the dialogue.

SPEAKING Giving and responding to news

Giving news
I'm learning (how to) …
I'm spending a lot of time with/in …
I'm feeling annoyed/excited because …
I'm working on …
He/She isn't feeling well.

Responding to news
Well done!   Good for you!   Awesome!   Great!   Cool!
That's terrible!   What a shame!   Poor you!
No way!   I don't believe it!   You're kidding!

3 🔊 2.15 Choose the correct option. Listen and check.
1 A: My exams are going well.
  B: ____
  a Poor you!   b No way!
  c Well done!
2 A: I'm not sleeping well these days.
  B: ____
  a What a shame!   b Good for you!
  c No way!
3 A: I'm learning how to speak Chinese.
  B: ____
  a You're kidding!   b What a shame!
  c That's terrible!
4 A: My phone isn't working.
  B: ____
  a Awesome!   b Poor you!
  c Great!

4 🔊 2.16 In pairs, respond to the news below. Use the correct intonation. Listen and check.
1 I'm writing a blog.
2 I can't find my phone. It has all my photos on it!
3 I'm winning the game!
4 My mum says I can't go out this weekend!

YOUR WORLD

5 In pairs, give and respond to news about your life. Use the Speaking box to help you.
A: I'm doing well at school.
B: Great!

I can give and respond to news.

2.7 Writing
A semi-formal email

Dear Student,

Thank you for agreeing to this exchange visit. Here's a photo of our visitors!
Boys: Haru, fourteen, and Kota, fifteen
Girls: Emi, fifteen, and Asa, fourteen
Their arrival date is 5 November. Please tell them:
- some facts about you and your family.
- some information about a normal school day.
- some advice about what clothes to wear at school.

Thank you for your help,
Mrs Tanaka, Head Teacher

1 A group of students from Japan want to visit your school. In pairs, read the message from their head teacher and answer the questions.
1 What is the date of their visit?
2 What do they need to know?

2 Read the email. Who is it from?

Dear Haru,

I'm writing to tell you about myself and my family.

My name's Nina. I'm fifteen and I have two brothers. Ed is twelve and Luke is ten. They're funny and outgoing. We like listening to music, so the house isn't very quiet. Our school is Linwood High. Lessons start at 8.45 and finish at 3.15. I play volleyball after school on Wednesdays, and we have matches at the weekend. Some schools in the USA have uniforms, but we don't. Most people wear T-shirts and jeans with trainers.

I'm looking forward to meeting you on 5 November!

Best wishes,
Nina

3 Study the Writing box. Find examples of the phrases in the email.

WRITING A semi-formal email with information

1 Greeting
Dear (name)

2 Explain reason for writing
I'm writing to …

3 Give more information
My friends and I …   Our school is …
Some/Most people …

4 Close your email
I'm looking forward to …

5 Closing phrase
Best wishes   Kind/Best regards

4 Study the Language box. Complete the phrases below with the correct prepositions.

LANGUAGE Prepositions of time

AT the weekend   night   2 p.m.   New Year
ON 3 May   New Year's Eve   Saturday(s)
IN the morning   the evening   2020   October

1 <u>on</u> your birthday   4 _____ 1999
2 _____ Valentine's Day   5 _____ Tuesday
3 _____ half past five   6 _____ April

WRITING TIME

5 Choose one of the other Japanese students from Exercise 1 and write an email to him/her.

1 Find ideas
Make notes about:
- your family and friends.
- your normal school day.
- the clothes students wear in your school.

2 Plan
Organise your ideas into paragraphs. Use Nina's email to help you.

3 Write and share
- Write a draft email. Use the Language box and the Writing box to help you.
- Share your email with another student for feedback.
- Write the final version of your email.

4 Check
- Check language: are the prepositions of time correct?
- Check grammar: are most verbs in the Present Simple with some in the Present Continuous?

I can write a semi-formal email.

Vocabulary Activator

WORDLIST 🔊 2.17

Clothes and accessories
baseball cap (n)
belt (n)
boots (n)
coat (n)
dress (n)
earrings (n)
(fancy-dress) costume (n)
glasses (n)
gloves (n)
handbag (n)
hat (n)
hoodie (n)
jacket (n)
jeans (n)
necklace (n)
scarf (n)
shirt (n)
shoes (n)
shorts (n)
sweater (n)
top (n)
tracksuit (n)
trainers (n)
trousers (n)
T-shirt (n)
underwear (n)
uniform (n)

Adjectives to describe clothes and accessories
baggy (adj)
checked (adj)
cotton (adj)
dark (adj)
leather (adj)
light (adj)
plain (adj)
striped (adj)
tight (adj)
woolly (adj)

Adjectives with -ed/-ing
annoyed (adj)
annoying (adj)
bored (adj)
boring (adj)
embarrassed (adj)
embarrassing (adj)
excited (adj)
exciting (adj)
frightened (adj)
frightening (adj)
interested (adj)
interesting (adj)
relaxed (adj)
relaxing (adj)

tired (adj)
tiring (adj)

Personality adjectives
bossy (adj)
chatty (adj)
cheerful (adj)
clever (adj)
confident (adj)
friendly (adj)
funny (adj)
helpful (adj)
kind (adj)
lazy (adj)
polite (adj)
quiet (adj)
rude (adj)
selfish (adj)
shy (adj)
tidy (adj)

Extra words
beard (n)
bracelet (n)
celebrate (v)
change clothes
feel (v)
festival (n)
footwear (n)

get fit
have a meal
have fun
hobby (n)
indoors (adv)
jewellery (n)
laces (n)
look cool
outdoors (adv)
outgoing (adj)
party (n)
person (n)
pocket (n)
protect from (v)
shopping trip (n)
snow boots (n)
socks (n)
spend time
style (n)
summer (n)
sunglasses (n)
walk a dog
wear (v)
wedding (n)
winter (n)

---

1 Use words from the wordlist to find these things.
  1 three items of jewellery *earrings, …*
  2 five things you can wear on your feet
  3 four negative adjectives that can describe personality
  4 three adjectives ending in *-ed* that describe positive emotions
  5 two words that describe materials for clothes

2 Complete the words in the sentences. Use the opposites of the words in bold. Use the wordlist to help you.
  1 Paul isn't **shy**, he's quite o*utgoing*.
  2 He isn't **rude**, he's very p_____.
  3 Paul isn't **quiet**, he's usually c_____.
  4 He isn't very **sad**, he's very c_____.

3 In pairs, replace the words in bold to make correct definitions. One sentence is correct. Use words from the wordlist to help you.
  1 You wear ~~boots~~ to keep your hands warm. *gloves*
  2 A **rude** person knows the right answers in class.
  3 **Dark blue** is a popular colour for jeans.
  4 A great party with all your friends is very **excited**.
  5 Teachers are **relaxed** when students talk in class.

4 In pairs, describe your favourite clothes. Use words from the wordlist to help you.
I like checked shirts and tight jeans.

5 In pairs, say what you think about these things. Use *-ing* adjectives from the wordlist.

> fancy-dress parties   jewellery   lazy people
> New Year   school uniforms   selfish people
> summer   tracksuits

I think fancy-dress parties are exciting.

6 🔊 2.18 **PRONUNCIATION** Listen to the underlined vowel(s) in each word and decide which sound you hear. Write the word in the correct column.

> b<u>a</u>ggy   b<u>e</u>lt   c<u>a</u>p   ch<u>a</u>tty   ch<u>e</u>cked   dr<u>e</u>ss
> f<u>a</u>shion   fr<u>ie</u>ndly   j<u>a</u>cket   l<u>ea</u>ther   rel<u>a</u>xing
> sw<u>ea</u>ter   tr<u>a</u>cksuit

/æ/	/e/
baggy	

7 🔊 2.19 **PRONUNCIATION** Listen, check your answers to Exercise 6 and repeat.

Revision

Vocabulary

1 Complete the words in the sentences. Then make the sentences true for you.
1. I don't like t r o u s e r s , I prefer jeans.
2. I don't usually wear a b____ with my jeans.
3. I never leave my socks and u_____ on the bedroom floor.
4. I love to wear my t_____ at the weekend.
5. I think hats are cool, but b_____ c___ are boring.
6. In my opinion, school u_____ is a great idea.

Trousers are OK, but I prefer jeans.

2 Complete the second sentence so that it means the same as the first one. In pairs, say if the sentences are true for you.
1. I'm not interested in family activities.
   I don't think family activities are *interesting* .
2. I get bored when I go shopping with my parents.
   I think shopping with my parents is _____ .
3. In my opinion, waking up early is annoying.
   I feel _____ when I wake up early.
4. I think it's relaxing to watch films with friends.
   I feel _____ when I watch films with friends.
5. When we have a big family party I feel tired.
   I think big family parties are _____ .

I don't agree. I think family activities are sometimes interesting.

3 Look at the pictures and complete the email with adjectives from the wordlist.

✉

Dear Fantastic Fashion,

I've got problems with my new clothes from your website. The jeans are dark blue, but I want ¹*light* blue ones. The T-shirt is baggy, but I like ²_____ T-shirts. The plain ³_____ hat is nice and warm, but it's very big. And the note says you don't have any more ⁴_____ shirts, so there's an awful striped one instead. It's really annoying!

Please help,
Sam

Grammar

4 Complete the questions with *is*, *are*, *do* or *does*. In pairs, ask and answer the questions.
1. *Are* you wearing a T-shirt today?
2. _____ the sun shining at the moment?
3. _____ the person next to you have a tidy desk?
4. _____ your friend wear a lot of jewellery?
5. _____ you like checked shirts?

5 Complete the message with the Present Simple or the Present Continuous form of the verbs in brackets.

17.18

Hey Max!
How are things with you? ¹*Are you going* (you/go) to your art classes these days?
My cousins ²_____ (visit) us at the moment. 😞
They ³_____ (come) to stay every summer, but I ⁴_____ (not like) it when they visit. They ⁵_____ (not like) any of the things I do. Now they're in the living room. They ⁶_____ (give) a concert for Mum and Dad. 😊 I'm sure my parents ⁷_____ (not enjoy) it. I ⁸_____ (not stay) here!
I ⁹_____ (leave) the house for a walk.
Message me soon!

6 Write answers to the questions. Use *at*, *in* or *on* with a time expression. Then compare with a partner.

When do you usually …
- have a shower?
- eat a lot?
- go on holiday?
- go out with friends?
- go to bed?
- wear T-shirts and shorts?

I usually have a shower in the morning.

Speaking

7 In pairs, role play the situation. Student A, look below. Student B, go to page 138.

Student A
- Think of some interesting news to tell Student B. Use the ideas below to help you.

a new hobby   a difficult test   wait for a friend

- Say hello to Student B.
- Ask what's new in Student B's life.
- Listen and respond to Student B's news.
- Give your news.

Dictation

8 🔊 2.20 Listen. Then listen again and write down what you hear during each pause.

33 Unit 2

SET FOR LIFE

Is everything OK?

1 In pairs, study the body language of the people in the photos and answer the questions.

Which person ...
1. is looking down?
2. is looking away?
3. is shouting?
4. is smiling?
5. has got wide eyes?
6. has got his/her head in his/her hands?
7. is moving his/her hands and arms?

2 How are the people in the photos feeling? In pairs, discuss how their body language shows their emotions. Use the adjectives below to help you.

| angry annoyed bored calm embarrassed |
| excited happy nervous shy stressed surprised |
| tired worried |

I think the girl in photo A is feeling angry because she's shouting.

3 In pairs, answer the questions.
1. Which of the emotions in Exercise 2 are positive and which are negative?
2. Think of situations when you feel the emotions. How do you usually react?

I'm angry when my sister uses my phone. I usually …

4 Read the messages between two friends. Why doesn't Ben want to come out?

> **Tamsin**
> Hey, Ben – do you want to come out for a pizza tonight?
>
> **Ben**
> No, I can't. I need to study tonight.
>
> **Tamsin**
> But it's Friday! 🙂
>
> **Ben**
> I know, but I've got a test on Monday.
>
> **Tamsin**
> You never come out with us anymore, Ben. ☹ Why not?
>
> **Ben**
> Don't you understand? I don't want a pizza. Stop messaging me, OK?

I can understand how people are feeling in difficult situations and offer help.

Understand other people's emotions

5 Why do you think Ben is behaving like this? In pairs, discuss possible reasons.
  a He doesn't like Tamsin any more.
  b He's worried about his schoolwork.
  c He prefers studying to going out.

6 🔊 2.21 Tamsin phones Ben. Listen to the conversation and check your answer to Exercise 5. What does Tamsin suggest doing tomorrow?

7 🔊 2.21 Study the Useful Phrases box. Then listen again and tick (✓) the expressions you hear in Ben and Tamsin's conversation.

8 In pairs, read the situations below. Discuss how the people are feeling and how they might show those emotions with their body language.
  a Emma is a new student in your class. She never speaks to the other students.
     She is feeling shy. She never smiles and often looks down.
  b Joe often makes mistakes when he speaks English. Some students in class laugh at him and make silly comments.
  c Most students in your class have got good marks for the year, but Harry has got bad marks.

9 Read the Useful Tips. In class, discuss the questions.
  1 Do you find it difficult or easy to talk about emotions with other people?
  2 Do you always follow the tips when you talk to your friends?

SET FOR LIFE

10 In pairs, role play a situation where one person offers help to another person in a difficult situation. Follow the instructions.

  1 Choose a situation from Exercise 8 or think of a situation from your own life.

  2 Write the scene. Use the expressions from the Useful Phrases box.
  Student A: Say how Student B looks and ask what is wrong.
  Student B: Explain how you feel and why.
  Student A: Offer help or advice.
  Student B: Thank Student A for his/her suggestions.

  3 Practise your dialogue. Remember to use body language and your voice to show emotions.

  4 Present the dialogue for the class or record it on your phone.

USEFUL TIPS
When you communicate with someone, try to read their emotions. This can help you to understand how people are feeling and offer help.

- Look at people's body language.
- Listen to their voice.
- Think about how you usually feel in the same situation.
- Ask how a person is feeling.

USEFUL PHRASES

Identifying emotions
☐ You seem (a bit/quite) unhappy.
☐ You look/sound (really) excited/bored.

Offering help
☐ Is everything OK?/Is something wrong?
☐ What's the matter?
☐ Can I do anything to help?
☐ Do you want to talk about it?

Offering advice
☐ When I feel …, I usually …
☐ Why don't you/I/we …?

Animal life

3

VOCABULARY
Animals | Animal body parts | Personality | Looking after pets

GRAMMAR
Past Simple: *was/were* | Past Simple: regular and irregular verbs

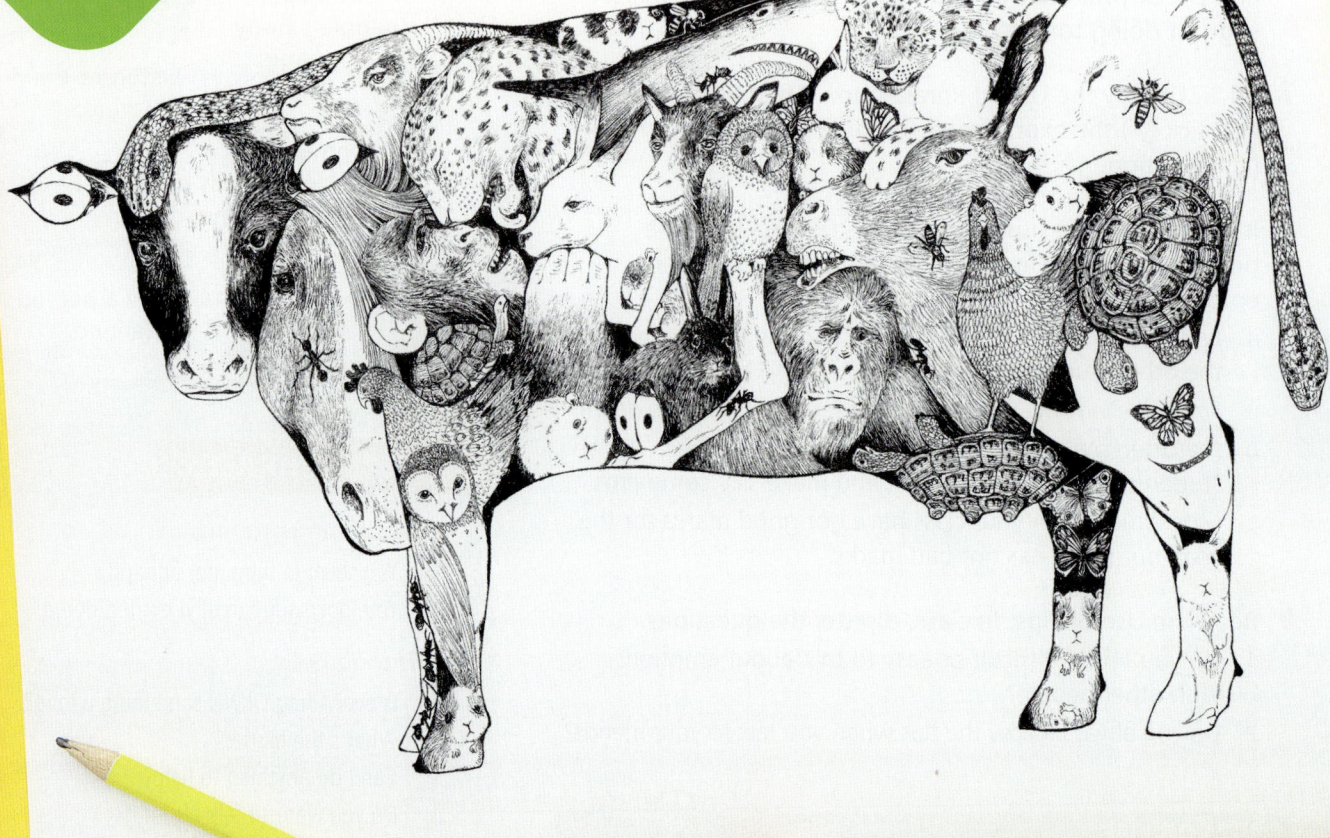

3.1 Vocabulary
Animals

1 🔊 **3.1** Study Vocabulary box A. How many of these animals can you find in the picture? Which animal is not in the picture?

VOCABULARY A ▶ Animals

ant   bee   butterfly   chicken   cow   donkey   goat
gorilla   guinea pig   horse   kangaroo   ladybird
leopard   owl   parrot   polar bear   rabbit   shark
snake   tortoise

2 🔊 **3.2** Put the animals from Vocabulary box A into the correct category. Listen and check.

pets	guinea pig
farm animals	
wild animals	
sea animals	
insects	

3 🔊 **3.3** Listen and write the animal you think you hear. Then listen and check.

Unit 3   36

4 **I KNOW!** In pairs, add more animals to each category in Exercise 2. How many words can you add in two minutes?

5 Think of two or more animals for each category below. In pairs, compare your answers.
  1 These animals don't have four legs. *chicken, …*
  2 These animals sleep all winter.
  3 These animals are good at climbing.
  4 These animals are good at running.
  5 We can ride these animals.
  6 These animals are very dangerous.

6 🔊 3.4 Study Vocabulary box B. Find examples of these things in photos A–F.

VOCABULARY B — Animal body parts

yellow **beak**   yellow **claws**   orange **feathers**
grey and white **fur**   white **paws**   black **tail**
blue **wings**

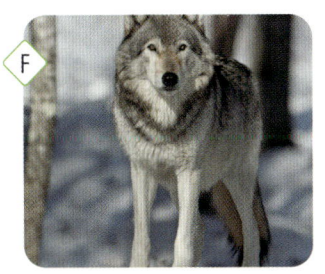

photo C – a yellow beak

7 Choose the correct option.
  1 Kangaroos use their *tails / fur* like an extra leg.
  2 Leopards' *wings / paws* help them to climb trees.
  3 Owls' wings are big with soft *fur / feathers*.
  4 Tortoises' mouths are *claws / beaks*, like a bird.

8 In pairs, tick (✓) the right sentences and cross (✗) the wrong ones. Go to page 138 to check your answers. Which fact do you find surprising?

RIGHT or WRONG?
What do you know about animals?

1 Penguins have fur, not feathers.
2 Polar bears have white fur but black skin.
3 Tigers have stripes on their fur and on their skin.
4 Cats' front paws have five toes, but their back paws have four toes.
5 Bees can beat their wings 200 times a second.
6 A brown bear's claws can grow to over fifteen centimetres.
7 Butterflies have two wings.
8 The tail of a giraffe can grow to over 2.5 metres.

9 🔊 3.5 Work in groups. Listen to five descriptions of animals. How quickly can you guess each animal?

10 Choose an animal from Vocabulary box A. In pairs, guess your partner's animal by asking questions. You can only answer *yes* or *no*.
  A: *Does it live on a farm?*
  B: *Yes, it does.*
  A: *Does it have a …?*

VIDEO ▶ **WIDER WORLD**

11 ▶ 14 Watch five people answering questions about animals. Write down any animals they mention.

12 In pairs, ask and answer the questions.
  • What's your favourite wild animal? Why do you like it?
  • Which dangerous wild animals live in your country?
  • Are you afraid of any animals? Why?
  My favourite wild animal is … because they're cute/funny …

I can talk about animals.   37   Unit 3

3.2 Grammar

Past Simple: was/were

Ella: You weren't at home yesterday.
Josh: That's right. I was out.
Ella: Where were you? Were you at the shops?
Josh: No, I wasn't. We were all at the zoo.
Ella: You were at the zoo! That's fantastic!
Josh: Yes. It was the twins' birthday.
Ella: Really? Was it fun?
Josh: Yes, it was. It was fantastic. There was a great café and there were lots of interesting animals.
Ella: Were the kids excited?
Josh: Excited? They weren't excited, they were crazy! The animals were shocked!

1 🔊 3.6 Read the dialogue. Why was Josh at the zoo?

2 Study the Grammar box. Find more examples of *was/were* in the dialogue.

GRAMMAR — Past Simple: was/were

+	I **was** out. She **was** excited. We **were** at the zoo.	
–	I **wasn't** at the shops. She **wasn't** shocked. We **weren't** at home.	
?	**Were** you at the shops? **Was** it fun? **Were** they excited?	Yes, I **was**./No, I **wasn't**. Yes, it **was**./No, it **wasn't**. Yes, we **were**./No, we **weren't**.
	Where **were** you?	
+	there is/are → there **was/were**	
–	there isn't/aren't → there **wasn't/weren't**	

Time expressions: last night/weekend, yesterday, this morning, two days ago, at ten o'clock

GRAMMAR TIME > PAGE 128

3 Choose the correct option.
1 There *wasn't / weren't* many people at the zoo yesterday.
2 There *was / were* a penguin in a pool.
3 The big leopard *was / were* asleep.
4 There *wasn't / weren't* any polar bears.
5 The gift shop *wasn't / weren't* open.

4 Complete the table with places below. In pairs, guess your partner's answers.

AT			
a concert	a friend's	a party	an aquarium
home	school	the cinema	the shops	the zoo
IN			
a café	a park	a pet shop	the classroom

Who	Where	When
your brother or sister		an hour ago
your friend		last weekend
your mother or father		yesterday at 7 p.m.
you		in the summer

A: Was your brother at home an hour ago?
B: No, he wasn't. He was in a park.

5 🔊 3.7 Listen and complete the dialogue. Then practise the dialogue in pairs.
A: Where were you last Saturday?
B: ¹*I was at a concert in the park.*
A: Was it fun?
B: ² _____
A: Were there many people there?
B: ³ _____
A: What was the weather like?
B: ⁴ _____

VIDEO — WIDER WORLD

6 ▶ 15 Watch four people talking about last Saturday. Write down where the people were and what the weather was like.

7 In pairs, use the questions in Exercise 5 to talk about last Saturday.
A: Where were you last Saturday?
B: I was at a party.

Unit 3 · 38 · I can use *was* and *were* to talk about the past.

3.3 Reading and Vocabulary
Animals and their personality

1 🔊 3.8 Read the blog. What are the animals in photos A–C?

2 Read the blog again and choose the correct answer.
   1 What does Alex learn about sloths?
      a They don't usually leave the trees.
      b They love being with people.
      c They enjoy climbing up and down trees.
   2 Raccoons are clever because they can
      a make friends.
      b drink from a bottle.
      c do difficult things with their paws.
   3 One of Alex's jobs at the centre is
      a to wash the birds' feathers.
      b to prepare food for the birds.
      c to play with the birds.
   4 Barbara pulls Alex's hair because she
      a likes him.
      b is ill.
      c is strange.

3 🔊 3.9 Study the Vocabulary box. Match the words with the sentences.

   VOCABULARY — Personality

   adventurous   aggressive   lively   playful   sociable

   1 Sharks can hurt or kill people. *aggressive*
   2 Monkeys move around energetically.
   3 Sam often plays with things and people.
   4 My friend's dog enjoys being with people.
   5 Maya enjoys doing new, exciting things.

   YOUR WORLD

4 Work in pairs. Think of an animal you like or dislike. Describe its personality. Say if you agree with your partner's opinion.
   A: *I don't like cats. I think they're lazy.*
   B: *I don't agree. Cats are cute and playful.*

A B C

Animal adventures

Last month, I was a volunteer at an animal rescue centre in Costa Rica. I met volunteers from all over the world and learned about animals' behaviour and their personalities. Here are some top moments from my blog.

Alex, 17, Birmingham

Day 1
My first day was hard work but fun. The most famous Costa Rican animals are probably the sloths. Mikey and Sarita are very slow, of course, but they're not lazy. These lovable animals spend most of their lives upside down in trees. Sloths only come down to the ground to go to the toilet.

Day 2
I love sloths, but now my favourite animals are raccoons, because they're adventurous and they enjoy making new friends. The two raccoons here have funny names: Rice and Beans! This morning they were lively and playful, as usual. These clever animals are unusual because they have five fingers. They can use their paws to open bottles … or to hold hands with volunteers. It's so cute!

Day 3
This morning my main job was to clean the birds' area and make their lunch. The parrots 'talk', so I think they're sociable, but they're noisy. I like their colourful wings and tails. I prefer the toucans, though, because they can catch grapes in their large beaks.

Day 4
The female spider monkey, Barbara, is very old. She was cute yesterday, but today she was aggressive. Her new game was to sit on my head and pull my hair. Her claws were sharp, so that was painful! The vet says that this behaviour shows Barbara loves me. How strange!

I can understand a blog about an animal rescue centre.

3.4 Grammar

Past Simple: regular and irregular verbs

VIDEO ▶ **A WEEKEND WITH A DRAGON**

Lena: Wow! So this is Rex. Where did you get him?
Mateo: A man left him at the animal rescue centre.
Lena: Really? Why did he do that?
Mateo: He didn't want Rex anymore. Mum liked Rex, so she phoned me. And of course, I wanted a bearded dragon.
Lena: Lucky you! Dragons are so cool!
Mateo: Thanks for looking after him. I wrote a list of things to do. Here you are.
Lena: Thanks. And don't worry! Have fun with your grandparents.

Next day

Lena: Hi Mateo. Yes, Rex is fine. Was fine. I played with him this morning, but then he suddenly escaped!
Mateo: No! What happened?
Lena: I went to the kitchen to get his food and when I came back, he wasn't there. I looked for him everywhere, but I don't know where he went.
Mateo: Is he on the sofa? Or under it?
Lena: No, he isn't. I'm so stressed! I can't find him! Oh, wait a minute. He's here!
Mateo: Hurray! Where is he?
Lena: Rex is back in the cage. He's eating his food. Phew!

1 Describe the animal in the photo. Would you like to have a pet like that?

2 ▶ 16 🔊 3.10 What problem did Lena have with the pet? Watch or listen and check.

3 Study the Grammar box. Find examples of the Past Simple regular and irregular verbs in the dialogue.

GRAMMAR — Past Simple: regular and irregular verbs

	Regular verbs	Irregular verbs
+	I **wanted** a bearded dragon.	I **went** to the kitchen.
–	He **didn't want** Rex.	She **didn't go** home.
?	**Did** she **want** a pet? Yes, she **did**./No she **didn't**.	**Did** she **go** to the kitchen? Yes, she **did**./No she **didn't**.
	What **did** Mateo **want**?	Why **did** he **do** that?

Past Simple verbs are irregular in the affirmative form only.

GRAMMAR TIME > PAGE 128

4 🔊 3.11 Write the Past Simple forms of these regular verbs. Then listen and add them in the correct column.

~~decide~~   ~~enjoy~~   happen   ~~like~~   listen
visit   walk   want   watch

/t/	/d/	/ɪd/
liked	enjoyed	decided

5 Complete the text with the Past Simple form of the verbs in brackets.

Mateo ¹*didn't stay* (not stay) at home last weekend. He ² _____ (visit) his grandparents. He ³ _____ (not take) his new pet, Rex, with him. Mateo ⁴ _____ (enjoy) his weekend. He ⁵ _____ (go) to the cinema and then ⁶ _____ (have) a special meal for his grandad's birthday.

6 In pairs, make questions from the prompts. Then answer the questions.
1 you / go / to the cinema last week / ?
2 your friend / phone you / last night / ?
3 you / have / a family meal yesterday / ?

VIDEO ▶ **WIDER WORLD**

7 ▶ 17 Watch four people answering questions about their day. Write down the activities they talk about.

8 In pairs, ask and answer the question.
What did you do this morning?
A: What did you do this morning?
B: I ate cold pizza.

I can use the Past Simple to talk about past events.

3.5 Listening and Vocabulary
Looking after pets

1. Read the text and decide which of the pets is good for Zara.

2. 🔊 3.12 **WORD FRIENDS** Check you understand the phrases below. Then listen to Zara's friend Jack talking about his pet and number the phrases in the order that you hear them.

   ☐ brush his/her fur
   ☐ buy food for him/her
   ☐ feed him/her
   ☐ put fresh water in his/her bowl
   ☐ spend time with him/her
   ☐ take him/her for a walk
   ☐ train him/her

3. 🔊 3.12 Listen again. Mark the sentences T (true) or F (false). Correct the false sentences.
   1. ☐ Jack's mum bought some fish for the cat.
   2. ☐ Jack fed Misty.
   3. ☐ Misty ate the fish.
   4. ☐ Jack put water in Misty's bowl.
   5. ☐ Anna took Misty for a walk.
   6. ☐ Jack and Anna spent a lot of time with Misty in the evening.

4. 🔊 3.13 Listen to four dialogues. Choose the correct answer.
   1. What kind of pet did Zara decide to get?
      a a cat   b a dog   c a snake
   2. How many animals did Jodie offer Zara?
      a one   b two   c four
   3. Zara's dad decided to buy something in a pet shop. How much was it?
      a £15   b £25   c £50
   4. What did Zara's dad want her to do?
      a take the cat outside
      b feed it
      c give it water

YOUR WORLD

5. Which animal would you like as a pet? Why? Discuss in groups. Use the phrases below to help you.
   They're fun/clean/quiet/boring/dirty/noisy …
   You can/can't …
   You need to/don't need to …

   I'd like to have a snake. They're quiet and they don't scratch the furniture.

QUESTION OF THE WEEK
What pet can I get?

Zara has a problem. She lives in a small city centre apartment, but she wants a pet. She doesn't have any allergies, but she hates getting up early! As a busy teenager, Zara doesn't have much free time, either.

Cats are cute and clean, but they scratch the furniture, and some people have an allergy to cats. They're fun to play with when they're little kittens, but they aren't so sociable when they grow up.

Dogs are fun. You can play with them, and they protect your home, but you need to train them and take them for a walk. They're great friends, but they feel bad if you don't spend time with them.

Snakes are quiet, and you don't need to take them for a walk. But you can't play with them much, and they eat live animals. They're beautiful, but some people are frightened of them.

I can understand a conversation about pets.

3.6 Speaking
Apologising and responding to apologies

VIDEO ▶ **WORKING WITH ANIMALS**

Mum: Hi! It's nice to see you! I'm glad you're here. We need more volunteers. You can clean these cages. Then feed the animals.
Mateo: Sure. OK, Mum. I'm good at cleaning cages. Lena, can you do the food?
Lena: Of course. So this is the guinea pig food and this is the rabbit food.
Mateo: Yes. Put two spoons in each bowl. Easy.

A few minutes later …

Mateo: Hang on, this looks like guinea pig food.
Lena: Oops! Did I put the wrong food bowls in the cages?
Mateo: You did? Honestly, Lena!
Lena: I'm really sorry. It all looked the same to me.
Mateo: Never mind. No problem. Just change the bowls now.
Lena: Good call.
Mateo: Right. Where is the clean bedding for the rabbits? Aha. Got it! This box's enormous!
Lena: Hey, mind out! Oh, now look. There's bedding all over the floor!
Mateo: Sorry, I didn't mean to do that.
Lena: Don't worry. Just be more careful.
Mateo: What a mess!
Lena: Mateo, do you really want to work with animals? It isn't easy, you know.

SOUNDS GOOD! Good call. • Mind out! • What a mess!

1 ▶ 18 🔊 3.14 Describe the photo. How do you think Mateo and Lena are feeling? Watch or listen and check.

2 Where are Mateo and Lena helping as volunteers? What activities do they do?

SET FOR LIFE

3 How can you help animals as a volunteer? Discuss in groups. Use the ideas below to help you.
- help in your local animal centre
- take your neighbour's dog for a walk
- organise a charity event

4 Study the Speaking box. Find examples of the phrases in the dialogue.

SPEAKING | **Apologising and responding to apologies**

Apologising
I'm (really/so) sorry.
I didn't mean to do that/it.
I feel terrible.

Responding to apologies
Never mind.
No problem.
Don't worry.
Honestly!
That's all right.
Just be more careful.

5 🔊 3.15 Use the Speaking box to complete the dialogues. Sometimes more than one answer is possible. Listen and check.

1 A: Excuse me. I think you're sitting in my seat. I have a reservation.
   B: _____ . I didn't realise!
   A: No problem!
2 A: _____ . I didn't hear you. Could you repeat that?
   B: No problem. It's J-O-R-G-E.
3 A: I'm sorry I'm late! My bus didn't arrive on time.
   B: _____ . The buses are terrible these days!

YOUR WORLD

6 In pairs, role play one of these situations. Use the Speaking box to help you.
- You forgot a friend's birthday.
- You lost someone's book.
- You took someone's pen by accident.

Unit 3 — I can make and respond to apologies.

3.7 Writing
A blog entry

My holiday memories by Patricia Gallego

1. Last year I went on holiday to South Africa with my family.

2. On the last day of our holiday, we went on a safari! I was very excited in the morning because I really wanted to see an elephant.

   The safari started after lunch. We saw lots of wild animals: giraffes, zebras, birds and many different insects. But there weren't any elephants, so I felt sad.

   Then, our guide pointed at a group of animals behind some trees. We all stopped and listened. There was a loud noise, then I saw them. Elephants! They didn't look happy or friendly, so I was frightened at first. But the guide explained everything to us. The elephants weren't aggressive, they were playful! I was surprised, but I took some great photos.

3. It was the best experience ever!

1 Read the blog quickly and answer the questions.
   1. Where was Patricia?
   2. Who was she with?
   3. What wild animals did she see?
   4. How did she feel when she first saw the elephants?

2 Look at the blog again. Find all the examples of verbs in the Past Simple. Are they regular or irregular?

3 Study the Writing box. Find examples of the phrases in the blog.

> **WRITING** — A blog entry (a personal account)
>
> 1. **Say when the situation/event happened**
>   In 2018, I was …   Last year/Two years ago, I …
>
> 2. **Describe what happened and how you felt**
>   We looked for …   I took photos.   We saw …
>   I was very excited.
>   After that, I felt sad.
>   The birds were beautiful.
>
> 3. **Say what you think about the situation/event**
>   It was the best experience ever!
>   We had an amazing time.

4 Study the Language box. Find examples of linking words in the blog.

> **LANGUAGE** Linking words
> - Use *and* to add information.
> - Use *or* to give two options.
> - Use *so* to show results.
> - Use *but* to contrast information.
> - Use *because* to give reasons.

5 Complete the sentences with the linking words in the Language box.
   1. I don't like spiders *or* snakes.
   2. I didn't have a camera, _____ I took some photos with my phone.
   3. I went to Africa _____ I wanted to see elephants.
   4. We saw parrots _____ monkeys in the trees.
   5. My dad hates cats, _____ they love him!

WRITING TIME

6 Write a blog entry about a special memory. Try to include an animal in your blog.

1. **Find ideas**
   Make notes about a special memory.
   - Where were you?
   - Who was there?
   - What happened?

2. **Plan**
   Organise your ideas into paragraphs. Use Patricia's blog to help you.

3. **Write and share**
   - Write a draft blog entry. Use the Language box and the Writing box to help you.
   - Share your entry with another student for feedback.
   - Write the final version of your blog.

4. **Check**
   - Check language: are the linking words (*and, or, so, but, because*) correct?
   - Check grammar: did you use a variety of verbs in the Past Simple?

I can write a blog entry.

Vocabulary Activator

WORDLIST 🔊 3.16

Animals
ant (n)
bee (n)
butterfly (n)
chicken (n)
cow (n)
donkey (n)
goat (n)
gorilla (n)
guinea pig (n)
horse (n)
kangaroo (n)
ladybird (n)
leopard (n)
owl (n)
parrot (n)
polar bear (n)
rabbit (n)
shark (n)
snake (n)
tortoise (n)

Animal body parts
beak (n)
claw (n)
feather (n)
fur (n)
paw (n)
tail (n)
wing (n)

Personality
adventurous (adj)
aggressive (adj)
lively (adj)
playful (adj)
sociable (adj)

Word friends
(looking after pets)
brush his/her fur
buy food for him/her
feed him/her
put fresh water in his/her bowl
spend time with him/her
take him/her for a walk
train him/her

Extra words
animal charity (n)
aquarium (n)
be frightened of
bedding (n)
behaviour (n)
brown bear (n)
cage (n)
cat (n)
catch (v)
clean (v)
colourful (adj)
cute (adj)
dangerous (adj)
elephant (n)
farm animal (n)
food bowl (n)
giraffe (n)
hamster (n)
insect (n)
kitten (n)
live (v)
live animal (n)
lizard (n)
look after a pet
lovable (adj)
monkey (n)
penguin (n)
pet (n)
pick up (v)
play with a pet
raccoon (n)
rescue centre (n)
safari (n)
scratch the furniture
sharp (adj)
skin (n)
sloth (n)
spider monkey (n)
stripe (n)
teeth (n)
tiger (n)
toe (n)
toucan (n)
vet (n)
volunteer (n)
wild animal (n)
work with animals
zebra (n)
zoo (n)

1 Use words from the wordlist to find these things.
1 six animals that have paws *guinea pig, …*
2 five animals that have wings
3 seven animals over one metre high or long
4 two things you do with a farm animal, but not with a wild animal

2 Choose the correct answer.

Animal QUIZ

1 Which animal has claws?
   a horse   b guinea pig   c shark   d goat
2 Which animal lives in very cold places?
   a shark   b polar bear   c bee   d snake
3 Which of these adjectives has a negative meaning?
   a aggressive   b adventurous   c lively   d playful
4 Which body part don't birds have?
   a beak   b feather   c claw   d fur
5 Which of these things don't you need to do with a pet cat?
   a feed it   b spend time with it
   c train it   d take it for a walk

3 In pairs, say the names of two animals from the wordlist that you think:
1 make good pets for a child.
2 are aggressive.
3 are easy to train.
4 are nice to spend time with.

4 Imagine you are looking after your friend's pet. Use words from the wordlist to say how you look after the animal.

I'm looking after Sofia's parrot. I'm cleaning its cage …

5 🔊 3.17 **PRONUNCIATION** Complete the sentences with the words below. Use the words that rhyme with the words in bold. Then listen, check and repeat.

| claws   ~~polar bear~~   sharks   snake   wing |

1 **There** was a *polar bear* on the **chair** over **there**.
2 A **tortoise** has _____ , but it doesn't have **paws**.
3 There aren't any _____ in our local **parks**.
4 A **butterfly's** _____ is a beautiful **thing**.
5 It's time for the _____ to take a **break**.

Revision

Vocabulary

1 Write the names of animals for the definitions.

1 It can jump more than nine metres. It's from Australia. *kangaroo*
2 It's a dangerous sea animal. It's got very sharp teeth.
3 It's a small animal. People often keep it as a pet. It looks like a mouse.
4 It's a small insect. It's got six legs and can carry very heavy things.
5 It's an insect. It can make honey.
6 It's a large cat. It can run at about sixty kilometres per hour.
7 It's an insect. Its wings can be many different colours.

2 Complete the adjectives in the sentences.
1 Judie enjoys taking risks and doing extreme sports. She's a *dventurous*.
2 Bob often shouts at people and starts fights. He's quite a _____.
3 Monica is very active and always has lots of energy. She's very l_____.
4 Sue likes fun things, for example games and jokes. She's p_____.
5 Chris enjoys spending time with other people. He's very s_____.

3 Complete the sentences with the verbs below. Then, in pairs, say if you agree with the sentences.

| buy   feed   put   spend   take   ~~train~~ |

1 It's difficult to *train* a dog to lie down.
2 You need to _____ a dog for a walk twice a day.
3 It's a good idea to _____ a lot of time with your pet.
4 Make sure you _____ fresh water in a bowl every day.
5 It isn't important to go to a pet shop to _____ pet food.
6 Always _____ your pet with the right food.

Grammar

4 Complete the sentences with *was*, *wasn't*, *were* or *weren't*.

Jonathan the giant tortoise

- ¹*Was* Jonathan born in the USA?
  No, he ² _____ . He ³ _____ born on the island of St Helena in the South Atlantic.

- ⁴ _____ there lots of very old tortoises on the island?
  No, there ⁵ _____ . The other tortoises ⁶ _____ young – between thirty and fifty.

- So how old ⁷ _____ Jonathan on his last birthday?
  He ⁸ _____ about 190 years old.

5 Complete the text with the Past Simple form of the verbs below.

| arrive   eat   ~~go~~   not enjoy   not explain   see   stay   watch |

On Saturday my friends and I ¹*went* to a wildlife park. We ² _____ there at 11 a.m. and we ³ _____ there all day. We ⁴ _____ birds, like owls and eagles, and wild animals like monkeys. Then we ⁵ _____ our picnic lunch by a lake. After lunch, we ⁶ _____ a film about animals in danger, but I ⁷ _____ it very much.

Speaking

6 In pairs, role play the situations. Student A, look below. Student B, go to page 138.

Student A
- Student B is sitting in your seat at the cinema. Respond to his/her apology.
- You are late to meet Student B. Apologise.
- Student B dropped your new guitar. Respond to his/her apology.
- You forgot to feed Student B's pet. Apologise.

Dictation

7 🔊 3.18 Listen. Then listen again and write down what you hear during each pause.

45 Unit 3

BBC CULTURE

Perfect pets

A

B

PETS AROUND THE WORLD

For a long time, people used animals for food and for work. Today, many of us keep animals in our homes as pets. Cats and dogs are very popular pets in many countries. For example, in the UK there are nearly eleven million pet cats! Here are some other popular pets from around the world that you might find surprising.

China
People in China like many different animals, but one very popular pet is the goldfish. For Chinese people, the colour gold means money, and they believe goldfish are lucky. Some people say that goldfish have a bad memory, but it isn't true! They can remember when it's time for their food.

Japan
In Japan, they like keeping rabbits. They're gentle animals with soft fur, but when they're angry or frightened, they get aggressive and tap their feet on the ground loudly! They're also very small, which is important for people who live in small apartments.

The USA
Snakes are popular in the USA. They can live up to forty years, and people don't need to feed them a lot. They don't usually move very much, and some snakes sleep all the time during the cold months of the year. Most pet snakes are born in special centres. They're not dangerous or poisonous – unlike the snakes in the wild!

gentle (adj) not strong or violent
in the wild (phr) living free in nature
tap (v) hit lightly

1 In pairs, discuss the questions.
  1 What is happening in the photos?
  2 Do you have a pet? If not, would you like one? Why?/Why not?
  3 Do any of your friends have an unusual pet? Can you describe it?
  4 Why do people keep pets?

2 Match pets 1–3 with countries a–c where you think they are popular.
  1 ☐ rabbit   a China
  2 ☐ snake   b Japan
  3 ☐ goldfish   c The USA

3 🔊 3.19 Read the article and check your answers to Exercise 2.

4 Read the article again and answer the questions.
  Which animal …
  1 brings you good luck?
  2 sometimes makes a noise with its feet?
  3 lives for a long time?
  4 knows when it's time for a meal?
  5 sleeps a lot?

5 In pairs, discuss the advantages and disadvantages of each pet. Which (if any) is the perfect pet for your family? Why?
  A goldfish doesn't cost much to feed, but it's a bit boring.

BBC Wild at heart

6 Look at the photo of another pet. In pairs, discuss the questions.
1 What is this pet?
2 What abilities does it have? What can it do?

7 ▶ 19 Watch a video about pet behaviour and check your answers to Exercise 6. Number the pets below in the order that you see them.
☐ puppy ☐ parrot ☐ hamster

8 ▶ 19 Watch again and choose the correct option.
1 Dogs always need to *work / fight* with other dogs in their group.
2 Hamsters run fast to *hunt / run away from* other animals.
3 Hamsters put a lot of food in their mouths to *share with other animals / eat later*.
4 Some birds copy the 'language' of *their / another* group of birds.

9 (VISIBLE THINKING) In pairs, follow these steps.
WHY DO YOU SAY THAT?
1 Study the discussion question and choose your opinion.

Do you think it's a good idea to keep a pet?

Opinion: *Yes, I do. / I'm not sure. / No, I don't.*

2 Tick (✓) the reasons that you can use to support your opinion about keeping a pet. Can you add two more reasons for your opinion?
a ☐ Pets can be like friends to people.
b ☐ Animals are happier in the wild.
c ☐ You can learn about animal behaviour.
d ☐ They are expensive.

3 In pairs, discuss if it's a good idea to keep a pet. Give your opinion and all your reasons.

A: Do you think it's a good idea to keep a pet?
B: Yes, I do.
A: Why do you say that?

PROJECT TIME

10 In groups of three, prepare a digital presentation about a popular pet in your country. Follow these steps.

1 In groups, choose a popular animal. Decide who in your group can find the answers to these questions.
- Where does the animal originally come from? What does it look like? What can it do?
- How many people have the animal as a pet? Why is it popular?
- How do you look after this animal? What does it eat? What does it like doing?

2 Individually, create your part of the presentation.
- Find the information and photos for the slideshow.
- Decide on a title for each slide.
- Write a short text for each slide and add the photos.

3 In your group, create your presentation. You can use a presentation program.
- Put the slides together and think of a title for the presentation.
- Check and edit your presentation.
- Practise giving the presentation as a group.

4 Show your presentation to the class.
- Answer other students' questions.
- Listen to the other presentations. Ask questions.

Progress Check Units 1–3

Vocabulary and Grammar

1 Complete the second sentence with the word in bold so that it means the same as the first one. Use no more than four words.

1 I think it's relaxing to watch films with friends. **FEEL**
   I _feel relaxed_ when I watch films with friends.
2 He was very interested in art and painting. **INTO**
   He _____ art and painting.
3 She found that reading poetry was boring. **GOT**
   She _____ when she read poetry.
4 Yesterday we went to the theatre, not the cinema. **GO**
   Yesterday we _____ to the cinema, we went to the theatre.
5 I watch soap operas on Fridays and Sundays. **TWICE**
   I watch soap operas _____ .

2 Complete the text with one word in each gap.

When I ^{1} _was_ twelve, my grandma gave me two baby rabbits for my birthday. They ^{2}_____ very small and really cute. Now they're bigger, but they're still amazing. Their names are Fluffy and Snowy. They're quite easy to look after. I feed them and I brush them ^{3}_____ day. I also have to clean their cage and buy food ^{4}_____ them. Mum has an allergy to fur, so she ^{5}_____ brushes them. My brother also wanted to get a pet. ^{6}_____ weekend Mum took him to the pet shop and got him a fish.

3 Complete the text with the correct form of the words in brackets.

Some people say teens are too much into technology, but I disagree. In my free time I watch video clips of my favourite ^{1}_musicians_ (**MUSIC**) like Lorde or Lana Del Rey on my phone. For school projects I watch ^{2}_____ (**DOCUMENT**) on my computer. I also use my computer for shopping. Last week I bought some new ^{3}_____ (**TRAIN**) from an online sports shop. I like talking to my friends on my phone. My best friend, Charlie, is a very ^{4}_____ (**CHAT**) person, so we talk for hours! I get ^{5}_____ (**ANNOY**) when people say teens use too much tech. It isn't true.

Speaking

4 Complete the dialogue with the words below. There is one extra word.

| ~~about~~ ask because believe |
| realise sorry worry |

A: How do you feel ^{1}_about_ game shows?
B: If you ^{2}_____ me, they're awful.
A: Don't say that! I really like game shows.
B: I'm ^{3}_____ . Maybe they are OK.
A: Well, I'm feeling excited ^{4}_____ my mum's on a game show today.
B: I don't ^{5}_____ it! You're kidding. Sorry again!
A: Don't ^{6}_____ . Do you want to come and watch the show?
B: OK. Maybe I'll like it after all!

5 In pairs, follow the instructions.
Student A: Go to page 138.
Student B: Go to page 144.

Listening

6 Does your school have a website? What things are interesting for a school website?

7 🔊 PC1–3.1 Listen to the dialogue. Match students 1–4 with things they do for the website a–f. There are two extra answers.

1 ☐ Julia   a design
2 ☐ Natalie   b chief editor
3 ☐ Theo   c photography
4 ☐ Arlo   d articles
                   e animal blog
                   f games blog

Reading

Wear it and feel it

Do you always wear black or white? Or do you choose clothes in different colours for different days? Maybe we don't know why we choose different colours, but read on to see how colours can change the way you feel.

Blue helps you to relax when you are stressed. It can also help your creativity. Put on a comfortable blue tracksuit and start painting or writing! But be careful. Blue is a cold colour, so if you feel sad, don't wear your blue hoodie. Choose a green one instead. The colour of trees is also relaxing and makes us think of nature.

Red and pink are the colours of love, but red is more energetic, so wear your favourite red dress when you go out with friends. Everyone will want to talk to you! But red can also make you hungry for junk food, so don't wear a red T-shirt every day!

Do you feel tired in the morning? Put on a yellow sweater. Yellow is the colour of the sun. It gives you energy and it can wake you up. Experts say yellow also makes us feel clever, so why not wear a yellow scarf or necklace when you have exams?

Finally, black and white. White helps you feel more confident. It is useful because it goes with everything! Black is a strong colour that can help a shy person feel confident too. Put on your black jeans when you are meeting someone new and match them with a white T-shirt.

8 Answer the questions. Then compare your answers with the class.
1 What are your favourite colours of clothes?
2 How do you feel when you wear clothes in these colours?

9 Read the article and complete the sentences with a word or a short phrase in each gap.
1 These two colours can help you feel more relaxed: *blue and green* .
2 These two colours make you feel full of energy: _____ .
3 If you go to an exam, wear something in this colour: _____ .
4 These colours can help you if you are shy: _____ .

10 Read the article again and choose the correct answer.
1 What does the writer say about clothes and colours?
   a We have too many choices.
   b They can change our feelings.
   c We always know why we choose them.
2 Why is it good to paint or write in blue clothes?
   a Because they make you creative.
   b Because blue is a colour of nature.
   c Because blue always makes you happy.
3 Why are red clothes a bad thing to wear every day?
   a They can make you fall in love.
   b They can take away your energy.
   c They can make you want to eat more.
4 What do experts say about the colour yellow?
   a It is good for us on sunny days.
   b It makes us feel tired.
   c It makes us feel intelligent.
5 Why is white a useful colour?
   a It is good for any meeting.
   b It matches all other colours.
   c It makes you feel strong.

Writing

11 Tick (✓) the shows and performances that you like.
☐ dance shows   ☐ street theatre
☐ films at the cinema ☐ plays at the theatre
☐ open-air concerts

12 Write a blog entry about a show or performance that you saw. Include the information below.
• where and when you went
• what you saw
• how you felt

Cool tech!

4

VOCABULARY
Digital devices | Using technology |
Computer equipment | Phrasal verbs |
Favourite websites | Computer problems

GRAMMAR
Used to | Verb patterns

Tech Users in My Family

What kind of tech users are your family members? Do they like using new gadgets or are they afraid of them? Read about the tech users in my family.

A The Influencer

Two years ago, I got a new smartphone with a great digital camera. I use it to make video clips that I post on my YouTube channel. I've got thousands of followers! If you'd like to hear more about my tech family, watch my video blog!

B The New User

My granny Betty is crazy about sport. She never used a lot of technology until she got a new smartphone. Now she makes workout videos herself!

C The Mindful User

My sister Lily hasn't got any social media accounts and she doesn't really use her smartphone. She prefers to meet her friends in town instead of sending messages. She only uses tech to join her online classes at college or look for information.

D The Players

My parents love playing video games. On Saturdays, they take out their games console and play different games. They always have a lot of fun! It's funny because my sister and I aren't into gaming so much.

4.1 Vocabulary
Technology

1 🔊 4.1 Study Vocabulary box A. Which of the devices can you find in photos A–D?

VOCABULARY A | **Digital devices**

Bluetooth® speaker   digital camera   games console
handsfree headset   phone charger   smartphone
smartwatch   wireless earbuds

2 Read the blog on page 50. In pairs, ask and answer the questions.
1. Which devices from Vocabulary box A do you and your family members use?
2. What kind of tech users are they? Think of tech names for them.

3 🔊 4.2 **WORD FRIENDS** Check you understand the phrases below. In pairs, ask and answer the questions.

charge your phone	look for information
check social media	make video clips
check the time	phone a friend
download apps	play online games
join an online class	send texts/messages
listen to music/podcasts	take photos

1. Which devices from Vocabulary box A can you use for these activities?
   You can use a smartphone to make video clips.
2. How often do you do these things?
   I check my social media a lot.
3. When did you last do them?
   I sent three messages before breakfast this morning.

4 🔊 4.3 Study Vocabulary box B. In pairs, find five of the words. Check you understand them.

VOCABULARY B **Computer equipment**

keyboard   memory   microphone   printer
scanner   screen   touchscreen   USB cable

WATCH OUT!
Do you play online games? – adjective
Do you play online? – adverb

5 Do the quiz in Exercise 4. Tick (✓) the sentences that are true for you. In pairs, compare your answers.

6 🔊 4.4 Complete the text with words from Vocabulary box B. Listen and check.

My favourite device

A few years ago, I had a desktop computer, a laptop and a tablet, but now I only use my smartphone. The ¹*touchscreen* has a great picture and it's easier to use than a computer mouse and ² _____ . The sound on my phone is great too. The ³ _____ is so good that I don't need to hold the phone next to my mouth when I speak. I can use a ⁴ _____ or Bluetooth® to connect my phone to a ⁵ _____ or scanner to print or scan documents. The phone has 512 GB of ⁶ _____ , so there's plenty of space. Who needs a computer?

Are you tech clever?

1. ☐ I can write messages without looking at the keyboard.
2. ☐ I stay calm when my computer (or printer or scanner) stops working.
3. ☐ I ask how much memory a phone or tablet has before I buy it.
4. ☐ I take regular breaks from looking at my computer screen or touchscreen.
5. ☐ I use a wireless headset to play games online.
6. ☐ I speak quietly when I use my phone in public.
7. ☐ I never play online games late at night.

Four or more ticks (✓) means you are tech clever.

YOUR WORLD

7 Which of the activities in Exercise 3 do you usually do on a computer and which do you do on your phone? Discuss in pairs.
I usually use my phone to check social media and to send messages, but I prefer to use a computer to make video clips.

4.2 Grammar

Used to

VIDEO ▶ **WE DIDN'T USE TO HAVE PHONES**

Gran: Here are your drinks.
Adam: Thanks.
Gran: Funny weather today, isn't it?
Lena: Mmm, thanks.
Gran: Are you listening to me? When you were little, we used to talk when you came to visit. You used to ask me questions. You were interested in the world!
Lena: We are interested in the world.
Gran: You didn't use to be on your phones all day.
Lena: That's because we didn't use to have phones.
Gran: When I was your age, we didn't have a phone in our house. We had to walk to the phone box at the end of the street. We didn't use to have emails or text messages or …
Adam: How did you use to communicate?
Gran: We used to write letters.
Adam: Did you use to send postcards too?
Gran: Yes, we did. The postman used to bring us letters almost every day. The problem today is you young people are addicted to your phones. OK, let's go to the shops!
Lena: What for?

Gran: Look at that! They've got the new model of this phone!
Lena: But you only got that phone last year!
Adam: Gran, you're addicted!

1 ▶ 20 ◆) 4.5 Describe the photo. Why is Gran unhappy? Watch or listen and check.

2 Study the Grammar box. Find more examples of *used to* in the dialogue.

GRAMMAR *Used to*

We use *used to* to talk about habits and states that were true in the past, but are not true anymore.

+	We used to talk when you came to visit.	
−	We didn't use to have phones.	
?	Did you use to send postcards?	Yes, we did. No, we didn't.
	How did you use to communicate?	

GRAMMAR TIME ▶ PAGE 129

3 ◆) 4.6 Rewrite the sentences with the correct form of *used to*. Listen and check.
1 Lena doesn't enjoy doing jigsaw puzzles anymore.
   Lena used to enjoy doing jigsaw puzzles.
2 Lena likes video games now, but she didn't before.
3 Adam has a tablet now, but he didn't before.
4 Mateo doesn't watch TV all the time anymore.
5 Mateo studies hard these days, but he didn't before.

4 Make questions from the prompts below and *used to*. In pairs, ask and answer the questions.
1 Lena and Adam / ask Gran questions / about the world / ?
2 Lena and Adam / have phones / ?
3 how / Gran / communicate / ?
4 the postman / bring a lot of letters / ?

A: *Did Lena and Adam use to ask Gran questions about the world?*
B: *Yes, they did.*

5 Write sentences with *used to* to explain why these sentences are false.
1 Marco Polo went to China in a helicopter in the 13th century.
   People didn't use to travel by helicopter then.
2 I have a photograph of the moment when Columbus first arrived in America in 1492.
3 Isaac Newton used an electronic calculator in the 1680s.
4 In 1898 Marie Curie sent a text to her husband saying 'I discovered radium! ☺'
5 Shakespeare wrote his plays on a tablet.

YOUR WORLD

6 How was your life different ten or five years ago? Write down three sentences with *used to*. Then tell your partner.

I used to play all the time ten years ago.

4.3 Reading and Vocabulary
Technological innovations

1 🔊 **4.7** The Mobile World Congress is the world's largest exhibition for the mobile phone industry. Do you know what these innovations are? Read the report and check.

> face recognition glasses   flexible screens   flying drone taxis
> long-lasting batteries   robot musicians   waterproof phones

2 Read the report again and choose the correct answer.
1. What did the writer of the text do at the MWC?
   a. She looked at the new technology.
   b. She bought some clothes there.
   c. She presented a new phone.
2. What kind of text is this?
   a. An advertisement for the MWC.
   b. Instructions for the visitors to the MWC.
   c. A report about the MWC.

3 Read the report again and complete the notes with a word or a short phrase in each gap.

1. Where: _Barcelona_
2. When: _____
3. Number of visitors: _____
4. How long it lasts: _____
5. A device that can identify people you see: _____
6. Thanks to this you can wear a phone on your body or clothes: _____
7. The length of time the phone battery lasts without charging: _____

4 🔊 **4.8** **WORD FRIENDS** Match the highlighted phrasal verbs in the report with the definitions. Listen and check.
1. Discovered something. _found out_
2. Ended a phone call.
3. Look at something to see what it's like.
4. Wore something to see what it was like.
5. Started an electrical device.

5 Complete the questions with the correct form of the phrasal verbs in Exercise 4. In pairs, ask and answer the questions.
1. What's the first electronic gadget you _switch on_ every morning?
2. What's the last thing you say on the phone before you _____?
3. What was the last video that you _____ online?
4. What's the best way to _____ information about the right phone for you?
5. Do you always _____ clothes before you buy them?

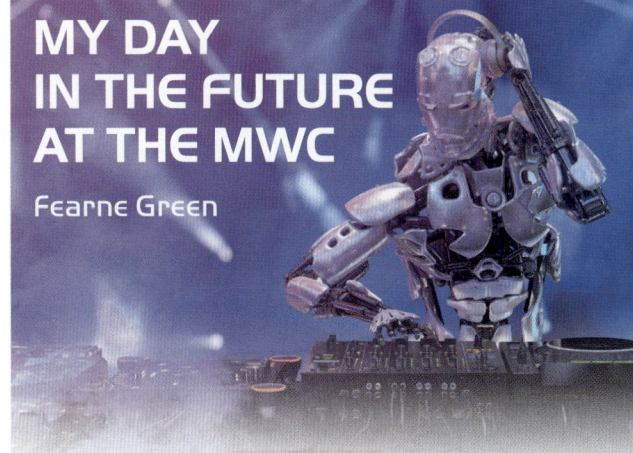

MY DAY IN THE FUTURE AT THE MWC
Fearne Green

Last week, I found out about the future of phones at the MWC.

The Mobile World Congress is the world's largest exhibition for the mobile phone industry. It used to take place in France, but now it takes place in Barcelona every February or March. This year I was one of 100,000 people there to check out the latest gadgets and technology.

It was a fantastic four-day-long experience. I heard robots playing music and I wore face recognition glasses that tell you the name of everyone you look at. I also flew in a flying drone taxi without a pilot. Scary!

Flexible screens that bend like paper were big again this year. I saw a phone that you wear around your arm and I tried on a T-shirt that can show videos on its screen.

In one place, they switched on a phone and put it in a tank full of water. It was one hundred percent waterproof. In another, they hit a phone with a hammer to show how tough the screen is.

The congress was amazing. I saw some wonderful innovations and others that are less practical. For example, I made a call on a phone with a battery that works for fifty days before you need to charge it! Unfortunately, it's three centimetres thick and really heavy, so I hung up and used my own, light phone to call a taxi home.

6 **YOUR WORLD** In groups, discuss one of the questions below. Then report your answers to the class.
- Which innovations in the report on the MWC do you really like? Which ones are not so interesting?
- What innovations would you like to see in mobile phone technology in the future?

I can understand a report about new technologies.

4.4 Grammar
Verb patterns

1. How do you feel when you do not have your phone with you?

2. 🔊 4.9 Read the text. Why does Jen think she is addicted to her phone?

Can you live without your phone?

Jen, 15

I use my phone from the minute I wake up. I don't mind talking to people face to face, but I prefer texting friends. I also enjoy following my favourite sports stars online. But I would like to spend less time on my phone. I don't know why I need to check my social media pages every few minutes. I try to switch it off sometimes. But the thing is, I can't stand being without my phone. I hate it when I forget to charge it and the battery dies. I think I'm probably addicted to my phone.

3. Study the Grammar box. Find more examples of these verb patterns in Jen's text.

GRAMMAR Verb patterns

- We use **to** + **the infinitive** after these verbs:
  agree, decide, forget, learn, need, remember, try, want, would/'d like
  I *try to switch* it *off* sometimes.

- We use **verb** + **-ing** after these verbs:
  can't stand, don't mind, enjoy, finish, hate, keep, like, love, prefer, stop
  I *prefer texting* friends.

GRAMMAR TIME ▶ PAGE 130

4. Choose the correct option. In pairs, say if the sentences are true for you.
   1. I enjoy *to try / trying* new apps on my smartphone.
   2. I hate *to be / being* without my phone.
   3. I would like *to buy / buying* a new smartphone.
   4. I sometimes forget *to charge / charging* my phone.
   5. I don't mind *to text / texting*, but I can't stand *to make / making* phone calls.

5. 🔊 4.10 Complete the text with the correct form of the verbs in brackets. Listen and check.

   I hate ¹*checking* (check) my phone all the time. That's why at New Year I decided ² _____ (stop) using it in the evenings. That was six months ago. Sometimes I still forget ³ _____ (switch) it off, but usually I remember ⁴ _____ (do) it. I used to be bored in the evenings, but now I enjoy ⁵ _____ (read) books and I'm trying ⁶ _____ (learn) how to dance. My sister agreed ⁷ _____ (teach) me. I like ⁸ _____ (have) a phone, but I love ⁹ _____ (spend) time offline too.

6. In pairs, complete the text with the correct form of the verbs in brackets. Which app do you like?

   Taylor describes her favourite new apps

   Noshinarush
   I don't like ¹*cooking* (cook) much, so I love ² _____ (order) food with this app. It's easy to use and it's quick!

   Sing Sweetly
   I'm learning ³ _____ (sing) – I want ⁴ _____ (be) the next Adele! This app is like a personal music teacher. I really enjoy ⁵ _____ (use) it. It's great!

   Chimp Notes
   I use this app when I need ⁶ _____ (organise) my notes. It isn't free, but I don't mind ⁷ _____ (pay) for good apps.

   Internet Bolt
   It isn't easy for me to stop ⁸ _____ (waste) time online. So this app is really useful. It's a shame I keep ⁹ _____ (forget) I have it!

7. In pairs, ask and answer the questions. **YOUR WORLD**
   - What are your favourite apps? Why?
   - Why are they useful?

   My favourite app is … It's fun. I use it to …

4.5 Listening and Vocabulary
Favourite websites

1 In pairs, read the Life Online survey and answer the question.

You can use YouTube to view videos. I use it a lot.

2 🔊 4.11 **WORD FRIENDS** Complete the text with the correct form of the highlighted verbs in the survey. Listen and check.

I needed to find a program for making films, so I ¹*searched* the web and found one. I ² _____ on the link and saw it was free, so I ³ _____ the program. After I finished making my film, I wanted to ⁴ _____ it with other people, so I ⁵ _____ my video clip to a video-sharing website. In the first week, 300 people ⁶ _____ my video. Now hundreds of people ⁷ _____ me on social media, and I enjoy ⁸ _____ online with some of them.

3 🔊 4.12 Listen to Part 1 of a radio programme. Complete the notes with a word or a short phrase in each gap.

YouTube
- It started in ¹*February 2005*.
- The first video was ² _____ long.
- In ³ _____ Google agreed to buy it for $1.65 billion.
- Every ⁴ _____ people watch over a thousand million hours of videos.
- Every minute people upload over ⁵ _____ hours of videos.
- There are YouTube websites in almost ⁶ _____ languages.

4 🔊 4.13 Listen to Part 2 of the programme and choose the correct answer.
1. Upload is a
   a computer program.   b radio programme.
   c website.
2. Alex likes YouTube because
   a it shows many different kinds of videos.
   b it's always funny.
   c he likes watching famous people.
3. What are the most popular kinds of videos on YouTube?
   a sports   b comedy shows   c music videos
4. How many views does one of the most popular YouTube music videos have?
   a 2 billion   b 7 billion   c 8 billion
5. What did Alex and his son make with the help of a video tutorial?
   a a computer program   b a speaker
   c a phone

Life Online

Which websites and social media sites can you use to do these things?

- **view** and **download** videos or **upload** your own videos
- buy and sell things
- keep in touch with friends and **chat** online
- **search** the web for other websites that interest you
- read articles and **click** on links to find out more information
- **share** photos and videos
- write micro blogs and **follow** people you like

VIDEO ▶ **WIDER WORLD**

5 ▶ 21 Watch three people talking about their favourite websites. Write down the names of the websites and why the people like them.

Michael's favourite website is Facebook. He likes it because …

6 In pairs, ask and answer the questions about your favourite websites.
- What kind of website is it?
- What can you do on it?
- How popular is it?
- Do you know how and when it started?
- How often do you visit it?
- Why do you like visiting it?

My favourite website is Instagram. You can use it to …

I can understand a radio interview about a popular website.

4.6 Speaking
Talking about technology problems

VIDEO ▶ THE COMPUTER CRASHED

Mateo: Aargh no! The computer crashed. It isn't working.
Noah: You need to press Control-Alt-Delete.
Mateo: OK, let's try … No, that didn't work.
Noah: Try switching it off and on again.
Mateo: No … the screen's frozen. How about calling Mia?
Noah: Good idea … Oh! No answer.
Mateo: Let's search online. What's your wi-fi password?
Noah: Em … Password.
Mateo: Seriously? … OK, shall we look for a blog, an online forum or the FAQs on this website?
Noah: Have a look at that video!

Twenty minutes later. Noah's phone rings.

Mia: Hi Noah, why did you call?
Noah: My computer crashed. We thought you could help, but we watched a video online and fixed it ourselves!
Mia: Good for you. So you don't need me?
Noah: No, thanks, we're fine … Oh no! The computer crashed again! Mia? Can you help us? Please!
Mia: OK. Give me ten minutes.

SOUNDS GOOD! • Good for you. • Seriously?

1 ▶ 22 ◀)) 4.14 Watch or listen. What problems did the boys have and what solutions did they find?

SET FOR LIFE

2 What can you do when you have a problem? In groups, order the ideas. Is it a good plan?
- ☐ ask someone for help
- ☐ choose the best idea
- ☐ decide what the problem is
- ☐ think of possible solutions together

3 Study the Speaking box. Find examples of the phrases in the dialogue.

SPEAKING Talking about technology problems

You need to switch it off and on again/charge it.
You need to press Control-Alt-Delete.
Let me/Let's try (something).
Look at the FAQs (Frequently Asked Questions) on this website.
Let's search online (for a solution).
How about calling …?
Shall we look for a blog or an online forum?

4 ◀)) 4.15 **WORD FRIENDS** In pairs, check you understand the sentences below.
The battery died.
The computer crashed/isn't working.
The internet connection is slow.
The mouse/printer doesn't work.
The screen's frozen.

5 ◀)) 4.16 Complete the dialogues with one word in each gap. Listen and check.
1. A: The screen's *frozen*.
   B: Let me _____ something … No, that didn't work. Shall we look _____ a blog?
2. A: The internet _____ is slow. I can't download this video.
   B: Let's _____ online for a solution.
3. A: Oh no! My computer _____ !
   B: You need to _____ it off and on again.
   A: I tried that, but it isn't _____ .
   B: How about _____ a computer helpline?

6 Work in pairs. Student A, go to page 139. Student B, go to page 144.

YOUR WORLD

7 In pairs, think about three problems with technology. Talk about them and suggest solutions.
A: I broke the screen on my phone.
B: Let's search online for a solution.

Unit 4 · 56 · I can talk about technology problems.

4.7 Writing
A review of a gadget

A personal blog on the digital world

CONNECT WITH CALLUM

Read my reviews of apps, games and gadgets.

1. Today, I'm reviewing a useful new gadget – Beezer's Audio Shades.

2. **What is it?** It's a combination of two gadgets: cool sunglasses and hi-tech earphones. The shades are great for protecting your eyes. You can also connect the earphones to your phone to listen to music.

3. **Good points** The glasses are light and perfect for looking cool. I love the audio speakers too. The sound is fantastic.

4. **Bad points** They are expensive. And it wasn't easy to connect the shades to my phone.

5. **Do you recommend it?** I recommend buying this gadget, but be sure to get an extra battery!

1. Read Callum's review. What does he like and not like about the gadget? What is his recommendation?

2. Study the Writing box. Find examples of the phrases in Callum's review.

WRITING A review of a gadget

Introduction
1. Today/This week, I'm reviewing a new device/gadget.
   This game/app is exciting/practical/useful.

Say what it is
2. It's a new app for learning to paint.
   You can use it to edit videos/text your friends.

Mention good points
3. The glasses are light and look great/fantastic/cool.
   The battery lasts for ages/twenty hours.

Mention bad points
4. It's/They're (a bit) slow/expensive/heavy.
   The battery doesn't last very long/died after one week.

Say if you recommend it
5. I recommend (buying) this gadget. It's great fun/easy to use.
   I don't recommend spending any money on it.

3. Study the Language box. Find examples of expressions of purpose in the review.

LANGUAGE Expressions of purpose

Use **for + -ing** or **to + infinitive** to express purpose.
This app is great **for sharing** your photos.
You can use the app **to edit** videos.

4. Complete the sentences with *for* and *to*. Use the Language box to help you.
   1. You can use the console *to* watch films.
   2. I use the app _____ buying food.
   3. I often go to the library _____ use the internet connection.
   4. This is a good blog _____ finding answers to computer problems.
   5. Can I use this cable _____ connect my phone to yours?

WRITING TIME

5. Write a review of a device, gadget, game or app.

   1 Find ideas
   Make notes for a review.
   - What is the product/its name/the price?
   - What is it for?
   - What are its good/bad points?
   - Do you recommend it?

   2 Plan
   Organise your ideas into paragraphs. Use Callum's review to help you.

   3 Write and share
   - Write a draft review. Use the Language box and the Writing box to help you.
   - Share your review with another student for feedback.
   - Write the final version of your review.

   4 Check
   - Check language: are the expressions of purpose (*for* + -ing, *to* + infinitive) correct?
   - Check grammar: did you use the correct verb patterns?

I can write a review of a gadget.

Vocabulary Activator

WORDLIST 🔊 4.17

Digital devices
Bluetooth® speaker (n)
digital camera (n)
games console (n)
handsfree headset (n)
phone charger (n)
smartphone (n)
smartwatch (n)
wireless earbuds (n)

Word friends
(using technology)
charge your phone
check social media
check the time
download apps
join an online class
listen to music
listen to podcasts
look for information
make video clips
phone a friend
play online games
send messages
send texts
take photos

Computer equipment
keyboard (n)
memory (n)
microphone (n)
printer (n)
scanner (n)
screen (n)
touchscreen (n)
USB cable (n)

Word friends
(phrasal verbs)
check out (v)
find out (v)
hang up (v)
switch on (v)
try on (v)

Word friends
(favourite websites)
click on links
chat online
download videos
follow people
search the web
share photos
share videos
upload videos
view videos

Word friends
(computer problems)
The battery died.
The computer crashed.
The computer isn't working.
The internet connection is slow.
The mouse doesn't work.
The printer doesn't work.
The screen's frozen.

Extra words
app (n)
be addicted to
buy and sell things
call a helpline
charge (v)
communicate (v)
connect to (v)
desktop computer (n)
device (n)
document (n)
drone (n)
edit videos
electronic (adj)
extra (adj)
fix a problem
gadget (n)

hi-tech (adj)
innovation (n)
install a computer program
keep in touch
laptop (n)
last (v)
offline (adj)
online forum (n)
password (n)
phone battery (n)
phone box (n)
read articles
recommend (v)
save photos
social networking site (n)
sound (n)
stay calm
switch off (v)
tablet (n)
take (regular) breaks
technology (n)
text (v)
waterproof (adj)
website (n)
wi-fi (n)

---

1 In pairs, complete the sentences with words from the wordlist.
1 You need a *keyboard* to write emails and messages on a PC.
2 A _____ is a device for playing games online.
3 You don't need a _____ to connect a Bluetooth® speaker to your phone.
4 _____ are great for listening to music while running.
5 All modern smartphones use a _____ to type information.

2 Match verbs 1–6 with words a–f to make phrases. Use the wordlist to check your answers.
1 ☐ listen to   a apps
2 ☐ check   b podcasts
3 ☐ download   c your friends
4 ☐ send   d online classes
5 ☐ join   e the time
6 ☐ phone   f texts

3 Complete the sentences with one word in each gap. In pairs, say if the sentences are true for you.
1 I enjoy listening *to* podcasts.
2 I once got a virus after I _____ on a bad link.
3 My computer is very good. It never _____ .
4 I _____ a few famous sportspeople on social media.

4 🔊 4.18 **PRONUNCIATION** Listen to how you pronounce the underlined letters in each word and repeat.

> ca**b**le cam**era** charg**er** comput**er**
> digit**al** mem**ory**

5 🔊 4.19 **PRONUNCIATION** In pairs, practise saying these words with the /ə/ sound. Then listen and check.

> article internet microphone printer
> scanner social media

Revision

Vocabulary

1 Complete the words in the sentences.
1. You need a lot of m<u>emory</u> on your phone to save photos.
2. I can't make a copy of the picture for you. The s_____ doesn't w____ .
3. A s_____ is small, so you can wear it on your wrist.
4. My battery d____ . Can I use your phone c_____?
5. I dropped my laptop, and now the s_____ is f_____ .
6. We couldn't play o_____ games today because the internet c_____ was too slow.

2 Complete the texts with the words below. Which gadget do you prefer? Why?

> digital   ~~headset~~   link   make   microphone
> photos   view

BUY THIS!
Are you bored with your old earphones? I'm selling my handsfree ¹<u>headset</u> for £10. You can click on this ²_____ to see photos. It's great for people who chat online a lot because the ³_____ is very good.

Only £65!
I've got a new ⁴_____ camera, so my old one is for sale. You can take great ⁵_____ with it and ⁶_____ amazing video clips. Do you want to see how to use it? You can ⁷_____ a short video here.

3 Replace the words in bold with the phrasal verbs below.

> ~~check out~~   find out   hang up
> switch on   ~~try on~~

1. My old headphones are terrible. Can I **wear** your headphones for a minute?
   try on
2. I'm not surprised you can't print. You forgot to **press the 'on' button on** the printer.
3. He started shouting, so I decided to **end the phone call**.
4. Wow! **Have a look at** the prices of these games consoles.
5. I don't know which charger to buy. I need to **get** some more information.

Grammar

4 Complete the text with the correct form of *used to* and the verbs in brackets.

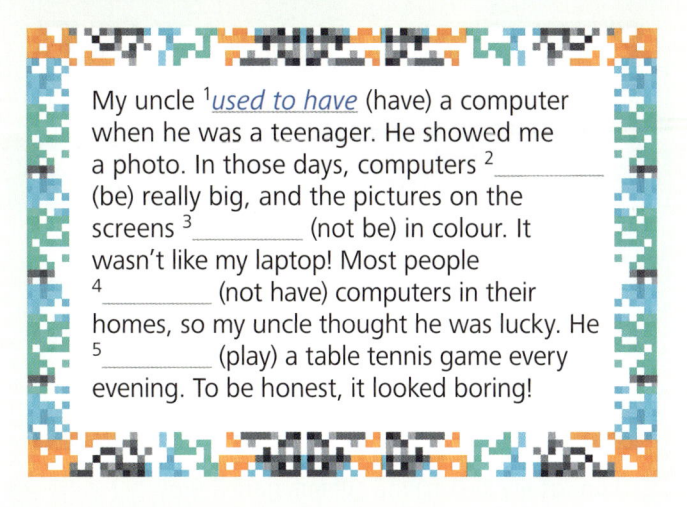

> My uncle ¹<u>used to have</u> (have) a computer when he was a teenager. He showed me a photo. In those days, computers ²_____ (be) really big, and the pictures on the screens ³_____ (not be) in colour. It wasn't like my laptop! Most people ⁴_____ (not have) computers in their homes, so my uncle thought he was lucky. He ⁵_____ (play) a table tennis game every evening. To be honest, it looked boring!

5 Choose the correct option. In pairs, compare your answers.

> **Picture This** is a great photography app. I use it when I need ¹*to make / making* my photos look amazing. I don't mind ²*to share / sharing* natural photos on social media, but I usually try ³*to post / posting* interesting photos. I enjoy ⁴*to change / changing* the colours so that everything looks dramatic. It's good for people who would like ⁵*to learn / learning* how to create great photos. I want ⁶*to tell / telling* all my friends about it!

6 Complete the sentences with the correct form of the verbs in brackets. In pairs, say which sentences are true for you.
1. I stopped <u>using</u> (use) my old games console a long time ago.
2. I sometimes write messages and then forget _____ (send) them.
3. I really hate _____ (get) a virus on my computer.
4. I need _____ (spend) more time offline.
5. I keep _____ (lose) my phone charger.

Speaking

7 In pairs, role play the situation. Then change roles and talk about a different technical problem.
- **Student A** – Ask Student B what the problem is.
- **Student B** – Describe the technical problem.
- **Student A** – Offer a solution.

Dictation

8 🔊 4.20 Listen. Then listen again and write down what you hear during each pause.

SET FOR LIFE

My digital life

A Look at my best friend @emmajane here! She's fun and very cute. Looking good here, right?! 😂

B On holiday in Hendon Bay with my parents. 😢 This place is SO boring! The weather is terrible, and there's nothing for teenagers to do (not even a cinema)! Stay away from here!!

C Happy Birthday, Tom. It's your big day – sixteen today! See you later at the party. (4, Pendle Road, Chadbury, right?)

D My friend Daz is an amazing graffiti artist! This is some of his work from last week – at those old buildings near the station. Shhh!! 🤔

1 In groups, discuss the questions.
1. How often do you use social media?
2. Which apps do you use for social media?
3. How many contacts/followers do you have?
4. What sort of things do you post?
5. Do you ask other people for permission before you write about them?

2 Read posts A–D and match them with questions 1–4.

Which post …
1. ☐ gives a personal view of a place?
2. ☐ talks about a celebration?
3. ☐ shows something that a friend did?
4. ☐ has a funny photo of another person?

3 In groups, discuss the four posts. Is it OK to post things like that?

I can communicate with people on social media in a respectful and safe way.

Behave well on social media

4 🔊 **4.21** Listen to four people talking about the posts in Exercise 2. Match speakers 1–4 with posts A–D.
1 ☐ 2 ☐ 3 ☐ 4 ☐

5 🔊 **4.21** Listen again. Choose the correct answer.
1 What is the boy worried about?
 a His party wasn't a success.
 b His name and address appeared online.
2 What is the girl's reaction to the post?
 a She found it funny.   b She's upset about it.
3 What mistake did the speaker make?
 a He posted a photo on a public account.
 b He sent a photo to his head teacher.
4 Why are the boy and girl annoyed?
 a The information in the post is false.
 b The post includes some negative opinions.

6 Tick (✓) the statements which are true for you. In pairs, compare your answers.
1 ☐ A lot of my posts are public.
2 ☐ I know who is looking at my posts.
3 ☐ I think about other people before I post photos or comments.
4 ☐ I always use polite language in my posts.
5 ☐ All the information that I put on social media is true.
6 ☐ I try to present myself in a positive way.

7 Read the Useful Tips. In class, discuss the questions.
1 Which tip is the most important and why?
2 Can you add another tip to the list?

SET FOR LIFE

8 In groups, prepare a social media post. Follow the instructions.

1 Choose one of the situations below or think of a situation from your own life.

> party   school trip   special day at school

2 Write a short message and describe what happened. Take a photo of your group or find a photo online.

3 Check your post. Does it follow the rules of posting online? Use the questions below to help you.
• Are the facts true?
• Is it kind?
• Does the post give any personal details about other people?
• Do you need to ask anyone before you post the photo?
• Do you want the post to be public or private?

4 Share your posts in class.

USEFUL TIPS

When you use social media, it is important to follow some rules to keep safe and avoid hurting other people's feelings.

NO!
- Don't share photos of other people without asking.
- Don't share details that tell other people who you are.
- Don't post photos that show bad behaviour.
- Don't make unkind comments.

YES!
- Think about other people's feelings.
- Keep your posts private, not public.
- Present a positive image online.
- Remember that things on the internet are there forever!

My place, my space

5

VOCABULARY
Things in the home | Prepositions of place | Housework | Adverbs of manner | Places in town

GRAMMAR
Defining relative clauses | Modal verbs: *can*, *have to* and *must*

5.1 Vocabulary

Things in the home

1 Look at the picture. Which rooms can you see?

2 🔊 5.1 Study Vocabulary box A. Find these things in the picture.

VOCABULARY A	Things in the home
living room	armchair bookcase coffee table sofa
kitchen	cooker dishwasher fridge iron microwave washing machine
bedroom	bedside table wardrobe
bathroom	shower sink
around the house	ceiling cupboard curtains floor hall light mirror plant roof rug vacuum cleaner

3 🔊 5.2 Study Vocabulary box B. Look at the picture again and choose the correct option.

VOCABULARY B Prepositions of place

above   behind   between   in   in front of   near   next to   on   opposite   under

1 The dishwasher is *near / opposite* the window.
2 There's a mirror *above / under* the sink.
3 The sink is *behind / next to* the bath.
4 The plant is *under / behind* the armchair.
5 The bed is *between / on* the bedside table and the window.

Unit 5   62

4 In pairs, make more sentences with prepositions about the picture on page 62.

5 🔊 5.3 **WORD FRIENDS** Find these phrases in the Housework Survey and write the missing words. Listen and check.
1 clean/vacuum the *floor*
2 do the cooking/the _____
3 do the ironing/the washing/the _____
4 dry the _____
5 make your _____
6 put on the _____
7 sort/take out the _____
8 tidy your _____

HOUSEWORK SURVEY

In your house
- who does the washing and the ironing?
- who makes your bed and tidies your room?
- who vacuums or cleans the floor?
- who takes out the rubbish?
- who sorts the rubbish for recycling?
- who does the shopping and the cooking?
- who puts on the dishwasher?
- who does the washing up or dries the dishes?

6 In pairs, ask and answer the questions in the survey.
A: *Who vacuums the floor in your house?*
B: *In my house, my dad vacuums the floor. I …*

7 🔊 5.4 Complete the text with the words below. Listen and check.

clean   cleaning   do (x 2)   make   puts on   sort   taking out   tidies   ~~vacuuming~~

Who likes housework?

Coco
I love ¹*vacuuming* the rugs and the floors. It's fun! My mum doesn't like ²_____ the rubbish, so I do it once or twice a week.

George
I often ³_____ the rubbish because I think it's important to recycle. My sister usually ⁴_____ the dishwasher every evening after dinner, and I take out the dishes when they're dry. Oh, and I always ⁵_____ my bed, of course.

Altam
To be honest, I don't mind ⁶_____ the bathroom mirror and the sink and the shower too. But I never ⁷_____ the floor. My parents do that.

Priya
In our house everyone ⁸_____ their own room at the weekend. I don't usually ⁹_____ the shopping, but I enjoy cooking. I can ¹⁰_____ the ironing too, but I can't stand it! I burned a hole in my T-shirt once!

8 Complete the sentences about housework to make them true for you. Use words from Exercise 5 to help you.
1 I don't like *taking out the rubbish*.
2 I don't usually _____ .
3 I _____ every day.
4 I never _____ .
5 I sometimes _____ at the weekend.
6 I don't mind _____ , but I can't stand _____ .

9 In pairs, discuss your answers **YOUR WORLD** to Exercise 8.
A: *I never do the shopping or the cooking.*
B: *Really? I don't mind doing the shopping, but I can't stand cooking.*

I can talk about things in the home and housework.

5.2 Grammar
Defining relative clauses

The ups and downs of my home
Judy Brown

🙂 Here are some things which I love about my home.

- **Flat 5B.** This is the flat where we live. It isn't very big, but it's comfortable and bright. It's a place where I feel happy.
- **The view.** I love the view that I have from my bedroom window. I can see the park where I play football.
- **Mrs Kerr.** She's the woman who lives next door. She's eighty-six, but she's lots of fun! I like the people that live downstairs too. They're really friendly, but Mrs Kerr is special.

☹️ And now some things that annoy me.

- **The bathroom.** This is the only room which I don't like. It's too small!
- **The stairs.** In our building there's a lift that never works! So we have to walk up five floors!
- **Noisy neighbours!** I don't like the people who live in the flat upstairs. There's a man who vacuums the floor at midnight! And there's someone that plays really loud music all the time!

1 🔊 5.5 Read the blog post. What does Judy like and dislike about her home? Why?

2 Study the Grammar box. Find more examples of relative clauses in the blog post.

GRAMMAR Defining relative clauses

- We use **who** or **that** for people.
  She's the woman *who* lives next door.
- We use **which** or **that** for things.
  Here are some things *which* I love about my home.
  There are some things *that* annoy me.
- We use **where** for places.
  This is the flat *where* we live.

GRAMMAR TIME > PAGE 130

3 Complete the sentences with the correct relative pronouns.
1 The house *where* I live has six rooms.
2 I like the people _____ live next door.
3 The bus _____ goes past my house is the number 11.
4 This is the room _____ we eat.
5 I have a neighbour _____ puts on the dishwasher at 6 a.m.
6 I love the place _____ I live.

4 Combine the sentences with relative pronouns.
1 I live in a house. It's 100 years old.
   I live in a house that/which is 100 years old.
2 I live in a flat. It has two bathrooms.
3 This is the cupboard. We keep the glasses and plates there.
4 From my window I can see a road. It's always busy.
5 I've got a sister. She shares a room with me.
6 I like the people. They live next door.

5 Complete the sentences with relative pronouns and your own ideas. In pairs, compare your sentences.
1 The room *where* I spend most of my time is …
2 The person _____ annoys me the most is …
3 The thing _____ I love about my home is …
4 One place _____ I feel really happy is …
5 The people _____ live next door are …
6 The housework _____ I dislike the most is …

YOUR WORLD

6 Write about the things that you love about your home and the things that annoy you. Use relative clauses.
The people who live next door are really friendly.
The flat where we live has two bathrooms.

7 In groups, talk about your home. Use the sentences from Exercise 6 to help you.

Unit 5 — I can use defining relative clauses to describe people, things and places.

5.3 Reading and Vocabulary

Storytelling

1 Describe the photo. Do you ever go to summer camp?

2 🔊 5.6 Read the story and answer the questions.
1 Where is the old house?
2 What does the storyteller find?
3 What is inside?

3 Read the story again. Complete gaps 1–4 with sentences a–e. There is one extra sentence.
a So I went inside and put the light on quickly.
b There were stories of wild animals that he saw.
c The man who built it was a farmer, Jacob Green.
d Another group took the rubbish out.
e It's a really popular activity for teenagers across the USA.

4 🔊 5.7 How do you think the story ends? Answer the questions. Listen and check. Were you right?
1 Do the campers read the last page?
2 What does it say?

5 🔊 5.8 Study the Vocabulary box. Find three more examples in the story.

VOCABULARY — Adverbs of manner

Adverbs which end in -ly
badly   carefully   nervously   noisily   perfectly
quickly   quietly   slowly

Adverbs which are the same as the adjectives
early   fast   hard   late   right   wrong

WATCH OUT!
The adverb for *good* is *well*.

---

6 Complete the sentences with adverbs formed from the adjectives in brackets.
1 I put things in the dishwasher *slowly* (slow).
2 Our dog eats really _____ (noisy).
3 I can't cook very _____ (good).
4 In the shower Dad sings _____ (bad).
5 My sister vacuums the living room _____ (fast).
6 I sometimes get up _____ (late).

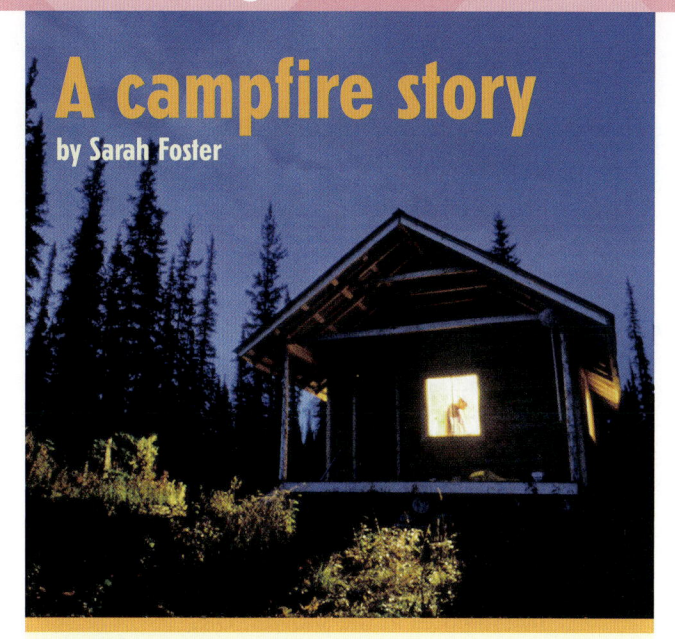

A campfire story
by Sarah Foster

Summer Camp is always cool because we stay in tents in a forest. At the centre of the camp there's an old, dark, wooden house where we have our evening meals. ¹____

I love evenings at camp because we sit outside and tell stories and funny jokes around the fire. One night last summer, we finished dinner early. In the kitchen, my friend and I did the washing up carefully in the big sink, then some campmates put the dishes away tidily. ²____ Mike, a camp leader, started playing his guitar by the fire outside. One by one, we sat down happily and sang songs.

Later, Mike asked me to get some marshmallows from a large cupboard at the end of the dark hall. ³____ In a corner of the shelf, next to the marshmallows, I saw a strange old book: *Diary 1905*. 'Look at this!' I called excitedly.

Of course, everyone wanted to see the old diary. We took it in turns to read about Jacob Green's life in his old-fashioned writing. In 1905, he wrote about bad weather and how he worked hard to finish the roof on his house. ⁴____ There were funny poems and jokes too. It was my turn to read a page which said 'Warning!' I read the next words nervously. 'Do not read the last page. I have a terrible secret.'

7 Write five sentences about things you and your family did last week. Use adverbs of manner.
Last week, I got up early on Monday …

YOUR WORLD

I can understand a story about a personal experience.   65   Unit 5

5.4 Grammar

Modal verbs: *can, have to* and *must*

VIDEO ▶ **RULES TO FOLLOW**

Gran: OK, girls. Thank you very much. Dinner's in five minutes.
Lena: Your gran's lovely.
Mia: Yes, but she has some rules we have to follow.
Lena: Like what?
Mia: We have to do the washing up.
Lena: That's fine.
Mia: And, you can't use your phone near her.
Lena: Seriously?
Mia: What else? You mustn't spend more than five minutes in the shower, OK?
Lena: Yeah.
Mia: Oh! And you mustn't say 'yeah'. You have to say 'yes'. And you mustn't forget to say 'please' and 'thank you'.
Lena: Is that all?
Mia: No, em … we can't wear jeans at dinner.
Lena: What do we have to wear?
Mia: A nice dress.
Lena: I don't have a dress. Can I borrow one of yours?
Mia: Of course you can. This one will look nice. One more thing … You have to 'sing for your supper'.
Lena: What? Do I have to sing a song?
Mia: No, you don't have to sing a song, but you have to do something. You can read a poem or dance or … You don't have to be good, but you can't refuse.
Lena: Why didn't you tell me this before, Mia? Oh! I see. Very funny.

1 ▶ 23 ◀) 5.9 Describe the photo. Watch or listen. How does Lena feel about Mia's gran's rules?

2 Study the Grammar box. Find more examples with *can't, have to* and *mustn't* in the dialogue.

GRAMMAR — Modal verbs: *can, have to* and *must*

Can I borrow one of your dresses? (Is it OK?)
You **can** read a poem. (It's OK.)
You **can't** refuse. (It isn't OK.)

Do I **have to** sing a song? (Is it necessary?)
You **have to** try. (It's necessary.)
You **don't have to** sing a song. (It isn't necessary.)
You **mustn't** say 'yeah'. (Don't!)

GRAMMAR TIME ▶ PAGE 131

3 What things do you have to do at home? What don't you have to do? Discuss in pairs.

I have to make my bed, but I don't have to …

4 ◀) 5.10 Choose the correct option. Listen and check.

Ali: You ¹*can / have to* remember some rules when you visit my house. You ²*can't / don't have to* wear your shoes. Take them off at the front door. And you ³*don't have to / mustn't* talk with your mouth full during dinner.
Jan: ⁴*Do I have / I have* to eat everything on my plate?
Ali: No, you ⁵*can / can't* leave some food if you want. You ⁶*don't have to / mustn't* eat everything.

5 Complete the sentences to make them true for you. In pairs, compare your sentences.
1 I *have to* take a bus to go to school.
2 I _____ go to school on Saturdays.
3 You _____ go shopping on Sundays in my town.
4 I _____ do a lot of housework at home.
5 I _____ go to bed before 10 p.m.
6 In my house I _____ stay up late at weekends.

A: *Do you have to take a bus to go to school?*
B: *No, I don't. I can walk or ride my bike.*

VIDEO ▶ **WIDER WORLD**

6 ▶ 24 Watch four people talking about rules for children. Write down what they say.

7 Imagine you look after two little children. Write down rules for them using modal verbs. In pairs, compare your ideas.

You have to go to bed at half past seven.

I can use *can, have to* and *must* to talk about rules.

5.5 Listening and Vocabulary
Describing your town

1 In pairs, look at the photos. Do you think Keswick is an interesting place to visit? Why?/ Why not?

2 🔊 5.11 **I KNOW!** Study the Vocabulary box. How many words can you add in two minutes?

> **VOCABULARY** Places in town
>
> art gallery   café   castle   church   cinema   estate
> hotel   library   museum   park   police station
> post office   shopping centre   station
> tourist information centre   town hall

3 Work in pairs. Give the name of a local place for your partner to guess.
   A: *Odeon.*   B: *That's a cinema!*

4 🔊 5.12 Listen to the telephone information line. Complete the notes with a word or a short phrase in each gap.

> *Trip to Keswick*
> • *For maps and leaflets go to: the* ¹tourist information centre; *open every day, in the old* ² _____
> • *Top attraction:* ³ _____ *(history of pencil making!)*
> • *Small* ⁴ _____ *with a popular arts* ⁵ _____

5 In pairs, read the results of a survey about Keswick and find the three:
   1 biggest problems for young people there.
   2 most popular reasons why it's a good place to live.

6 🔊 5.13 Listen and decide which answers from the survey each person mentions.

	Declan	Louise	Annie	Brett
Likes	*friendly people*			
Dislikes				

7 🔊 5.13 Listen again and match statements a–e with speakers 1–4. There is one extra statement.
   1 ☐   2 ☐   3 ☐   4 ☐

   a He/She doesn't ride a bike in town anymore.
   b He/She enjoys riding a bike.
   c He/She lived in another town before.
   d He/She is planning to live in a different place.
   e He/She lives outside the town.

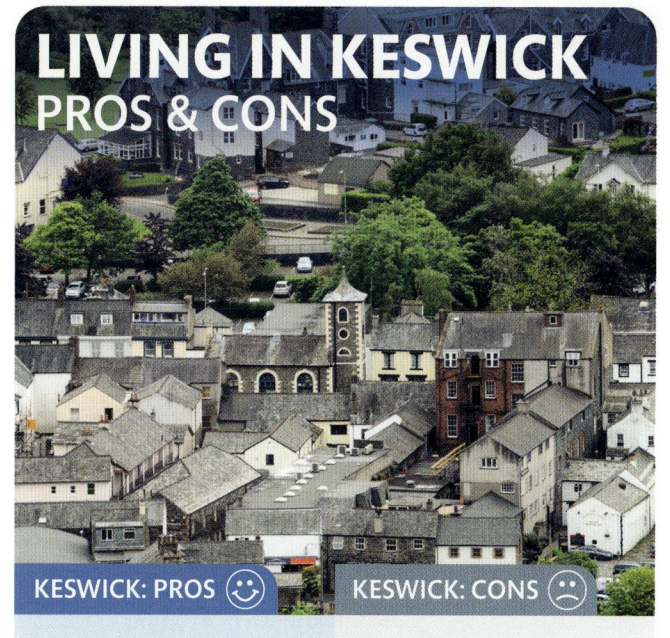

LIVING IN KESWICK
PROS & CONS

KESWICK: PROS 🙂
1 Friendly people
2 The beautiful countryside
3 Nice old buildings
4 Great cafés and shops
5 The film festival
6 Nice lakes

KESWICK: CONS 🙁
1 Nothing to do in the evenings
2 Not enough shops
3 No public transport in the evenings
4 Too much traffic in the town centre
5 Everybody knows who you are

VIDEO ▶   **WIDER WORLD**

8 ▶ 25 Watch five people talking about the places where they live. Write down what they like and don't like about each place.

9 What do you like and what don't you like about the place where you live? Tell the class.
   I like the music festival, but I don't like …

I can understand a conversation about a town.

5.6 Speaking
Asking for, giving and receiving advice

VIDEO ▶ **NOAH'S NEW ROOM**

Mia: Hi Noah! What's up?
Noah: I feel a bit sad.
Mia: Lying in bed doesn't help. Why don't you do something?
Noah: I don't want to do anything. I'm fed up.
Mia: No wonder. It's depressing here. You really should redecorate this room.
Noah: Hmm, that's not a bad idea. What do you think I should do?
Mia: I think you should tidy up, make your bed, put away the clothes that are on the floor …
And I think you should take down the posters that are on this wall too.
Noah: Yeah? What should I put up instead?
Mia: Something cheerful. Some cute kittens? Or puppy dogs?
Noah: That's a terrible idea! Oh! You're joking.
Mia: You shouldn't have any posters. Keep it simple. Put up one of your drawings.
Noah: Yeah, that's a good idea!
Mia: OK, let's do it! Come on!
Later
Mia: It's like a new room! … What's wrong? Are you still sad?
Noah: No, I'm happy. But I'm exhausted!

SOUNDS GOOD! I'm fed up. • No wonder. • Keep it simple.

1 ▶ 26 ◀» **5.14** Describe the photo. Watch or listen and answer the questions.
1. How does Noah feel at the beginning? Why?
2. What advice does Mia give to Noah?
3. How does Noah feel at the end?

SET FOR LIFE

2 What can you do when you feel sad? Discuss in groups. Use the ideas below to help you.
- create something
- do a sport
- eat something healthy
- do something useful
- find something to laugh about

3 Study the Speaking box. Which phrases are NOT in the dialogue?

SPEAKING | Asking for, giving and receiving advice

Asking for advice
Where/What should I …?
What do you think I should …?
Can you give me some advice?

Giving advice
You (really) should/shouldn't …
I think/don't think you should …
Why don't you …?

Accepting advice
That's a good/brilliant idea.
That's not a bad idea.

Rejecting advice
That's a terrible idea!
I don't think that's a good idea.

4 ◀» **5.15** Complete the dialogue with one word in each gap. Listen and check.
A: I ¹*think* you should change your curtains.
B: Hmm. That's ² _____ a bad idea. What colour ³ _____ I get?
A: Well, I ⁴ _____ think you should get black ones. They're depressing. And you ⁵ _____ get white curtains. They let too much light in. Why ⁶ _____ you take my old curtains? They're nice.
B: That's a ⁷ _____ idea. Thanks.

YOUR WORLD

5 In pairs, think of advice you can give to a new student in your town. Then take turns to ask for and give advice.

Where should I go to meet friends?

Unit 5 | 68 | I can ask for, give and receive advice.

5.7 Writing
An informal email

> SUBJECT: Big news!
>
> ① Hi Gemma,
> ② How are you? I hope you're well. Big news! My mum changed jobs last month, so we had to move to a new flat!
> ③ Now we're in Swanford, a town in the south of England, not far from London. It's quite small with some old-fashioned buildings, but it seems nice. There's a beautiful park, a modern shopping centre and a sports centre where I can go swimming.
> Our new flat isn't big, but it's comfortable. It's got big windows too, so it's very bright. It's on the second floor, so there's a great view over the park from the living room.
> ④ I have to go now because our new neighbours are coming for dinner. The kitchen's untidy, so I have to help Mum.
> ⑤ Take care!
> Maisie

1 In pairs, read the email. What is the big news? What good things does Maisie say about her new home?

2 Study the Writing box. Find examples of the phrases in the email.

WRITING An informal email describing a place

① **Greeting**
Hello,   Hi,   Hi there,

② **Ask for/Give news**
How are you?   How are things?
I hope you're well.
Everything's fine here.
Guess what!   Big news!

③ **Describe the place**
It's in the south of England/near …/not far from …
It's quite small.   It isn't very big.
It seems nice/interesting.
There's a beautiful park.   There are some cool shops.
Our new flat/house is comfortable/big/modern.
It's on the second floor.   It's in a quiet street.

④ **Close your email**
It's time to finish.
I have to go now because …

⑤ **Closing phrase**
See you soon!   Best wishes,   Love,   Take care!

3 Match the adjectives with their opposites from the email.

LANGUAGE Adjectives to describe places

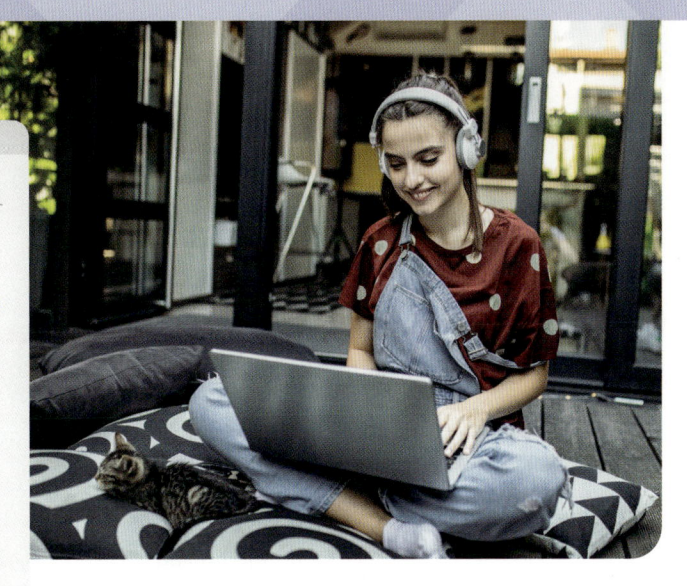

dark – ¹*bright*
old-fashioned – ² _____
small – ³ _____
tidy – ⁴ _____
ugly – ⁵ _____
uncomfortable – ⁶ _____

4 🔊 5.16 Complete the description of the house with words from the Language box. Listen and check.

My gran's house isn't ¹*modern* like ours, it's really ² _____ . The house is very ³ _____ – there are six bedrooms. In Gran's living room the curtains are always closed, so it's really ⁴ _____ ! The armchairs are quite ⁵ _____ because they're very old and small. Luckily, outside is great! Gran's garden is full of ⁶ _____ flowers and plants, so it's my favourite place to sit.

WRITING TIME

5 Imagine you moved to your home town last week. Write an email to a friend. Describe your new home.

① **Find ideas**
Make notes for an email. Think about:
• the town or village where you live.
• some interesting places and what they look like.
• your home and the things that you like about it.

② **Plan**
Organise your ideas into paragraphs. Use Maisie's email to help you.

③ **Write and share**
• Write a draft email. Use the Language box and the Writing box to help you.
• Share your email with another student for feedback.
• Write the final version of your email.

④ **Check**
• Check language: did you use adjectives to describe places?
• Check grammar: did you use the correct relative pronouns?

I can write an informal email.   69   Unit 5

Vocabulary Activator

WORDLIST 🔊 5.17

Things in the home
armchair (n)
bathroom (n)
bedroom (n)
bedside table (n)
bookcase (n)
ceiling (n)
coffee table (n)
cooker (n)
cupboard (n)
curtains (n)
dishwasher (n)
floor (n)
fridge (n)
hall (n)
iron (n)
kitchen (n)
light (n)
living room (n)
microwave (n)
mirror (n)
plant (n)
roof (n)
rug (n)
shower (n)
sink (n)
sofa (n)
vacuum cleaner (n)
wardrobe (n)
washing machine (n)

Prepositions of place
above (prep)
behind (prep)
between (prep)
in (prep)
in front of (prep)
near (prep)
next to (prep)
on (prep)
opposite (prep)
under (prep)

Word friends (housework)
clean the floor
do the cooking
do the ironing
do the shopping
do the washing
do the washing up
dry the dishes
make your bed
put on the dishwasher
sort the rubbish
take out the rubbish
tidy your room
vacuum the floor

Adverbs of manner
badly (adv)
carefully (adv)
early (adv)
fast (adv)
hard (adv)
late (adv)
nervously (adv)
noisily (adv)
perfectly (adv)
quickly (adv)
quietly (adv)
right (adv)
slowly (adv)
well (adv)
wrong (adv)

Places in town
art gallery (n)
café (n)
castle (n)
church (n)
cinema (n)
estate (n)
hotel (n)
library (n)
museum (n)
park (n)
police station (n)
post office (n)
shopping centre (n)
station (n)
tourist information centre (n)
town hall (n)

Extra words
beautiful (adj)
big (adj)
bright (adj)
building (n)
comfortable (adj)
depressing (adj)
dining room (n)
downstairs (adv)
excitedly (adv)
flat (n)
garden (n)
happily (adv)
house (n)
live next door
modern (adj)
neighbour (n)
old-fashioned (adj)
place (n)
redecorate (v)
room (n)
rule (n)
shelf (n)
small (adj)
summer camp (n)
tent (n)
tidily (adv)
tidy (adj)
ugly (adj)
uncomfortable (adj)
untidy (adj)
view (n)
window (n)

1 Use words from the wordlist to find these things.
1. seven electrical devices *cooker, …*
2. five housework chores you usually do in the kitchen
3. two housework chores you do outside the house
4. seven pieces of furniture
5. seven places where people often spend their free time

2 Look at the picture and complete the sentences with prepositions from the wordlist.

1. The bed is <u>opposite</u> the wardrobe.
2. The posters are _____ the bookcase.
3. The rug is _____ the floor.
4. The bedside table is _____ the bed.
5. The wardrobe is _____ the bookcase and the window.
6. The chair is _____ the table.

3 In pairs, describe public places in your town. Use words from the wordlist to help you.
In my town, there's one big shopping centre. It's near the station.

4 Order the words to make sentences. In pairs, say if the sentences are true for you. How do you do housework?
1. my room / I / tidy / perfectly / usually
   I usually tidy my room perfectly.
2. do / sometimes / the cooking / quickly / I
3. badly / I / bed / my / make
4. enjoy / the floor / I / vacuuming
5. always / rubbish / carefully / sort / I / the

5 🔊 5.18 **PRONUNCIATION** In pairs, choose the odd one out. Use the underlined letters to help you. Listen, check and repeat.

1. ab<u>o</u>ve   c<u>u</u>pboard   (<u>a</u>rmchair)
2. r<u>u</u>bbish   c<u>a</u>stle   b<u>a</u>throom
3. r<u>u</u>g   p<u>a</u>rk   ab<u>o</u>ve
4. fl<u>oo</u>r   c<u>o</u>ffee table   w<u>a</u>rdrobe
5. m<u>o</u>dern   sh<u>o</u>pping   fl<u>oo</u>r

Revision

Vocabulary

1 Complete the sentences with names of places in town.
1. When I lost my passport, I completed a report at the _police station_.
2. I need to collect a parcel from the _____.
3. There are some good clothes shops and a cinema in the new _____.
4. That _____ has some of my favourite paintings.
5. I got a map and some hotel addresses from the _____.

2 Choose the correct option.
1. You can find a *shower / fridge* in a café.
2. You can find a wardrobe in a *hotel / station*.
3. You can find a *microwave / bookcase* in a library.
4. You can find a *mirror / plant* in a park.
5. You can find a hall in a *castle / park*.
6. You can find a *bath / cooker* in the kitchen.

3 Complete the text with the Past Simple form of the correct verbs.

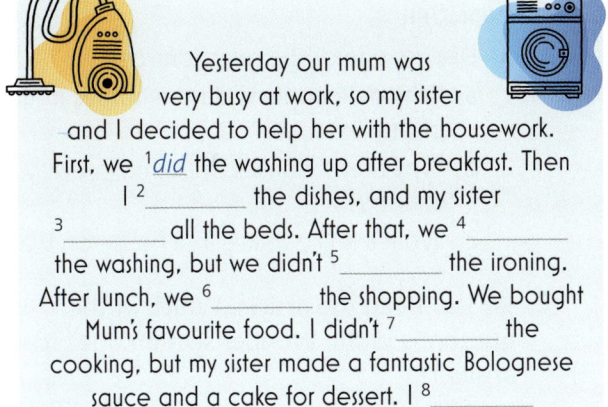

Yesterday our mum was very busy at work, so my sister and I decided to help her with the housework. First, we ¹_did_ the washing up after breakfast. Then I ²_____ the dishes, and my sister ³_____ all the beds. After that, we ⁴_____ the washing, but we didn't ⁵_____ the ironing. After lunch, we ⁶_____ the shopping. We bought Mum's favourite food. I didn't ⁷_____ the cooking, but my sister made a fantastic Bolognese sauce and a cake for dessert. I ⁸_____ the kitchen floor. Mum was very surprised when she came home!

4 Complete the questions with the correct form of the words in brackets. In pairs, ask and answer the questions.
1. Do you usually work _hard_ (hard) at school?
2. Do you eat _____ (quick) or _____ (slow)?
3. Do you usually get Maths problems _____ (right) or _____ (wrong)?
4. Do you write text messages _____ (fast) or _____ (careful)?
5. Can you think of one thing you usually do _____ (perfect)?

Grammar

5 Complete the sentences with *who*, *where* or *which*. Which of these pronouns can you replace with *that*?
1. The people in the street _where_ I live are very friendly.
2. Some new neighbours moved into the house _____ is next door to ours.
3. The boy _____ lives next door is older than me.
4. My sister often walks the dog _____ lives at number ten.
5. The park _____ I play basketball is on the corner.
6. The team _____ I play for is called the Park Rangers.
7. The woman _____ lives opposite us has got two cats.
8. The bus stop _____ I meet my friends is in the next street.

6 Choose the correct option.

My room, my rules

For Mum, Dad and Samir.

- You ¹*have to / can* come in, but remember you ²*have to / mustn't* knock first.
- You ³*don't have to / mustn't* touch my laptop.
- You ⁴*can't / have to* stay in my room when my friends are here.
- You ⁵*have to / mustn't* talk to me when I've got homework.
- You ⁶*can't / must* be quiet when I'm on the phone.

Thanks, Serena

Speaking

7 In pairs, role play the situations. Student A, look below. Student B, go to page 139.

Student A
- You want to change the decoration in your bedroom. Ask Student B for advice. Then accept or reject the advice.
- Give Student B advice for the surprise party he/she wants to organise. If he/she rejects your ideas, give him/her different advice.

Dictation

8 5.19 Listen. Then listen again and write down what you hear during each pause.

BBC CULTURE

Home sweet home

Houses around the world

In the UK, people often live in brick houses with two floors and a garden. In the USA and Australia, people's houses are often made of wood. Why are houses different around the world? The shape and the size of our houses depends on what we need. People everywhere build houses to protect them from different dangers, like the weather, enemies and animals. Here are some of the world's unusual homes.

Rock houses
People in North Africa and southern Europe started to live in underground houses over a thousand years ago. These houses kept them safe from enemies and the hot sun. Today in the south of Spain, some people still live in rock houses that are hundreds of years old. When the weather is very hot in the summer, these houses are nice and cool.

Yurts
In Mongolia and other parts of central Asia people still have a nomadic lifestyle. They live in large round tents which they build from wood and special cloth or skins. It only takes between thirty minutes and three hours to build a yurt or take it down. They are very comfortable and protect people from strong winds outside.

Stilt houses
In some parts of Asia, South America and West Africa, people live in stilt houses. The stilts lift the houses above the ground or the water. On land, the stilts stop animals, like rats and mice, getting into the house. On water, the stilts stop dangerous animals, like crocodiles. Sometimes, in bad weather, the sea gets very high. The stilts protect the houses when the sea level rises.

brick (n) a hard material for building walls
nomadic (adj) moving often from place to place
protect (v) keep something safe
stilt (n) a long stick made of wood that supports something
wood (n) the material that we take from trees

1 **VISIBLE THINKING** In pairs, follow these steps.
   SEE
   1 Describe the photo. Where in the world do you think these houses are?
   THINK
   2 Why are the people travelling on a boat? Why are the houses on water?
   WONDER
   3 Discuss one of the questions below.
      a Why did people build the homes in the photo like that?
      b Why aren't houses the same in every country?
      c What's it like to live in a house on water?

2 🔊 5.20 Read the article. Which of the questions in the Wonder section does it answer?

3 Read the article again and answer the questions.
   Which house …
   1 is good when you don't live in one place for a long time?
   2 is good when the weather is hot?
   3 is safe from animals?
   4 is good for rainy and stormy weather?

4 In pairs, discuss the questions.
   1 What types of homes are usual in your country?
   2 Are there any unusual houses in your country?
   3 How do houses in your country protect people from the weather?

BBC ▶ I want my own room!

5 Look at the photo. Which room in a house do you think this is? Why is it in a TV programme?

6 ▶ 27 Watch Part 1 of the programme. Check your answers to Exercise 5.

7 ▶ 28 Watch Part 2 of the programme. Who does these tasks? Match people a–d with questions 1–4.
Who …
1. ☐☐ paints a plan for the room?
2. ☐☐ takes the old things out of the front room?
3. ☐ chooses the wallpaper?
4. ☐ chooses old photos for the wall?

a girls   b mum   c sister   d designer

8 ▶ 29 Watch Part 3 of the programme. Tick (✓) the things that are in the room.
1. ☐ cupboards   5. ☐ cushions
2. ☐ wardrobe   6. ☐ plants
3. ☐ armchair   7. ☐ sofa bed
4. ☐ rug   8. ☐ TV

9 In pairs, discuss the questions.
1. Have you got your own room?
2. What is there in your bedroom?
3. Describe your dream room.

PROJECT TIME

10 In groups of four, create a mood board with style ideas for a teenager's room. Follow these steps.

1 In groups, decide on the overall feel of your room. Discuss the questions below.
- What is the style of your room? (modern/traditional/hi-tech/simple/original/comfortable)
- How big is the room?
- What makes it special?

Plan your mood board. Decide who in your group can find more information for each point.
- furniture in the room
- things on the walls and the floor
- gadgets and special features
- colours and patterns

2 Individually, create your part of the mood board.
- Take pictures or collect images of furniture, gadgets, colours and fabric designs for the mood board.
- Write a few sentences about your part of the board.

3 In your group, create your mood board. You can use a mood board creator.
- Combine the best pictures, colours and designs into a single mood board.
- Put your sentences together to describe the mood board.
- Practise describing your mood board.

4 Show your mood board to the class.
- Answer other students' questions.
- Look at the other mood boards. Ask questions.

Look after yourself

6

BODY CHALLENGE
Can you do these things?

VOCABULARY
Parts of the body | Sports and fitness | Accidents and injuries | Sleep | Symptoms, illnesses and allergies

GRAMMAR
Countable and uncountable nouns | Quantifiers | Past Continuous and Past Simple

1. Raise one eyebrow and not the other.
2. Touch your toes without bending your knees. 
3. Touch your ankle with your elbow. 
4. Touch your neck with your shoulder. 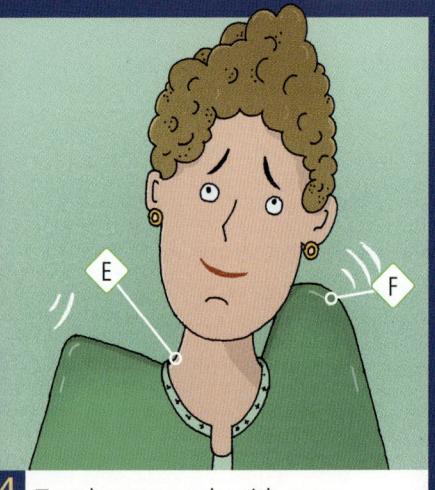
5. Touch your elbow with your lips. 
6. Touch your eyebrow and your throat with the fingers of one hand. 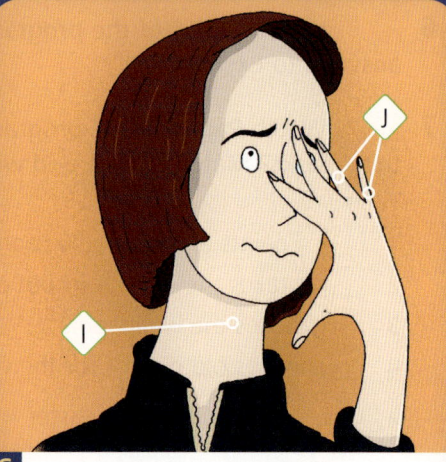

6.1 Vocabulary

The body

1 **I KNOW!** Work in pairs. How many parts of the body can you name in a minute?

2 🔊 6.1 Study Vocabulary box A. Match the words with parts of the body A–J in the pictures. Listen and check.

VOCABULARY A ▶ Parts of the body 1

☐ ankle ☐ elbow ☐ eyebrow ☐ fingers
☐ knee ☐ lips ☐ neck ☐ shoulder
☐ throat ☐ toes

3 🔊 6.2 Read and listen to the Body Challenge quiz. In pairs, ask and answer the questions.

A: *Can you raise one eyebrow and not the other?*
B: *Yes, I can.*

4 🔊 6.3 Study Vocabulary box B. In pairs, find the words in the fact box in Exercise 5. Check you understand them.

VOCABULARY B ▶ Parts of the body 2

bone   brain   heart   muscle   skin   stomach   tongue

Unit 6   74

5 In pairs, read the fact box. Which of the facts do you find most surprising?

PHYSICAL FACTS

1. Your largest organ is not inside your body, it's your skin – it can be fifteen percent of your body weight!
2. The human stomach can stretch to hold up to four litres of food!
3. A human brain is three to four times smaller than an elephant's.
4. Twenty-five percent of your bones are in your feet – there are twenty-six in each foot.
5. Your heart beats about 100,000 times a day to move the blood around your body.
6. Your tongue has eight muscles. It's very strong. (Perhaps because we talk a lot!)

6 🔊 6.4 **WORD FRIENDS** Complete the table with the words below. Listen and check.

badminton cycling exercises healthy
hockey rugby surfing yoga

play	¹*badminton* basketball football ²_____ ³_____ (team) games
do	⁴_____ sport weight-training ⁵_____
go	⁶_____ running ⁷_____ swimming walking
keep	fit ⁸_____

7 🔊 6.5 Listen to Alfie and Chloe talking about how they keep fit. Choose the correct option.
1. To keep *fit / sport* Chloe does *yoga / exercises* before breakfast every morning.
2. She also goes running *three / five* times a week.
3. She used to play *football / hockey* at school.
4. Alfie doesn't go *swimming / climbing* because he thinks it's boring.
5. He *plays badminton / does weight-training* with his friend Tim.

8 How do you keep fit? Discuss in pairs.
A: *How do you keep fit? Do you do a lot of sport?*
B: *Yes, I go running at weekends, I play football for the school team and I do judo.*

9 🔊 6.6 **WORD FRIENDS** Listen to Chloe and Alfie talking about accidents and injuries. Complete the sentences with body parts.
1. When Alfie fell, he hit his *head* and hurt his _____ .
2. One time he broke his _____ during a football match.
3. Last week, Chloe cut her _____ and burned her _____ in the kitchen.

10 Label photos A–E with the highlighted injuries in Exercise 9.

A *broke his leg*
B _____
C _____
D _____
E _____

YOUR WORLD

11 In pairs, talk about a time you had an injury. Use the phrases in Exercises 6 and 9 to help you.
A few years ago, I went skiing and I broke my leg.

I can talk about the body, sport and keeping fit.

6.2 Grammar

Countable and uncountable nouns | Quantifiers

VIDEO ▶ GOOD FOR YOU

Mia: Hi, what's for lunch?
Noah: First, a salad with a lot of tomatoes.
Lena: Don't put too many tomatoes in it!
Mia: But tomatoes are good for your skin.
Mateo: There isn't enough salt.
Mia: Too much salt isn't good for you.
Noah: OK … Now some crisps … How many crisps do you want in the salad?
Mia: Crisps in a salad?
Noah: Yeah, but not many … I'm kidding!
Mateo: After the salad there's some chicken.
Lena: That smells good! Are there any chips?
Mateo: No, there weren't enough potatoes.
Mia: Good, I don't want any chips.
Noah: I'm making a dessert, but it's healthy. There isn't much sugar in it. Mateo, how much chocolate do I need?
Mateo: 200 grams.
Mia: That's a lot of chocolate!
Lena: Can we have some cream with it?
Mateo: Sorry, we don't have any cream. Mia, are you eating the chocolate?
Mia: Oh! Oops!
Noah: Don't worry. Chocolate's good for you!

1 ▶ 30 🔊 6.7 Describe the photo. Why is Mia smiling? Watch or listen and check.

SET FOR LIFE

2 Do you have a healthy lifestyle? In groups, say how often you do these things.
- drink two litres of water
- eat five pieces of fruit and vegetables
- have a good breakfast
- sleep for eight hours
- walk or exercise for thirty minutes

3 Study the Grammar box. Find more quantifiers with nouns in the dialogue.

GRAMMAR | Quantifiers

Countable	Uncountable
how many crisps?	how much chocolate?
too many tomatoes	too much salt
a lot of tomatoes	a lot of chocolate
some crisps	some chicken
not many crisps	not much sugar
not any chips	not any cream
not enough potatoes	not enough salt

GRAMMAR TIME ▶ PAGE 131

4 In pairs, add words from the dialogue to the lists below. Then add more examples of food and drink.
Countable: *tomatoes, crisps, …*   Uncountable: *salt, …*

5 Complete the sentences with the quantifiers below.

| ~~many~~   enough   too many   too much |

1 There aren't *many* crisps, but I don't need any more.
2 There isn't _____ rice for four people. Add some more.
3 Don't put _____ butter on your toast.
4 I've got _____ olives. Do you want some?

WATCH OUT!
We usually ask questions with **any**. Are there **any** chips? But we can use **some** in questions when we make an offer or a request. Can we have **some** cream?

6 Choose the correct option.
1 My brother doesn't eat *many / some* vegetables.
2 Don't eat *enough / too much* salt – it's bad for you.
3 *How many / How much* sugar did you put in my tea?
4 Is there *any / many* jam in the cupboard?
5 Would you like *any / some* of this cake?

YOUR WORLD

7 In pairs, discuss your bad eating habits.
I don't eat enough vegetables. What about you?

Unit 6   I can talk about quantities of food.

6.3 Reading and Vocabulary

Sleep

1 Are these sentences true for you?
1. It's hard to get up in the morning.
2. I sleep more than my parents.
3. I never want to go to bed before 11 p.m.

2 🔊 6.8 Read the letter and answer the questions.
1. Who did Carla write to?
2. What is the letter about?
3. What does she want her parents to stop doing? Why?

3 Read the letter again. Choose the correct answer.
1. Teenagers can't fall asleep until it's late because
   a. they feel tired in the morning.
   b. they have less melatonin than adults.
   c. their brains work differently from adult brains.
2. Teenagers shouldn't play video games at night because
   a. blue light can stop you sleeping.
   b. their parents don't think it's a good idea.
   c. video games are bad for you.
3. Teenagers can't get enough sleep during the week because they
   a. are growing.
   b. have to go to bed before 10 p.m.
   c. have to get up early for school.
4. Carla thinks it's a good idea that
   a. schools start later.
   b. students can sleep at school.
   c. teenagers get up early.

4 🔊 6.9 **WORD FRIENDS** In pairs, find these phrases in the letter and write the missing words. Listen and check.
1. fall *asleep*
2. feel _____/tired
3. get enough _____
4. get up/wake up _____ / late
5. go to _____/sleep
6. keep you _____
7. remember your dreams
8. sleep badly/_____

5 🔊 6.10 Choose the correct option. Listen and check. Then ask and answer the questions in pairs.

BEDTIME QUESTIONS
1. What time do the people in your house usually *go / sleep* to bed?
2. Do you usually start to *fall / feel* sleepy before or after your parents?
3. Do you usually *fall / sleep* well at night?
4. What time do you *feel / get* up on school days? Is that too early?
5. What time do you usually *go / wake* up at the weekend?
6. Do you ever find it difficult to *fall / wake* asleep? Why?

TeenSpace
About us Lifestyle Health and fitness **Teenagers talk**

An open letter
by Carla Lee

Dear Mum and Dad,

I know you don't like it when I go to bed late and I can't wake up early in the morning. But it's not my fault. I'm a teenager, and teenagers are different.

Human brains make a hormone called melatonin, which makes us feel sleepy. But teenagers don't start producing melatonin until about 11 p.m., two hours after adults or younger kids. That's why we can't fall asleep early and we play video games or go on our phones. But that's not a good idea because the blue light from screens reduces the melatonin in our brains and keeps us awake!

The problem is that teenagers are growing, so we need more sleep than adults: eight to ten hours a night! But if we can't sleep before midnight and we have to get up at 7 a.m. to go to school, then one thing is clear: we don't get enough sleep during the week. In some places schools start later, which is great! But our school starts at 8 a.m.! ☹

So what happens? At weekends we sleep late, sometimes very late. ☺ Sleep is important. If you don't sleep well, you feel tired. Your memory fails. You can't concentrate. You get angry more easily. You have more accidents. And you fall ill more often.

So please don't open my curtains too early. I'm not lazy. I just need to sleep.

Love, Carla

VIDEO — WIDER WORLD

6 ▶ 31 Watch four people talking about sleeping and getting up. Write down the sleep habits they mention.

7 In pairs, talk about your sleep habits.
   A: *What time did you go to bed last night?*
   B: *I went to bed at …*

I can understand an open letter about sleep.

6.4 Grammar

Past Continuous and Past Simple

Tell us about your accidents!
What happened to you? What were you doing when it happened?

Yesterday afternoon I was cycling in the park. Some kids were playing football, so I wasn't paying attention to where I was going. While I was watching the match, a dog ran in front of me. I fell off my bike. I broke my arm, hurt my back and cut my knee. It was really painful. *Arlo*

My basketball team was playing a match on Friday. We weren't playing well, and the other team was really good. They were winning 34–21 when I got the ball. Unfortunately, when I was trying to score a basket, I hurt my ankle and fell. I hit my head and broke my nose. I was lucky I didn't break my neck. *Jodie*

1 🔊 **6.11** Describe the photo. Read the text and answer the questions.
1. What was Arlo doing yesterday afternoon?
2. What happened to him when he fell?
3. What was Jodie doing on Friday?
4. What happened to her?

2 Study the Grammar box. Find more examples of the Past Continuous in the text.

GRAMMAR	Past Continuous and Past Simple
+	I was cycling in the park. She was jumping. They were playing football.
–	I wasn't running. She wasn't swimming. We weren't playing well.
?	Were you cycling? Yes, I was./No, I wasn't. Was she jumping? Yes, she was./No, she wasn't. Were they playing? Yes, they were./No, they weren't. What was she doing yesterday at 5 p.m.?

Past Simple and Past Continuous
While/When/As I was watching the match, a dog ran in front of me.
I was watching the match when a dog ran in front of me.

GRAMMAR TIME > PAGE 132

3 In pairs, ask and answer the questions below.
What were you doing …
- at 8 p.m. last Friday?
- an hour ago?
- at six o'clock this morning?
- on Sunday at 12.30?
- last week at this time?
- 24 hours ago?

A: *What were you doing at 8 p.m. last Friday?*
B: *I was watching a film. What about you?*

4 Choose the correct option.
1. My cousin *had / was having* an accident when he *rode / was riding* a motorbike.
2. My mum *hit / was hitting* her head as she *got / was getting* into the car.
3. As my dad *did / was doing* weight-training, he *hurt / was hurting* his back.
4. We *fell / were falling* when we *danced / were dancing*.
5. I *hurt / was hurting* my ankle when I *ran / was running* to school.

5 🔊 **6.12** Complete the dialogue with the correct form of the verbs in brackets. Listen and check.

A: What ¹<u>were you doing</u> (you/do) when the accident ²_____ (happen)?
B: I ³_____ (drive) my kids to school. They ⁴_____ (make) a lot of noise, so I ⁵_____ (tell) them to be quiet. I ⁶_____ (not look) at the road and I ⁷_____ (drive) into a tree. Fortunately, nobody was hurt.

VIDEO — **WIDER WORLD**

6 ▶ **32** Watch three people talking about accidents they had. Write down what happened to them.

7 Work in groups. Describe an accident you had when you were younger.
- How old were you?
- What were you doing at the time of the accident and what happened next?

I was ten. I was walking to school when …

Unit 6 — I can use the Past Continuous and the Past Simple to tell a story about past events.

6.5 Listening and Vocabulary

Symptoms, illnesses and allergies

1 Look at the picture. Why is tomorrow a big day for Mansewood United?

2 🔊 6.13 Study the Vocabulary box. In pairs, match the symptoms with the illnesses and allergies.

> **VOCABULARY** Symptoms, illnesses and allergies
>
> **Symptoms**
> cough   feel ill   feel sick   have a cough   have a headache
> have a high temperature   have a sore throat
> have a stomachache   sneeze
>
> **Illnesses and allergies**
> have a cold   have a food allergy   have hay fever   have the flu

When you have hay fever, you can sneeze.

3 🔊 6.14 What symptoms have the players in the picture got? Complete the sentences. Listen to Jerry and check.
1 Nathan is *sneezing* .
2 James has got a _____ .
3 Ben has got a _____ throat and a high _____ .
4 Chris has got a _____ .

4 🔊 6.15 Listen to a dialogue. In pairs, answer the questions.
1 Why couldn't Ben play?
2 Why was Nathan sneezing?
3 Why did James have a stomachache?
4 Why couldn't Chris play?
5 What did the coach get at the end?

5 🔊 6.16 Listen to Jerry talking to a friend about the football match. Choose the correct answer.
1 They played the match on
  a Wednesday.
  b Saturday.
  c Sunday.
2 While Jerry was visiting friends,
  a he got a cold.
  b he got the flu.
  c he got hay fever.
3 On the day of the match, Jerry felt
  a great.
  b ill.
  c very well.
4 Ben didn't finish the match because
  a he hurt his ankle.
  b he broke his leg.
  c he hurt his back.
5 Jerry's team won the match
  a 2–1.
  b 3–1.
  c 3–2.

YOUR WORLD

6 In pairs, talk about a time when you were ill. Describe your symptoms.

I had a really bad cold last month.

I can understand a conversation about health problems.

6.6 Speaking
Talking about health problems

VIDEO ▶ **WHAT'S THE MATTER?**

Noah: Hi Lena, how are you feeling?
Lena: I've got a sore throat and a headache. I think I've got the flu.
Noah: Have you got a temperature?
Lena: No, I haven't. Perhaps it's just a cold.
Noah: Maybe you should take some medicine.
Lena: I took some an hour ago.
Noah: You probably need to stay in bed for a day or two … Oh! Is this your model for Technology? Can I help you with it?
Lena: Sure.
Noah: Ow!
Lena: What's the matter?
Noah: My fingers are stuck! Ow! It hurts!
Lena: Let me see. How did you do that?
Noah: I was using this glue and …
Lena: That's the wrong glue! It's really strong! You should be more careful. Here, have some water.
Noah: I don't need water! My fingers are stuck together! It's really painful! Ow!
Mum: Hi! What's going on? Why were you shouting? What's wrong?

Lena: Noah's got his fingers stuck together.
Mum: Let me have a look. You need to see a doctor. Come on!

SOUNDS GOOD! Sure. • What's going on? • Let me have a look.

1 ▶ 33 🔊 6.17 Describe the photo. What is Noah's problem? How do you think it happened? Watch or listen and check.

2 Study the Speaking box. Find examples of the phrases in the dialogue.

SPEAKING **Talking about health problems**

Asking what the problem is
What's the matter? What's wrong?
How are you feeling?

Talking about symptoms
I feel sick/ill/terrible.
I've got a stomachache/a headache/toothache/
a temperature/a sore throat/a cold/the flu.
My leg/back hurts.
It's sore/painful.

Giving advice
Sit down.
Have some water.
You should/need to lie down/stay in bed/keep calm/
see a doctor/be more careful/go to hospital.
You should take a tablet/some medicine.

---

3 🔊 6.18 Complete the dialogues with one word in each gap. Listen and check.
1 A: What's the *matter* ?
   B: I've got a _____ temperature.
   A: You should stay in _____ and take some _____ .
2 A: _____ wrong with you?
   B: I _____ terrible, and my leg _____ . Perhaps it's broken.
   A: I think you _____ go to hospital.

4 Suggest what the people should do. Use the Speaking box to help you.
1 Lena's got the flu. *She should take some medicine.*
2 Mateo's got hay fever.
3 Mia broke her arm.
4 Noah's stomach hurts.
5 Adam fell down the stairs and hurt his shoulder.

YOUR WORLD

5 In pairs, follow the instructions. Use the Speaking box and Exercise 4 to help you.
- Student A – ask how Student B is feeling. Listen and give advice.
- Student B – you feel ill. Tell Student A about your symptoms.
- Change roles.

Unit 6 80 I can talk about health problems.

6.7 Writing
A narrative

1 Read Sophia Grey's story and answer the questions.
1. Why was Sophia in Cardiff last Sunday?
2. What was the weather like at first?
3. What happened to Sophia?
4. Who helped her?
5. Why did she feel so happy?

WRITING **A narrative**

1. **Write when and where the event happened**
   Last Sunday in Cardiff, I ran my first half marathon.
2. **Describe the scene**
   The sun was shining.
3. **Describe the action**
   I was running towards the 20 km sign.   I fell.
4. **Write what happened in the end**
   I crossed the finishing line.

2 Match sentences a–d with sections 1–4 in the Writing box.
- a ☐ As I was running, a young man fell in front of me.
- b ☐ I took part in a race in my home town last weekend.
- c ☐ In the end, we finished the race together.
- d ☐ It was a beautiful day and I felt good.

3 Study the Language box. Find four examples of narrative linkers in the story.

LANGUAGE **Narrative linkers**

Use narrative linkers with the Past Simple and Past Continuous to connect ideas: *next, suddenly, then, when, after that, while, a few minutes later, the next day.*

4 Complete the text with the narrative linkers below.

| a few minutes later | suddenly |
| the next day | then | when | ~~while~~ |

¹*While* I was shopping in Cardiff on Sunday, I stopped to watch the half marathon. Just ² _____ , I saw my friend Sophia. ³ _____ she was running past me, I called out, but she didn't hear me. ⁴ _____ , she fell. I was worried, but ⁵ _____ someone helped her up, and she finished the race. ⁶ _____ at school, she told me all about it.

An unforgettable day
Sophia Grey

1. Last Sunday in Cardiff, I ran my first half marathon. 21.097 kilometres!

2. The sun was shining. I didn't go fast at first, but after ten kilometres, I felt fit and strong. While we were running through the city centre, the crowd began to cheer. I started to run faster.

3. I was running towards the 20 km sign when it started raining. I didn't slow down. That was a mistake because the ground was wet. Suddenly, I fell. I hurt my back and cut my hand. It was bleeding. My knee was sore too.

4. Another runner stopped and helped me to get up. Then we ran the last 200 metres together. I was crying when I crossed the finishing line, but I felt wonderful. It was an unforgettable day.

WRITING TIME

5 Write a narrative with the title: *An unforgettable day*.

1. **Find ideas**
   Make notes for a narrative.
   - Where and when did the story happen?
   - What was happening when the story began?
   - What happened?
   - How did it end?

2. **Plan**
   Organise your ideas into paragraphs. Use Simon's story to help you.

3. **Write and share**
   - Write a draft narrative. Use the Language box and the Writing box to help you.
   - Share your narrative with another student for feedback.
   - Write the final version of your narrative.

4. **Check**
   - Check language: did you use linkers to connect your sentences?
   - Check grammar: did you use the Past Simple and the Past Continuous?

I can write a narrative.

Vocabulary Activator

WORDLIST 🔊 6.19

Parts of the body 1
ankle (n)
elbow (n)
eyebrow (n)
fingers (n)
knee (n)
lips (n)
neck (n)
shoulder (n)
throat (n)
toes (n)

Parts of the body 2
bone (n)
brain (n)
heart (n)
muscle (n)
skin (n)
stomach (n)
tongue (n)

Word friends
(sport and fitness)
do exercises
do sport
do weight-training
do yoga
go cycling
go running
go surfing
go swimming
go walking
keep fit
keep healthy
play badminton
play basketball
play football
play hockey
play rugby
play (team) games

Word friends
(accidents and injuries)
break your leg
burn your hand
cut your finger
hit your head
hurt your ankle

Word friends (sleep)
fall asleep
feel sleepy
feel tired
get enough sleep
get up early
get up late
go to bed
go to sleep
keep you awake
remember your dreams
sleep badly
sleep well
wake up early
wake up late

Symptoms, illnesses and allergies
cough (v)
feel ill
feel sick
have a cold
have a cough
have a food allergy
have a headache
have a high temperature
have a sore throat
have a stomachache
have hay fever
have the flu
sneeze (v)

Extra words
accident (n)
adult (n)
advice (n)
bleed (v)
break your arm
break your nose
careful (adj)
concentrate (v)
cry (v)
cut your hand
doctor (n)
exercise (v)
fall (v)
finish the race
half marathon (n)
healthy (adj)
hormone (n)
hospital (n)
human (adj)
hurt your back
keep calm
lie down (v)
medicine (n)
memory (n)
my fingers are stuck
my leg/back hurts
painful (adj)
pay attention
see a doctor
sit down (v)
stay in bed
suddenly (adv)
take a tablet
take some medicine
teenager (n)
toothache (n)

---

1 Use words from the wordlist to find these things.
1 three parts of the bottom part of your body that you use when you walk *ankle, …*
2 three sports that are team games
3 two sports you can do in water
4 three body parts that are in/on many areas of your body
5 two symptoms ending with *-ache*
6 two body parts that are part of your mouth

2 Complete the sentences with words from the wordlist.
1 You have an *eyebrow* above each eye.
2 Your _____ is in the middle of your leg.
3 You feel _____ when you're not well.
4 You _____ a lot when you have hay fever.
5 When you've got the flu, your _____ can be high.
6 Weight-training is good for the _____ in your arms and back.

3 Complete the sentences with the words below. In pairs, say which sentences are true for you.

> ~~allergy~~   broke   burned   feel   remember   sleep

1 I don't have a food *allergy*, so I can eat everything.
2 I usually _____ my dreams when I wake up.
3 I sometimes _____ sleepy in class.
4 I get hay fever in the summer, so I don't _____ well.
5 Las year I _____ my hand on the hot oven.
6 I went to hospital when I _____ my leg.

4 🔊 6.20 **PRONUNCIATION** Listen to the words below and decide if you hear the underlined letters. Listen again and repeat.

> feel ti<u>r</u>ed   go wa<u>l</u>king   hea<u>d</u>ache   <u>k</u>nee   mus<u>c</u>le   temp<u>e</u>rature   tong<u>ue</u>   wake up ear<u>l</u>y   wei<u>gh</u>t-training

Unit 6

Revision

Vocabulary

1 Choose the correct answer.
1 Which of these things can you break?
   a muscles   b brain   c bones
2 Which of these things isn't very important for being healthy?
   a keeping fit   b waking up early
   c getting enough sleep
3 Which of these things makes you sneeze?
   a hay fever   b a cough   c feeling sick
4 Which of these things can't you do on your own?
   a do yoga   b go running
   c play badminton
5 Which of these things is not near your head?
   a neck   b ankle   c shoulder
6 Which of these things hurts if you eat too much?
   a tongue   b stomach   c brain

2 Match phrases 1–6 with a–f to make sentences.
1 ☐ I think I've got the
2 ☐ Our neighbour's loud TV keeps
3 ☐ My sister likes to
4 ☐ My friends often play
5 ☐ I can't write because I burned
6 ☐ I enjoy doing

a go running after school.
b my hand on the oven.
c flu, so I'm staying at home.
d weight-training to keep fit.
e football in the park.
f me awake at night.

3 Choose the correct option. Then think of some advice you can give to Archie.

✉

Dear Problem Pete,

My problem is that I often feel ¹*tired / tiring*. A few days ago I ²*kept / fell* asleep on the bus for a minute or two. When I woke ³*up / at* my friend was looking at me, but she didn't say anything.

I'm worried because I don't get ⁴*enough / too* sleep. I never go ⁵*in / to* bed late, but I don't sleep very ⁶*good / well*. I want to have a good night's sleep. What can I do?

Thanks for your help,

Archie

Grammar

4 Choose the correct option.
A: I'm so hungry! Is there anything to eat?
B: Well, we've got ¹*any / some* cheese.
A: Good! Have we got ²*any / some* bread for a sandwich?
B: No, we haven't got ³*any / some*. But we have got ⁴*any / some* eggs.
A: Excellent! How ⁵*many / much* eggs?
B: Two.
A: That's ⁶*not much / not many*!
B: But we've got ⁷*a lot of / any* potatoes.
A: Great! So, we can have fried eggs and chips!
B: No, I don't have ⁸*much / many* time to cook. And anyway, we eat ⁹*too many / too much* chips! There are ¹⁰*a lot of / too many* vegetables, so you can have a vegetable omelette!

5 Complete the text with the Past Simple or the Past Continuous form of the verbs in brackets.

Last weekend I ¹*was sitting* (sit) in my room when I ²_____ (hear) a noise from outside. I ³_____ (get up) and opened the window. My brother ⁴_____ (lie) in the garden. He ⁵_____ (not look) at me, so I ⁶_____ (shout) 'Jack! Are you OK?'
'My knee hurts. I fell off the chair,' he answered.
'Why? What ⁷_____ (you/do) on the chair?'
'I ⁸_____ (help) the cat to get down from the tree! I ⁹_____ (stand) on the chair when the cat ¹⁰_____ (jump) suddenly, and I fell. It's very painful!'

Speaking

6 In pairs, role play the situation. Student A, look below. Student B, go to page 139.

Student A
- Say hello to Student B.
- Ask Student B how he/she is.
- Ask Student B what happened.
- Give some advice.
- Reply that you aren't feeling well. Describe your symptoms.
- Listen and react to Student B's advice. Say thank you.

Dictation

7 🔊 6.21 Listen. Then listen again and write down what you hear during each pause.

SET FOR LIFE

Let's sort this out!

Mum:	Sam, can you tidy and vacuum the living room, please? And do the ironing?	Sam:	But washing up's really easy – and it's quick! Why do I have to do all the boring jobs?
Sam:	Again? But I did some ironing at the weekend. Why can't Alice do something?	Mum:	That's not true, Sam.
		Sam:	It's always me! Alice never has to vacuum the floors, or do the ironing. It's not fair!
Mum:	She did the washing up this morning.		

1 In groups, study the list of things which usually cause arguments between teenagers and their parents. Discuss the questions below.

> clothes/hair/make-up   coming home late   friends
> housework   mobile phones   schoolwork

1. Do you ever disagree with your parents on these topics? Give examples.
2. What other things do teenagers argue about with their parents?

2 🔊 6.22 Read the dialogue and answer the questions.
1. What are Sam and his mum arguing about?
2. What does Sam have to do?
3. Why doesn't he want to do it?
4. What does he feel about his sister, Alice?

3 How do you think the dialogue ends? Choose an answer.
   a Sam agrees to do the work.
   b Sam's sister has to do the housework.
   c Sam and his mum get angry.

4 🔊 6.23 Listen to the ending of the dialogue and check your answer to Exercise 3.

5 In pairs, discuss the questions.
   1 What happened at the end of the dialogue?
   2 Did Sam and his mum solve the problem?
   3 Are they both happy?

6 🔊 6.24 Listen to another possible ending to the dialogue. What do Sam and his mum do differently this time? Choose the correct option.
   1 They *listen / don't listen* to each other's arguments.
   2 They *make / don't make* personal comments.
   3 They *talk / don't talk* about their feelings.
   4 They *resolve / don't resolve* the problem.

Units 5–6   84   I can work with other people to resolve an argument.

Resolve arguments with other people

7 🔊 **6.24** Listen again. Number the expressions in the Useful Phrases box in the order that you hear them. Which expression is not in the dialogue?

8 In pairs, discuss the situations below. Decide how both people feel and how they can resolve the problem in a positive way.

Situation 1

A: Your younger brother/sister always takes your things without asking. Yesterday you found your expensive new camera in his/her room.

B: You are the younger brother/sister. You're interested in photography, so you took your brother's/sister's camera for a quick look.

Situation 2

A: You want to go to a party at the weekend and you'd like your mum/dad to collect you at midnight.

B: You are the parent. You think that midnight is too late, but you don't mind coming at ten o'clock.

9 Read the Useful Tips. In class, discuss the questions.
1. What do you do when you are feeling angry or annoyed with another person?
2. Do you think the tips can help? Why?/Why not?

SET FOR LIFE

10 In pairs, role play a situation where two people have an argument and find a way to resolve it. Follow the instructions.

1 Choose one of the situations in Exercise 8 or think of a situation from your own life.

2 Write the scene. Use the expressions from the Useful Phrases box. Decide:
- how both people in the situation feel
- what they should say in the dialogue
- how they can resolve the problem in a positive way

3 Practise your dialogue. Remember to stay calm and show that you understand another person's position.

4 Present the dialogue for the class or record it on your phone.

USEFUL TIPS

When you have an argument with another person, it is important to find a way to resolve it in a positive way.

- Stop for a moment and think.
- Stay calm. Use sentences with the pronoun *I* to explain your feelings.
- Don't use phrases like *You never … You always …*
- If you are wrong, apologise!
- Try to find a good solution for everyone.

USEFUL PHRASES

Stopping an argument
- [ ] Let's stop and think for a minute.
- [ ] Let's sort this out.
- [ ] What's the basic problem here?

Explaining your position calmly
- [ ] I (don't) feel that …
- [ ] I (don't) think that …

Seeing another person's point of view
- [ ] I understand that …
- [ ] I see what you mean.
- [ ] (Maybe) you've got a point.

Working together to find a solution
- [ ] If you like, I can …
- [ ] Perhaps I/you/we could …

Progress Check Units 1–6

Vocabulary and Grammar

1 Choose the correct option.
 1 I'm really interested ___ technology.
  a in   b into   c with
 2 Please remember to wear your ___ on school sports day.
  a costume   b uniform   c tracksuit
 3 Do you want to ___ yoga? Contact Marie for more information.
  a do   b go   c make
 4 No talking please. All students ___ be quiet during the exam.
  a can   b must   c don't have to
 5 I was listening to music when my little brother ___ into my room.
  a was coming   b came   c used to come
 6 Please put your coffee cups in the ___ before leaving the office. Thank you.
  a dishwasher   b washing machine   c wardrobe

2 Complete the text with one word in each gap.

Your bedroom is the place where you study, sleep and relax, so if you ask me, it's important to feel comfortable in it. We ¹*used* to live in a flat and I had a bedroom ²_____ was very small. In fact there wasn't ³_____ space for a table and chair, so I studied in the kitchen. Now we live in a big house, so I don't ⁴_____ to study in the kitchen. I've got a very big room ⁵_____ I can do my homework. I like a clean and tidy room, so I ⁶_____ my bed every day. At the weekend, I vacuum the floor and I take ⁷_____ the rubbish. In fact, everyone likes my room.

3 Complete the second sentence with the word in bold so that it means the same as the first one. Use no more than four words.
 1 Did you watch many horror films when you were little? **USE**
  Did you *use to watch* many horror films when you were little?
 2 Falling over in the basketball game was very embarrassing. **FELT**
  I _____ when I fell over in the basketball game.
 3 It isn't polite to finish a telephone conversation without saying goodbye. **HANG**
  It is rude _____ without saying goodbye.
 4 It's OK with me to do homework at the weekend. **MIND**
  I _____ homework at the weekend.
 5 We do lots of Maths tests – and I hate it! **STAND**
  I _____ lots of Maths tests.
 6 George is a very good dancer. **DANCES**
  George _____ .

Speaking

4 Choose the correct option.
 1 A: What do you think of comics?
  B: ___
   a I think they're cool.
   b I agree with you.
   c Sounds good.
 2 A: What should I do about my room?
  B: ___
   a Sit down.
   b That's a terrible idea!
   c I think you should redecorate it.
 3 A: ___
  B: My back hurts.
   a What's the matter?
   b Can you give me some advice?
   c What happened in the end?
 4 A: My computer crashed.
  B: ___
   a That's not a bad idea.
   b You need to switch it off and on again.
   c You have to charge it.

5 In pairs, follow the instructions. Go to page 139.

Listening

6 In pairs, discuss what can go wrong on a camping weekend. Use the photos to help you.

A

B

C

7 🔊 PC1–6.1 Listen and choose the correct answer.
1 Why didn't Amy go on the camping trip?
  a She had too much homework to do.
  b Her mum didn't let her go because she was ill.
  c She decided to stay at home.
2 What did Amy have for lunch?
  a pasta   b cheesecake   c soup
3 When did Frank get back from the camping trip?
  a On Monday.   b On Sunday.   c On Saturday.
4 Why did Amy's friends come home early?
  a They didn't feel well.
  b A family member came for a visit.
  c The weather was bad.

8 Tell your partner about a weekend that went wrong. What happened? What did you do?

Reading

9 Read the blog and complete the sentences with a word or a short phrase in each gap.

Emily's tech blog

Are you excited about new tech gadgets? Check out these amazing smart gadgets for your home!

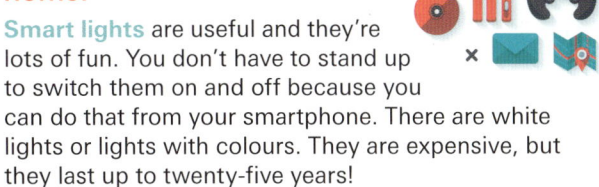

Smart lights are useful and they're lots of fun. You don't have to stand up to switch them on and off because you can do that from your smartphone. There are white lights or lights with colours. They are expensive, but they last up to twenty-five years!

Smart vacuum cleaners are popular with people who don't have enough time to clean their houses. There are different prices – you have to pay over £2,000 for a very expensive vacuum cleaner, but you can also get one for only £300. The vacuum cleaners that cost more have a camera that helps them move around the house. On a full battery they can work for ninety minutes and vacuum a big apartment or one floor of a house.

The **clock rug** is my favourite gadget. It's a smart alarm clock. I put my clock rug on the floor next to my bed, and it wakes me up at seven in the morning, or at ten at weekends! It uses my favourite songs from my smartphone when it turns on the alarm. The only way to make it stop is to get up and stand on it! So it works!

1 You can control smart lights with your _smartphone_ .
2 You can use smart lights for _____ years.
3 A cheaper smart vacuum cleaner costs _____ .
4 To move around the house, expensive smart vacuum cleaners use a _____ .
5 Emily gets up at _____ during the week.
6 To switch off the clock you must _____ .

10 What gadget from Emily's blog would you like to have? Why?

Writing

11 Write a narrative about a strange house. Include the information below.
- when and where the story began
- what was happening when the story began
- what happened in the story
- what happened in the end

87

Spending and saving

7

VOCABULARY
Types of shops | Containers | Shopping centres | Eco-friendly shopping | Money | Pocket money

GRAMMAR
Comparatives and superlatives of adjectives | *Going to* and Present Continuous for the future

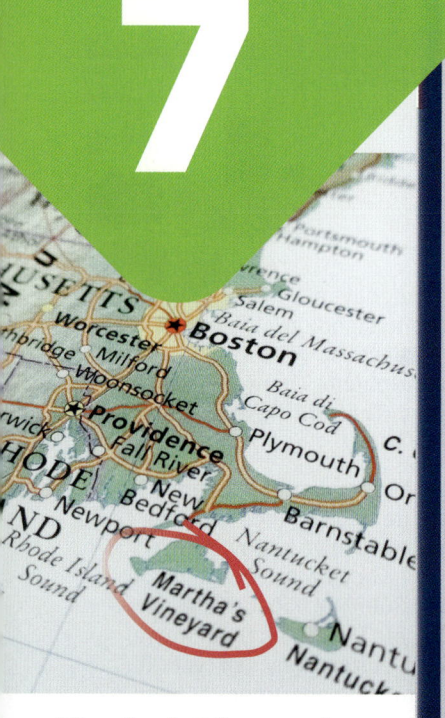

US TRAVEL GUIDE

Shopping | Places to stay | Where to eat | Things to do

Shopping in Martha's Vineyard is a special experience. There are no large out-of-town shopping centres or chain stores. The residents and visitors can enjoy their coffee in local cafés, get fresh bread and doughnuts in small bakeries and buy almost anything at Alley's General Store. (It's a greengrocer's, florist's and newsagent's all in one and a popular meeting place for people on the island.)

Martha's Vineyard
Located just off the coast of Massachusetts, USA, Martha's Vineyard is a great place to spend your summer break. This small island has got lots to offer for everyone: beautiful beaches, amazing countryside and quiet seaside towns.

7.1 Vocabulary

Shopping

1 In pairs, ask and answer the questions.
1. When was the last time you went shopping?
2. Did you go to a shopping centre or a small local shop?
3. What did you buy?

2 Read the text. Why is Martha's Vineyard different from other cities and towns?

3 🔊 7.1 **I KNOW!** Study Vocabulary box A. Which of the shops are mentioned in the text? Can you add more words?

VOCABULARY A **Types of shops**

bakery   bookshop   butcher's   café   clothes shop
florist's   greengrocer's   newsagent's   pharmacy
shoe shop

4 Which shops in Vocabulary box A have you got in your neighbourhood? Which shops haven't you got? Discuss in groups.

We've got a bakery, but we haven't got a bookshop.

Unit 7

5 🔊 **7.2** Listen to six recordings. Write the correct names of the shops from Vocabulary box A.

1 *shoe shop*   4 _____
2 _____   5 _____
3 _____   6 _____

6 🔊 **7.3** **WORD FRIENDS** Complete Karim's shopping list with the words below. Listen and check.

bottle   box   ~~bunch~~   packet   pair

- A ¹*bunch* of flowers and a ² _____ of chocolates for Mum's birthday
- Fresh bread
- Apples
- A ³ _____ of tissues, a ⁴ _____ of shampoo
- A ⁵ _____ of socks
- A photo album

7 🔊 **7.4** Listen to a dialogue. What did Karim forget to buy?

8 🔊 **7.5** Study Vocabulary box B. Find these things in the picture.

VOCABULARY B **Shopping centres**

car park   department store   escalator
food court   lift   multi-screen cinema
public toilets   shop assistant   shopper
trolley

9 🔊 **7.6** Look at the picture. Complete the sentences with words from Vocabulary box B. Listen and check.

1 There's a *shopper* with four bags outside the department store.
2 Some teenagers are going up the _____ .
3 An old man is waiting for the _____ .
4 A man has got lots of boxes in his _____ .
5 There's a big _____ behind the shopping centre.
6 You can choose a film to watch at the _____ .
7 There are some _____ near the exit.

10 🔊 **7.7** Match questions 1–4 with answers a–d. Listen and check.

1 ☐ Firstly, what's your favourite shop?
2 ☐ And where is it?
3 ☐ What does it sell?
4 ☐ Why do you like it?

a It's in the new shopping centre.
b They've got a good choice of games, and the shop assistants there are really helpful.
c My favourite shop is Game World.
d It sells computer games – new and second-hand.

VIDEO ▶   **WIDER WORLD**

11 ▶ **34** Watch five people talking about their favourite shops. Write down the places they mention and why they like them.

12 In pairs, ask and answer questions about your favourite shop.

A: What's your favourite shop? And where is it?
B: My favourite shop is …

I can talk about types of shops and shopping centres.

7.2 Grammar

Comparatives and superlatives of adjectives

1 Imagine that you want to buy some fragrance. Where do you buy it? Why?

> market   online   shopping centre
> small local shop

2 🔊 7.8 Read the comments. Where did each person buy the fragrance? Use the places from Exercise 1.

What are the best places to buy fragrance? Online, local shops or a shopping centre?

The NEW unisex fragrance!

Azra – I love wearing the new Wow! fragrance. I always buy it online. I love internet shopping because it's the quickest way to shop and it's easier to find the cheapest price. I can shop online in the evening, so it's more relaxing.

Marcel – Our local shops have the friendliest shop assistants! So when I need advice on a new fragrance, I go to a great pharmacy close to my flat. The people who work there are more helpful than the shop assistants at the shopping centre. Prices aren't as cheap at the pharmacy, but it's nearer to my home, so I don't pay for bus tickets!

Zoe – For me, the most important thing is to have fun. The shopping centre is the most enjoyable experience because there are many great shops. I go to the pharmacy there to choose a perfume. It's bigger than my local one, and there are more products. The area is nicer too, with lots of cafés.

3 Study the Grammar box. Find more examples of comparatives and superlatives in the comments.

GRAMMAR: Comparatives and superlatives of adjectives

quick	quicker	the quickest
nice	nicer	the nicest
big	bigger	the biggest
friendly	friendlier	the friendliest
important	more important	the most important
good	better	the best
bad	worse	the worst

They are bigger than my local shops.
They are not as cheap as the shopping centre.

GRAMMAR TIME > PAGE 133

WATCH OUT!
We don't use *the* after *my/your/their*, etc.
She's my ~~the~~ best friend.

4 Complete the comment with the comparatives or superlatives of the adjectives in brackets.

Ben – I bought this Wow! fragrance from the market, and that was my ¹*biggest* (big) mistake! It was ²_____ (cheap) than in the pharmacy, but I think my bottle is ³_____ (small) than my friend's. Also, the smell is ⁴_____ (bad) than the real one. The ⁵_____ (annoying) thing is that I can't take it back to the market!

5 Rewrite the sentences with *not as … as* and the adjectives in brackets.
   1 This shoe shop is smaller than the one near my flat. (big)
     This shoe shop isn't as big as the one near my flat.
   2 The prices in the bookshop are higher than online. (low)
   3 These shoes are cheaper than those trainers. (expensive)
   4 Inside the shopping centre it's colder than outside! (hot)
   5 The fruit in this shop is worse than at the market. (good)

VIDEO **WIDER WORLD**

6 ▶ 35 Watch three people talking about shopping centres. Write down the reasons why they like shopping there.

7 In pairs, ask and answer the questions.
   • Do you like shopping centres? Why?/Why not?
   • What's the best/worst thing you bought last year?

Unit 7   I can use the comparative and superlative of adjectives to describe things.

7.3 Reading and Vocabulary
Planet-friendly shopping

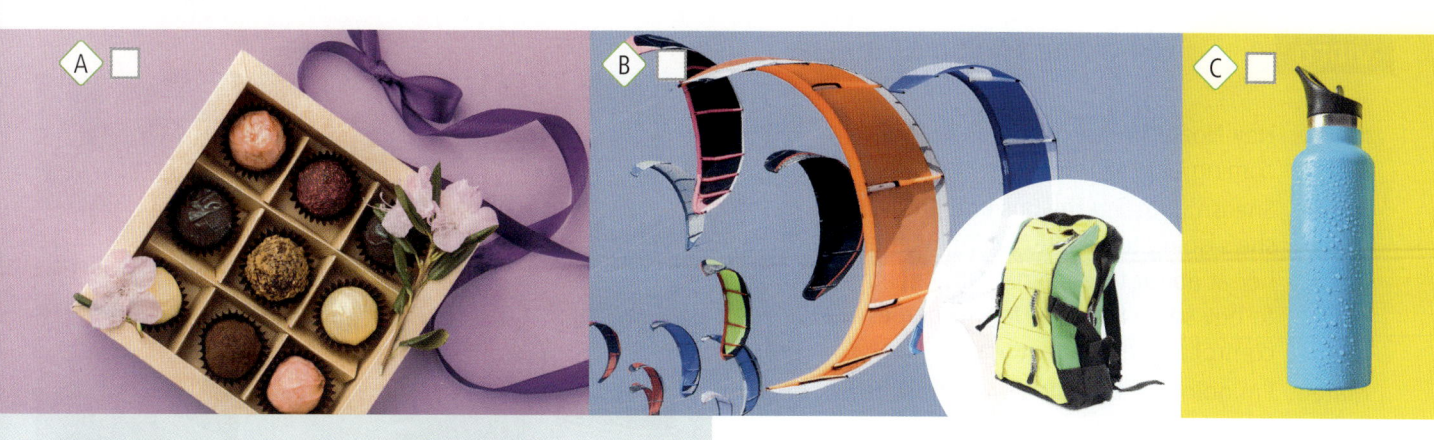

A ☐   B ☐   C ☐

Planet-friendly shopping

Can you think of good shopping habits to help the planet? We asked three people for ideas.

Idea 1 – Hasan, Turkey
I live in a seaside town where my parents run a popular kitesurf school. When kite sails are old, we don't throw them away. We keep them because we had a simple, planet-friendly idea. I recycle the old sails and make them into backpacks which are light, bright and stronger than normal bags. I sell them at the kitesurf school and online. I sometimes make different sizes or styles, but that's usually a bit more expensive. My customers love my backpacks, and they're better for the environment.

Idea 2 – Natalia, Spain
I stopped using plastic bottles last year. I found my metal water bottle on special offer at a local supermarket. Now I use it for my lunchtime drink every day. It's kinder to the environment than plastic bottles. It looks nicer too! My friends liked it and bought their own. Now we all share our small ideas. We usually take cloth bags when we go shopping, so we don't buy fruit and vegetables wrapped in plastic. Sometimes the smallest ideas can be the most important.

Idea 3 – Tomasz, Poland
A few years ago, our family decided to stop buying plastic things. Now we give presents that are more interesting and personal. So, on Mum's birthday I gave her a box of chocolates that I made myself. They weren't as good as chocolates from a supermarket, but Mum was happier with them! For my brother's birthday I'm buying old books from second-hand charity shops. They're cheaper than new ones, so you get more for the same price. And of course, we're going to go out for a meal. It's more important to have fun together than to have things!

1 How often do you buy clothes? Do you ever buy used clothes or sell old clothes? Why?/Why not?

2 🔊 7.9 Read the article and match ideas 1–3 with photos A–C. Which idea do you think is best?

3 Read the article again. Match people 1–3 with questions a–f. Each person can match with more than one question.
Which person …
a ☐ believes big ideas aren't always the best?
b ☐ made a homemade present?
c ☐ started to use something different?
d ☐ keeps and reuses old things in a new way?
e ☐ thinks family time is better than buying things?
f ☐ makes money from helping the world?

4 🔊 7.10 Study the Vocabulary box. In pairs, find the words in the article. Check you understand them.

VOCABULARY ▸ Eco-friendly shopping

charity shop   cloth bag   customer   environment
planet-friendly   price   recycle   special offer

5 Match words from the Vocabulary box with the definitions.
1 A person who buys something. *customer*
2 You can reuse this to put your shopping in.
3 To reuse something to help the environment.
4 The amount of money you pay for something.
5 A cheaper price than the usual price.
6 The natural world.

6 In groups, discuss the questions. **YOUR WORLD**
- Can you suggest three ideas for planet-friendly presents?
- Which idea is the best? Why?

I can understand an article about shopping habits.

7.4 Grammar

Going to and Present Continuous for the future

VIDEO ▶ **WHAT ARE YOU GOING TO BUY?**

Mateo: Hey Noah! Where is Mia? Is she coming or not?

Noah: She isn't getting the bus until three, so she's going to be late. We're meeting her at about three thirty. OK, I need to buy some batteries for my games controller. What about you?

Mateo: I'm going to look for a present for my dad. He's coming home next week.

Noah: Really? Where is he now?

Mateo: He's in Denver, on a music tour.

Noah: That's cool. What are you going to get him?

Mateo: I'm not sure. I'm going to look in the new joke shop. Dad's got a great sense of humour.

In the joke shop

Mateo: Hmm. Crazy socks? No. This remote-control spider is funny, but Dad doesn't need it.

Noah: Yeah. It's just a piece of stupid plastic. It's best to avoid it. Why don't you buy him a concert ticket? Or make something? It's kinder to the planet!

Mateo: You're right! I'm not going to buy it. Do you know what? I'm going to write a song for Dad. He loves my songs.

1 ▶ 36 ◀) 7.11 Describe the photo. Watch or listen and tick (✓) the things Noah and Mateo are planning to do.
- ☐ buy a games controller
- ☐ buy a present
- ☐ buy batteries
- ☐ listen to some music
- ☐ meet Mia
- ☐ phone Mia

2 Why doesn't Mateo buy the spider?

SET FOR LIFE

3 How can you be kind to the planet when you are shopping? Discuss in pairs.
- avoid plastic
- buy less
- buy local fruit and vegetables
- walk to the shops

4 Study the Grammar box. Find more examples of *going to* and the Present Continuous in the dialogue.

GRAMMAR — Going to and Present Continuous for the future

- **Fixed arrangements**
  He's *coming* home next week.
  She *isn't getting* the bus until three.
  Is she *coming* or not?

- **Intentions and future plans**
  She's *going to look for* a new book.
  I'm *not going to buy* it.
  Are you *going to buy* a present?

GRAMMAR TIME > PAGE 133

5 Use the Present Continuous to write about three arrangements for next week. In pairs, compare your sentences.

My sister's singing in a concert on Friday night.

6 ◀) 7.12 Complete the sentences with *going to* and the verbs in brackets. Listen and check.
1. I *'m going to buy* (buy) something to drink.
2. He _____ (come) with me to the shoe shop.
3. _____ (you/come) with us?
4. I _____ (go) to the bookshop first.
5. We _____ (buy) a really nice present for Gran.
6. I _____ (not spend) all my money.

YOUR WORLD

7 Use *going to* to write three or four intentions for the future. In groups, compare your sentences.

I'm going to invite some friends to my house at the weekend.
I'm not going to use plastic bags when I go shopping.

7.5 Listening and Vocabulary

Saving and spending money

1 Does money make people happy? Vote *yes* or *no* and say why.

A: Yes, you can buy things you dream about.
B: No, money can't buy friends or happiness.

2 🔊 7.13 Read the quiz. Then listen and choose Greg's answers, a or b. What does he ask Gemma for at the end?

BETEEN MAGAZINE

TO SAVE OR TO SPEND?

1 You get £10 pocket money and **earn** £20 babysitting. Do you put the money
 a in a money box?
 b in your purse/wallet/pocket?

2 You get £50 for your birthday. Do you
 a **save** some and **spend** the rest?
 b spend it all immediately?

3 You need new jeans. Do you
 a wait for the sales?
 b buy the pair you like without looking at the price?

4 A friend wants to **borrow** £20. Do you
 a say you never **lend** money?
 b agree and say they can **pay** you **back** any time?

3 🔊 7.14 Study the Vocabulary box. Which of the words can you find in the quiz? In pairs, complete the sentences.

VOCABULARY ▶ Money

change   money box   pocket money   purse
sales   wallet

1 My dad has a *wallet*, but I keep my money in my pocket.
2 The price of a book is £6.69, and you pay £10. How much _____ do you get?
3 How much _____ do you get a week?
4 Prices are lower in the summer _____ .
5 I have a _____ on a shelf in my room.

4 🔊 7.15 **WORD FRIENDS** Complete the sentences with highlighted verbs from the quiz in Exercise 2.
1 It's better to *save* money than to *spend* it.
2 Teenagers should _____ pocket money for doing housework.
3 I sometimes _____ money to my friends.
4 When I _____ money, I always *pay it back*.
5 I think teenagers should work to _____ their pocket money.

⚠ WATCH OUT!
lend – to give something to somebody for some time
borrow – to take something from somebody and give it back later

5 In pairs, do the quiz in Exercise 2. Go to page 144 to check your answers.

6 🔊 7.16 Listen to a radio phone-in and complete the notes with a word or a short phrase in each gap.

- The interviewer is asking listeners about ¹*pocket money*.
- Penny usually gets ² _____ pocket money each week.
- She saves her money in ³ _____ .
- Penny's friends sometimes borrow ⁴ _____ pounds from her.
- Penny saved enough money to buy ⁵ _____ last year.

7 🔊 7.17 Listen to the interviewer talking to an expert about saving money. Choose the correct answer.
1 The expert thinks Penny
 a is intelligent.   b should spend money.
 c isn't telling the truth.
2 The expert thinks it's good to
 a make a list.   b earn more money.
 c spend more than you earn.
3 The expert says it's a good idea to
 a stop using your mobile phone.
 b buy things you don't need.
 c find the lowest prices.

8 In pairs, discuss the statements in Exercise 4.

YOUR WORLD

A: Is it better to save money or to spend it?
B: I think …

I can understand a radio interview about money.

7.6 Speaking
Shopping for clothes

VIDEO ▶ SHOPPING IS HARD

SA: Good afternoon. Can I help you?
Mateo: Yes, I'm looking for a hoodie. How much is this one?
SA: That's £99.99.
Mateo: I'm looking for something cheaper than that.
Mia: What about these ones, Mateo? They're in the sale.
Mateo: Oh, that's a better price. I like special offers! Can I try this on, please?
SA: Of course. Just a moment ... here. The changing rooms are over there.
Mateo: Aargh, it's too big ... Excuse me! Have you got it in a smaller size?
SA: I think so … Here you are.
Mateo: This looks good. It's really comfortable …
Mia: Great! Now hurry up. The film's starting soon.
Mateo: I'm not sure about the colour.
Mia: Mateo! Are you buying it or not? I'm off. The film starts at four.
Mateo: Yes! I'll take it. Mia! Wait for me!
SA: Sir? Don't forget your hoodie!

SOUNDS GOOD! Hurry up. • I'm off. • Wait for me!

1 ▶ 37 🔊 7.18 Describe the photo. Why isn't Mia happy? Watch or listen and check.

2 Study the Speaking box. Find examples of the phrases in the dialogue.

SPEAKING — Shopping for clothes

Helping a customer
Can I help you?
They're in the sale.
What size are you?
The changing rooms are over there.
Here's your change.

Buying clothes
I'm looking for ...
How much is this one/are these?
Can I try this/these on, please?
It's/They're too big/small.
Have you got it/them in a smaller/bigger size?
Have you got it/them in another colour?
I'll take it/this one.
I'll take them/these ones.

3 🔊 7.19 Complete the dialogue with phrases from the Speaking box. Listen and check.

SA: Hello, can I help you?
C: ¹<u>I'm looking for a T-shirt</u>.
SA: This one's in the sale.
C: ²_____?
SA: Nine pounds ninety-nine.
C: ³_____?
SA: Yes, of course. The changing rooms are over there … Oh! It's too small.
C: ⁴_____?
SA: Yes, here you are. Oh, yes, that's better.
C: ⁵_____.
SA: Great. Here's your change. Goodbye.

4 🔊 7.20 Complete the sentences with *one* or *ones*. Listen and check.

WATCH OUT!
one/ones
Which **T-shirt** do you like best? – The blue **one**.
Which **trainers** are the right size? – These **ones**.

1 Do you want the white trainers or the blue <u>ones</u>?
2 This belt is too small. I need a bigger _____.
3 I'll take the black shirt, not the purple _____.
4 My sunglasses aren't as good as these _____.

5 **YOUR WORLD** In pairs, choose three items of clothing and role play three dialogues in a shop. Remember to change roles.

A: Good morning! Can I help you?
B: Yes, I'm looking for …

Unit 7 94 I can shop for clothes.

7.7 Writing
A message

A Hi Amy,
1. I'm going into town to buy some football boots.
2. Would you like to come?
3. Shall we meet at 2.30?
4. Let me know!

Sam

B Hi Mum,
1. I'm going to the sports shop to buy some new football boots!
4. I'm going to be back at about 5.00. See you soon!

Sam xxx

C Hi,
I'm organising a party at the new climbing wall to celebrate the end of exams. Would you like to come? We're going to meet outside the shopping centre at 7 p.m. on Friday. Let me know.
Amy

D Hi,
Sorry, but I'm really busy right now. Perhaps we could meet later? Good luck at the shop! See you soon.
Amy

1 Read Sam's messages. Which one includes an invitation and a plan? Which one did Sam write only to give information?

2 Read Amy's messages and answer the questions.
1. Which message is a reply to Sam's invitation?
2. What is Amy planning?

3 Study the Writing box. Find examples of the phrases in Sam's and Amy's messages.

WRITING — A message (making arrangements)

Give information
1. I'm having a party.
   I'm going into town.
   The bus is really late.

Make a request, offer or invite
2. Would you like to …?
   Can you help?

Make arrangements
3. Let's meet at …
   I'm going to be outside the cinema at 2.30.
   The party's starting at ten.

End the message
4. See you there.   See you soon.
   Let me know.

4 Study the Language box. Complete the sentences with one word in each gap.

LANGUAGE — Polite phrases

Would you like to go/meet/see …
Please come/meet me/wait …
Shall we meet after school?/**Perhaps we could** meet …?

1. Sandra, _____ meet me at the café after school.
2. _____ we go to the cinema?
3. Hi Charlie, _____ you like to see the *Avengers* movie with us?

WRITING TIME

5 Write a message to a friend, inviting them to go shopping or watch a film with you.

1 Find ideas
Make notes for a message.
- What do you want to do?
- Who are you going to invite?
- When and where are you going to meet?

2 Plan
Organise your ideas. Use Sam's and Amy's messages to help you.

3 Write and share
- Write a draft message. Use the Language box and the Writing box to help you.
- Share your message with another student for feedback.
- Write the final version of your message.

4 Check
- Check language: did you use polite phrases in your message?
- Check grammar: did you use the Present Continuous or *going to* for your arrangements?

I can write a message to make an arrangement.

Vocabulary Activator

WORDLIST 🔊 7.21

Shops
bakery (n)
bookshop (n)
butcher's (n)
café (n)
clothes shop (n)
florist's (n)
greengrocer's (n)
newsagent's (n)
pharmacy (n)
shoe shop (n)

Word friends (containers)
bottle of shampoo
box of chocolates
bunch of flowers
packet of tissues
pair of socks

Shopping centres
car park (n)
department store (n)
escalator (n)
food court (n)
lift (n)
multi-screen cinema (n)

public toilets (n)
shop assistant (n)
shopper (n)
trolley (n)

Eco-friendly shopping
charity shop (n)
cloth bag (n)
customer (n)
environment (n)
planet-friendly (adj)
price (n)
recycle (v)
special offer (n)

Money
change (n)
money box (n)
pocket money (n)
purse (n)
sales (n)
wallet (n)

Word friends (pocket money)
borrow money
earn your pocket money
get pocket money

lend money
pay (money) back
save money
spend money

Extra words
backpack (n)
be in the sale
busy (adj)
buy online
changing room (n)
cheap (adj)
climbing wall (n)
concert ticket (n)
Excuse me.
expensive (adj)
fresh (adj)
gift shop (n)
give presents
go into town
go out for a meal
good choice of
homemade (adj)
hurry up (v)
internet shopping (n)
keep money in your pocket

kind to the planet
local shop (n)
look for (v)
make a list
market (n)
out of town (adv)
pay for (v)
present (n)
quality (n)
reuse (v)
sail (n)
second-hand (adj)
sell online
sense of humour (n)
shop around (v)
shop online
shopping list (n)
size (n)
throw away (v)
water bottle (n)

---

1 Use words from the wordlist to find these things.
1 five places where you can buy food *bakery, …*
2 two names of people who buy things in a shop
3 two machines which can carry people up and down
4 three places where you can keep your money

2 Use words from the wordlist to answer the questions. Then write two more questions for your partner to guess.
1 Where can you buy medicine? *pharmacy*
2 What do you get when you pay cash in a shop?
3 Where can you buy different types of products?
4 What can you do with plastic, paper or old clothes?
5 What do you need to take with you to carry your shopping?
6 What do you do when you give someone money they need to return?
7 What tells you how much you have to pay?

3 Complete the sentences with one word in each gap. In pairs, say if the sentences are true for you.
1 I think it's a good idea to earn your *pocket* money.
2 I usually have a _____ of tissues in my school bag.
3 I sometimes _____ money on things I don't need.
4 I want to _____ a lot of money when I'm older.
5 I think it's important to pay money _____ if you borrow it.
6 I think a _____ of chocolates is a great birthday present.

I earn my pocket money. I help with the housework.

4 🔊 7.22 **PRONUNCIATION** Listen and find the words with a weak sound (/ə/). Listen again and check.
1 They're in (the) sale.
2 A bottle of shampoo.
3 What size are you?
4 A packet of tissues.
5 I'm looking for trainers.

Revision

Vocabulary

1 Complete the sentences with the words below. There are three extra words.

> borrow   butcher's   florist's   lift   newsagent's
> save   shop assistant   ~~wallet~~

1. I usually leave my *wallet* at home because I pay with my phone.
2. Dad went to the _____ to buy roses for Mum.
3. I read the news online, but I sometimes buy a magazine at the _____ .
4. I _____ my pocket money, but my sister always spends hers.
5. Gemma always buys chicken at the local _____ .

2 Choose the correct option.

Today's family shopping trip was terrible! First, my pocket money fell out of my ¹___ somewhere, and I lost £5. At the shopping centre, the ²___ wasn't working, so we had to climb the stairs. We went to lots of shops and a big ³___ , but I didn't find any nice clothes. The ⁴___ was busy, so we didn't have any lunch. And at the supermarket there weren't any ⁵___ , so we had to carry a heavy basket. Finally, it took a very long time to find our car in the ⁶___ !

1. a change   b purse   c sales
2. a escalator   b clothes shop   c environment
3. a special offer b greengrocer's
   c department store
4. a bakery   b bookshop   c café
5. a shoppers   b trolleys   c customers
6. a car park   b food court
   c multi-screen cinema

3 Choose the correct option. Then read the conversation in pairs.

A: I'd love to come for a pizza, but can you ¹*borrow / lend* me £5?
B: What? But you ²*borrowed / lent* £10 from me last week!
A: I know, but I ³*spent / saved* it on your birthday present, remember?
B: Oh yes! Why do you always ⁴*earn / spend* all your money? You should try to ⁵*save / pay* some money for something special.
A: I know, but I haven't got a job, so I don't ⁶*earn / lend* any money and I don't get much ⁷*wallet / pocket* money from my parents. I promise to pay you ⁸*up / back* tomorrow.

Grammar

4 Compare the shops with the words in brackets and *than* or *as … as*.

	Shoe Market	Shoe Shed	Sam's Shoes
How big is it?	large	medium	small
Price of a pair of trainers?	£65.00	£40.00	£90.00
Is it popular?	★★★☆☆	★★★★☆	★★★★☆

1. Shoe Shed / Sam's Shoes (big)
   Shoe Shed is bigger than Sam's Shoes./Sam's Shoes isn't as big as Shoe Shed.
2. Shoe Shed / Shoe Market (small)
3. Sam's Shoes / Shoe Market (expensive)
4. Sam's Shoes / Shoe Shed (popular)
5. Sam's Shoes / Shoe Market (popular)

5 Complete the text with the correct form of *going to* and the verbs in brackets.

Our parents ¹*aren't going to give* (not give) my sister and me pocket money anymore. We ²_____ (earn) money by helping with the housework. I ³_____ (clean) the bathroom, and my sister ⁴_____ (do) the washing up. I think it's a good idea, but it ⁵_____ (not be) fun.

6 Complete the text with the Present Continuous form of the verbs in brackets.

10.20 a.m.

Mum, I ¹*'m going* (go) to football training after school. Marcus ²_____ (come) too. Then we ³_____ (get) a lift with Marcus's mum. I ⁴_____ (not eat) dinner at home because we ⁵_____ (have) takeaway pizza.

Speaking

7 In pairs, role play the situation in a clothes shop. Use the ideas below to help you.
- what you are looking for
- colour
- size
- try it on
- the price

Then change roles and role play a situation in a shoe shop.

Dictation

8 🔊 7.23 Listen. Then listen again and write down what you hear during each pause.

Unit 7

BBC CULTURE

Shopping experiences

Encouraging you in

In the UK, about twenty percent of all sales are now online, and that number is growing. For a lot of people, buying things online is easier than going to a shop. Shops need to work hard to encourage customers into their stores. Did you know that they use some special techniques for this?

For example, a good shop window display can make people stop and share a photo or enter the shop. Shop window designers can be very creative, and sometimes they have very unusual ideas! What about putting real people into windows instead of mannequins? A top London shop once paid eight people to 'live' in their window displays for a week. And a New York store once filled a window with old clothes and rubbish! They wanted to make people think about fashion and the environment.

To encourage you to come in, shops often use things that look or smell nice. They put products like fragrances, flowers or fruit near the door. When you're inside the shop, they want you to stay for as long as possible. That's why they play music – and that's why you don't often see a clock on a shop wall! The necessary products (like milk in a supermarket or medicines in a pharmacy) are always at the back of the shop. Why? Because then you have to walk past a lot of other products to get to them!

Next time you go shopping, see how many of these techniques you can spot!

display (n) a collection of things for people to look at
encourage (v) make people think that something is a good idea
mannequins (n) models of the human body (for showing clothes)

1 In pairs, describe the photo. What is the shop trying to sell? Does the window make you want to go into the shop?

2 🔊 7.24 Read the text. What is it about? Choose the correct answer.
   a how shops attract customers
   b why people prefer shopping online
   c how to stop buying things you don't need

3 Read the text again and answer the questions.
   1 How many sales now happen online?
   2 What did a London shop once put in its windows instead of mannequins?
   3 Which products do shop designers often put near the door?
   4 Why do shops play music?
   5 Where can you often find medicines in a pharmacy?

4 In pairs, discuss how some shops you know use the techniques from the text.

BBC ▶ Fashion for all

5 In pairs, look at the photo and discuss the questions.
1 Who do you think the women are?
2 Where are they?
3 What is unusual about the mannequin?

6 ▶ 38 Watch a video and check your answers to Exercise 5.

7 ▶ 38 Watch again and choose the correct option.
1 Sophie's design is *a shop window / a wheelchair for mannequins*.
2 In 2012, her design appeared *at the London Paralympics / in a London fashion store*.
3 An 'accessible' shop *is easy for disabled people to visit / sells products for disabled people*.
4 Twenty-three percent of British fashion shops *are / aren't* accessible to disabled people.

8 In pairs, think of a shop you know and choose the correct option. Is the shop accessible?
1 You *can / can't* park near the shop.
2 You *can / can't* get a wheelchair through the shop door.
3 *Some / None* of the shelves are very high.
4 There *are some / aren't any* stairs in the shop.
5 There *is / isn't* a lift in the shop.

9 **VISIBLE THINKING** Which of these ideas for making shops more accessible do you think is the most important?
TAKE A DIFFERENT VIEW
1 Use images of disabled people in ads and shop windows.
2 Change the position of things in the shop.
3 Build lifts in shops.
4 Teach shop assistants more about disability.

PROJECT TIME

10 In groups of five, prepare a website for a new shop in your town. Follow these steps.

1 In groups, decide where your shop is and what it sells. Decide who in your group can prepare this information.
- the name of the shop
- what kind of products there are
- why the shop is special
- how your shop is eco-friendly
- how your shop is accessible for disabled people

2 Individually, prepare your part of the website.
- Find information and write your text.
- Find photos to go on the website.

3 In your group, create your website. You can use a website template.
- Choose the best photos to put on the website.
- Decide on a layout.
- Position the text, the logo and the photos.
- Check and edit your website.

4 Share your website with the class.
- Answer other students' questions.
- Look at the other websites. Ask questions.

Learning for the future

8

VOCABULARY
Jobs | Work collocations |
World of work | Tests | School
and education | Schoolwork

GRAMMAR
Will for future predictions |
First Conditional

8.1 Vocabulary
Jobs and work

QUIZ Personality and Career

PART 1 About you — It isn't easy to choose a future job. It's important to find work that matches your interests and personality. Think about these statements. Which one describes you best?

1. I'd like to help and take care of others.
2. I enjoy speaking to people and have good communication skills.
3. I'd like to work with tools, machines or cars and planes.
4. I'd like to have ideas, plan and make things.
5. I'd like to organise information, data, people or money.
6. I enjoy science and finding the answers to problems.

PART 2 Your results

1 You're a Helper
Think about these jobs:
care worker • firefighter •
nurse or doctor • police officer •
receptionist

2 You're an Influencer
Think about these jobs:
blogger • politician •
shop assistant • tour guide

3 You're a Doer
Think about these jobs:
builder • driver •
mechanic • pilot

4 You're a Designer
Think about these jobs:
architect • artist •
chef • gardener •
hairdresser

5 You're an Organiser
Think about these jobs:
accountant •
IT specialist • manager

6 You're a Thinker
Think about these jobs:
engineer • journalist •
lawyer • scientist

1 🔊 8.1 **I KNOW!** Study the Vocabulary box. In groups, say which of the jobs you can find in the photos on page 100. How many jobs can you add in two minutes?

VOCABULARY | **Jobs**

accountant   architect   artist   builder   care worker
chef   doctor   driver   engineer   firefighter   gardener
hairdresser   IT specialist   journalist   lawyer   manager
mechanic   nurse   pilot   police officer   politician
receptionist   scientist   tour guide   waiter/waitress

2 Read Part 1 of the quiz. Which statement is true for you?

3 Look at your results in Part 2 of the quiz. In pairs, compare your answers.

4 Match jobs from the Vocabulary box with the definitions.

This person …
1 works in a hospital. *doctor/nurse*
2 helps people on holiday.
3 draws pictures of buildings for builders.
4 makes parks look beautiful.
5 answers the phone in an office or a hotel.
6 writes articles for magazines.

5 🔊 8.2 Listen and guess what job each speaker has.
1 Nadia _____   3 Ethan _____
2 Scott _____   4 Amina _____

6 🔊 8.3 **WORD FRIENDS** Check you understand the phrases below. Then find a few possible jobs from the Vocabulary box for Cara and Trey.

be happy at work   work at the weekend
earn (good) money   work for a company
get to work on time   work in a team
work alone   work in an office
work as a (waitress)   work indoors/outdoors

WATCH OUT!
Work can be a noun as well as a verb.
I **work** hard. I enjoy my **work**.

7 🔊 8.4 Complete the text with words from Exercise 6. Guess the speaker's job. Listen and check.

One thing I like about my job is that I'm not inside all the time, I often work ¹*outside*. I might work on weekdays or at the ² _____ , day or night. I enjoy helping people. I don't ³ _____ much money, but I'm ⁴ _____ at work and I like my uniform. I really like working in a ⁵ _____ . My workmates are great. My job is dangerous and I must get to work on ⁶ _____ because people can die if you're late.

8 In pairs, discuss the questions.
1 Which job do you think is …
   • the most dangerous?
   • the easiest?
   • the best paid?
   • the most stressful?
2 Which job would you most like to have?

9 In pairs, choose a job from the Vocabulary box. Find out your partner's job in ten questions. You can only answer *yes* or *no*.
A: *Do you work in a team?*   B: *No, I don't.*

YOUR WORLD

10 Think of people you know. What jobs do they have? Do they like their jobs? Why?/Why not? Discuss in groups.
My aunt works outside quite often. She's a police officer. She loves her job because …

Cara, 17
I'm looking for a summer job. A part-time job is OK. I want to be happy at work. I enjoy working in a team or with other people. I don't mind working indoors or outdoors.

Trey, 18
I want to work in an office for a good company. I'd like to have a full-time job and work indoors, but the most important thing for me is to earn money. It's no problem for me to get to work on time.

I can talk about people and their jobs.

8.2 Grammar

Will for future predictions

School of the future

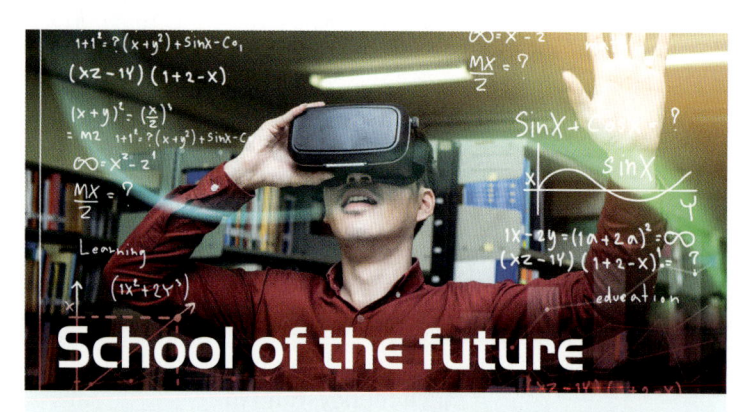

Education will still be very important in the future, but children won't be in classrooms all the time. They will also have online classes at home. There will be no central timetable for everybody. Students will choose their subjects and create their own learning plans.

In their lessons, students won't have paper coursebooks or whiteboards. They will use interactive walls to find information on the internet and watch videos. In some lessons, students will wear 'virtual reality' headsets. They will do a lot of experiments and work on projects with students from around the world. Will they have to take tests? Probably not!

They will still have teachers, but teachers will have AI robot assistants. The assistants will look like real teachers and help students learn.

But will pupils enjoy these lessons? We will have to see.

1 🔊 8.5 Read the text and find three examples of using technology at school.

2 Would you like to learn in a school of the future? Why?/Why not?

3 Study the Grammar box. Find more examples of *will/won't* in the text.

GRAMMAR — Will for future predictions

+	I **will** study abroad. She **will be** a teacher. They **will have** teachers.
–	I **won't have** homework. She **won't be** a nurse. They **won't have** coursebooks.
?	Will you study a lot? Will he play games? Will they have teachers? How will they learn?	Yes, I will./No, I won't. Yes, he will./No, he won't. Yes, they will./No, they won't.

Time expressions:
in 2040/twenty years' time/the next five years/the future
by (= before) 2040/New Year/my twentieth birthday

GRAMMAR TIME > PAGE 134

4 Complete the text with *will/won't* and the verbs in brackets.

Languages like English and German ¹*won't be* (not be) so popular in the future. But Chinese and Spanish ² _____ (become) very important. Students ³ _____ (not learn) with apps on their phones: instead, students ⁴ _____ (chat) to students their age in other countries and practise languages with AI teaching assistants. In the future, students ⁵ _____ (not have) a chance to meet their classmates every day, because they ⁶ _____ (often study) online at home.

> **WATCH OUT!**
> I **think** this **will happen**.
> I **don't think** this **will happen**.
> NOT ~~I think this won't happen.~~

5 In pairs, say if and when you think these predictions will come true. Use time expressions with *in* or *by*.
1 Schools will give laptops to all their students.
   I think this will happen by 2030./I don't agree. I don't think this will happen.
2 Students won't learn languages – everyone will use computers to translate.
3 Many people will decide to study abroad.
4 Most teachers will use social media to teach.
5 Students will play video games during lessons.

6 Tick (✓) the things you think you will do by your twentieth birthday.
☐ learn to drive ☐ get married
☐ go to university ☐ buy a house or flat
☐ start work ☐ buy a car

YOUR WORLD

7 In pairs, ask and answer questions about the things in Exercise 6.
A: Will you learn to drive before your twentieth birthday?
B: Yes, I will./No, I won't.

8.3 Reading and Vocabulary
Teenage role models

Mikaila and Mateusz: our role models

Last month we asked our readers who their role models are. Here are our favourite replies.

Who is your role model? Why?

Mikaila Ulmer, from the USA, is my role model because she's helping to save bees.

Mateusz Mach, from Poland, is my role model. He's a young entrepreneur whose best app helps deaf people.

Describe this person's career so far.

When two bees stung four-year-old Mikaila in one week, she decided to learn about them. She found out that bees help the environment, but they are in danger, so she sold home-made lemonade to make money for bee charities. It started as a small part-time job, but her business grew after she met a famous entrepreneur on a TV show. Now her company Me and the Bees is doing brilliantly. Mikaila is her own boss and she's still a teenager.

When Mateusz was at high school, he was interested in rappers' hand signs. This gave him the idea for his app. At first, Mateusz and his friends made funny new hand signs with the app. Then deaf people found that Mateusz's app was useful because it was like sign language. Mateusz worked hard to make his app better. Now the Five app is a popular way to send messages in sign language.

Will your career be similar?

Francesco, 13, Italy

I'd also like to work with food and drink. My mum's a chef, so she got me a temporary job as a waiter. I work well in a team, so I might be a manager for a food company one day, but I don't think I will have my own business.

Alexandra, 14, Russia

I'll probably study computer programming. I'd like to get a college diploma or a university degree. I'll be excited when I start my first full-time job as an IT specialist. But for now I'll probably get a part-time summer job as a lifeguard because I love swimming.

---

1 A role model is a person who you'd like to copy. Who is your role model and why?

2 🔊 8.6 Read the article. Which person helped people and which person helped the environment?

3 Read the article again and answer the questions.
  1. Why did Mikaila become interested in bees?
  2. What happened after Mikaila was on TV?
  3. Who helped Francesco get a temporary job?
  4. What gave Mateusz the idea for his app?
  5. Why did deaf people find the app useful?
  6. What full-time job will Alexandra do?

4 🔊 8.7 Study the Vocabulary box. In pairs, find the words in the article. Check you understand them.

VOCABULARY	World of work
qualifications	college diploma university degree
people	boss entrepreneur role model
types of work	full-time job part-time job summer job temporary job

5 🔊 8.8 Complete the text with words from the Vocabulary box. Listen and check.

This year I'm studying part-time for a ¹*college diploma* in tourism management. One day I'd like to have my own tour company. I don't think I'm an ²_____ because I don't have new ideas, but I'd like to be my own ³_____ . My aunt is my ⁴_____ . She's got a university ⁵_____ in tourism and she speaks four languages. She works ⁶_____ (eight hours a day) as a tour guide in Rome, Italy. I hope I can have a career like hers!

YOUR WORLD

6 In pairs, discuss three summer jobs you would both like to do in the future.

A: I'd like to work as a lifeguard at a swimming pool. What about you?
B: No, I can't swim very well.

I can understand an article about teenage ambitions.

8.4 Grammar
First Conditional

VIDEO ▶ IF YOU DON'T STUDY …

Mum: Mateo? It's 7 p.m. Are you going to study now?
Mateo: Er, sure. I'll text Noah first, then I'll study Science.
Mum: Hmm. The end-of-year exams start on Monday. Make sure you study for two hours every evening.
Mateo: Of course I will.
Mum: Great. Good for you.

One hour later

Mateo: Mum? I'm just going to see Noah.
Mum: Oh no, you're not, Mateo! Stay here. If you go to Noah's, you'll play online games.
Mateo: Mum, it's not fair! I need a break. I'll go crazy if I study all evening!
Mum: OK, well have a snack, then do some work.
Mateo: Fine. I guess if I don't do well in Science, I won't be a vet.
Mum: Exactly. It's your choice. You won't pass if you don't study.
Mateo: Very true. So, Mum, when's your driving test? If it's next week, it will be difficult for you to pass. You aren't studying very hard!

1 ▶ 39 🔊 8.9 Watch or listen. What is Mateo going to study? Why?

2 🔊 8.10 **WORD FRIENDS** Check you understand the phrases below. Then listen to a dialogue and tick (✓) the phrases you hear.

☐ cheat in a test ☐ have/take a test
☐ get a good/bad mark ☐ pass/fail a test
☐ get the results of a test ☐ study/revise for a test

3 In pairs, talk about your last big test. Use phrases from Exercise 2.

4 Study the Grammar box. Find more examples of the First Conditional in the dialogue.

> **GRAMMAR** First Conditional
>
> • *If* + Present Simple, *will* + verb
>   If I *don't do* well in Science, I *won't be* a vet.
>
> • *will* + verb *if* + Present Simple
>   You *won't pass* your tests if you *don't study*.

GRAMMAR TIME > PAGE 135

5 🔊 8.11 Choose the correct option. Listen and check.

Dad: Hi Rose! How's your revision going?
Rose: Terrible! And I'm really tired now.
Dad: So go to bed! If you ¹*get up / will get up* early tomorrow, you ²*feel / will feel* better and you'll remember more.
Rose: Yes, maybe. But I had a great idea. I can write notes on the back of my hand! If I ³*forget / will forget* something in the test, I ⁴*check / will check* it on my hand.
Dad: You can't do that! That's cheating! And if you ⁵*try / will try* to cheat, the teacher ⁶*is / will be* angry with you. Don't worry. I'll help you to revise.

6 Complete the sentences with the correct form of the verbs in brackets.

1 If I *pass* (pass) all my exams, I'll be so happy!
2 My gran _____ (help) me buy a laptop if I get good marks.
3 If Tiggy _____ (get) the results of the test, she'll phone me.
4 If I _____ (not get) a good mark, my mum won't be pleased.
5 We'll have to phone the doctor if she _____ (not feel) better soon.

VIDEO ▶ **WIDER WORLD**

7 ▶ 40 Watch seven people talking about the future. How do they complete these sentences?
 • If there's nothing good on TV tonight, I …
 • If I get some money for my birthday, I …
 • If my phone stops working, I …

8 Complete the sentences in Exercise 7 to make them true for you. In pairs, compare your sentences.

Unit 8 — I can use the First Conditional to talk about possible situations in the future.

8.5 Listening and Vocabulary
A modern school

1. Look at the photo of a classroom and answer the questions.
   1. What are the students doing? How are they feeling?
   2. Is it similar or different to your school?

2. 🔊 8.12 Listen to a podcast about an unusual school in Denmark. Choose the correct answer.
   1. Architects designed the school so that it
      a. has only one classroom.
      b. looks normal inside.
      c. has a lot of open spaces.
   2. On a normal school day, pupils can
      a. work in an office.
      b. use the library next door.
      c. eat lunch in a canteen with glass walls.
   3. The head teacher believes that pupils
      a. need good computer skills.
      b. don't like working on their own.
      c. must work hard.
   4. Pupils at Ørestad Gymnasium
      a. start school at half past eight.
      b. have helpful teachers.
      c. don't have any exams.

3. Would you enjoy going to a school like Ørestad Gymnasium? Why?/Why not? Discuss in pairs.

4. 🔊 8.13 **I KNOW!** Complete the Vocabulary box with the words below. Listen and check. Can you add more words?

   computer room   pupil   Science lab   ~~secondary school~~   sports hall   stairs

VOCABULARY — School and education

Places of learning
college   primary school   ¹secondary school   university

People in schools
classmate   form tutor   head teacher   Maths/English teacher   ²_____

Places in schools
canteen   classroom   ³_____   library   playground   ⁴_____   ⁵_____   staff room   ⁶_____

5. Complete the sentences with words from the Vocabulary box.
   1. Luke was late for school every day last week and had to see the _head teacher_.
   2. There's always a long queue for the _____ at lunchtime.
   3. I changed class last year – my new _____ are definitely nicer people!
   4. Sometimes we play basketball in the _____ in wet weather.
   5. The teachers relax in the _____ between lessons.

6. 🔊 8.14 **WORD FRIENDS** In pairs, complete the sentences with the words below. Listen and check.

   do (x2)   give   ~~make~~   write

   1. The best way to revise for a test is to _make_ notes.
   2. We _____ a lot of grammar exercises in English lessons.
   3. I'm quite shy, so I feel nervous before I _____ presentations.
   4. I always _____ my homework after I get home from school.
   5. It's hard to _____ essays in class.

YOUR WORLD

7. In pairs, ask and answer the questions.
   - How often do you talk to your head teacher and form tutor?
   - How often do you use the school library/computer room?
   - Do you prefer to give presentations or write essays? Why?

I can understand a podcast about a school.

8.6 Speaking
Expressing probability

VIDEO ▶ YOU'LL PROBABLY DO WELL

Noah: Are you guys ready for the History test?
Mia: Yes! I did some online practice tests.
Noah: So, you'll probably do well!
Mia: Fingers crossed! I may not get a hundred percent, but I think I'll pass.
Noah: I'm nervous, but I ate three bananas for breakfast! Bananas help you remember things.
Mia: Really? I might try that tomorrow.
Noah: It'll definitely help. I had a revision plan. I wrote lots of notes too, but it's difficult to remember dates.
Lena: I didn't revise enough because I was ill last week. I think I may fail. But I've got my lucky pencil case. Look!
Noah: Er, Lena? If you take your pencil case with you, you'll be in trouble! Look at the sign.
Lena: What sign?
Noah: 'Put your pens and pencils in a clear plastic bag or clear pencil case.'
Lena: No! What a nightmare! I won't pass now.

SOUNDS GOOD! Fingers crossed! • What a nightmare! • You'll be in trouble.

1 ▶ 41 ◀)) 8.15 Describe the photo. How do you think the kids feel about their test? Watch or listen and check.

SET FOR LIFE

2 What is your favourite revision tip? Discuss in pairs. Use these ideas and add your own tips.
- find a nice, quiet place to work
- write notes or draw mind maps
- revise together with your friends

3 Study the Speaking box. Find examples of the phrases in the dialogue.

SPEAKING Expressing probability

☺ ↑ I will **definitely** pass.
I will **probably** pass.
I **may/might** pass.
I **probably** won't pass.
☹ ↓ I **definitely** won't pass.

4 ◀)) 8.16 Order the words in brackets to complete the sentences. Listen and check.
1 Our teacher says the school trip *will definitely be* (be/will/definitely) to a chocolate factory.
2 I think we _____ (learn/will/probably) how to make chocolate.
3 Amy says she _____ (want/might) to be a chef or a chocolate taster.
4 Luke says he _____ (have/won't/definitely) money to buy lots of chocolate.
5 He _____ (want/won't/probably) to have dinner that evening.

5 In pairs, decide if these things will come true in your country in the next ten years. Use the Speaking box to help you.
1 Food will be more expensive.
2 Newspapers and magazines will still be popular.
3 Most people will work from home.
4 Everyone will use public transport – most people won't use cars.

Food will probably be more expensive.

VIDEO ▶ WIDER WORLD

6 ▶ 42 Watch four people making predictions about their future. Write down the ideas they mention.

7 In pairs, use the Speaking box to make predictions about your future.
I will definitely learn a new language.
I might still live in my home town.

Unit 8 · 106 · I can talk about things which will or won't probably happen.

8.7 Writing
A personal statement

1. Read the personal statement. Does Ana use full forms of verbs or short forms with an apostrophe (')? Why do you think she does that?

2. Read the personal statement again and complete the table about Ana.

Personal qualities	friendly and confident
Hobbies and interests	
Experiences	

3. Study the Writing box. Find examples of the phrases in Ana's personal statement.

   WRITING — A personal statement

   1. **Introduce yourself**
      My name is … I am …

   2. **Describe your personal qualities and give examples**
      I am friendly and confident.
      It is easy for me to make new friends.
      I am a very happy person.
      I look at the positive side of a situation.
      I am good at making people laugh.

   3. **Talk about your hobbies and interests**
      I am interested in learning languages/helping people.
      I like learning languages.
      I am crazy about sports.

   4. **Talk about your experiences**
      Last year, I went to Italy.
      I made new friends.

   5. **Talk about your hopes for the future**
      In the future, I think I will be …

4. Study the Language box. Find examples of the adjectives with prepositions in Ana's statement.

   LANGUAGE — Adjectives + prepositions

   After these phrases we add a verb + -ing:
   brilliant at   interested in
   crazy about   keen on
   fond of   not bad at
   (really/not very) good at

   Brad is **good at counting**.
   Wendy is **fond of talking**.

5. Write three sentences about your skills and abilities. Use the Language box to help you.

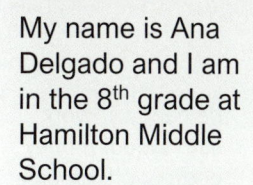

---

1. My name is Ana Delgado and I am in the 8th grade at Hamilton Middle School.

2. I am very friendly and confident. I think I am good at making people laugh too. I study hard at school, and on Thursday afternoons I read to children at the hospital.

3. I am interested in helping people. I am crazy about sports, especially volleyball and swimming. I am also keen on learning new things, so I would like to try new sports.

4. Last summer, I went on an adventure sports camp. It was a great experience – I learned new skills and made new friends. I am not very good at IT, but I work hard to get better at things I find difficult. So I am taking extra IT classes on Saturdays.

5. In the future, I think I will be a lawyer or a nurse.

WRITING TIME

6. Write a personal statement for a part-time job or a summer job.

   1. **Find ideas**
      Make notes for a personal statement.
      • What job would you like to have?
      • What are your personal qualities, your hobbies and interests?
      • What are your experiences? Talk about the skills that you can use in the job.

   2. **Plan**
      Organise your ideas. Use Ana's statement to help you.

   3. **Write and share**
      • Write a draft statement. Use the Language box and the Writing box to help you.
      • Share your statement with another student for feedback.
      • Write the final version of your statement.

   4. **Check**
      • Check language: did you use adjectives + prepositions correctly?
      • Check grammar: did you use the full forms of verbs?

I can write a personal statement.

Vocabulary Activator

WORDLIST 🔊 8.17

Jobs
accountant (n)
architect (n)
artist (n)
builder (n)
care worker (n)
chef (n)
doctor (n)
driver (n)
engineer (n)
firefighter (n)
gardener (n)
hairdresser (n)
IT specialist (n)
journalist (n)
lawyer (n)
manager (n)
mechanic (n)
nurse (n)
pilot (n)
police officer (n)
politician (n)
receptionist (n)
scientist (n)
tour guide (n)
waiter (n)
waitress (n)

Word friends (work collocations)
be happy at work
earn (good) money
get to work on time
work alone
work as a (waitress)
work at the weekend
work for a company
work in a team
work in an office
work indoors
work outdoors

World of work
boss (n)
college diploma (n)
entrepreneur (n)
full-time job (n)
part-time job (n)
role model (n)
summer job (n)
temporary job (n)
university degree (n)

Word friends (tests)
cheat in a test
fail a test
get a bad mark
get a good mark
get the results of a test
have a test
pass a test
revise for a test
study for a test
take a test

School and education
canteen (n)
classmate (n)
classroom (n)
college (n)
computer room (n)
English teacher (n)
form tutor (n)
head teacher (n)
library (n)
Maths teacher (n)
playground (n)
primary school (n)
pupil (n)
Science lab (n)
secondary school (n)
sports hall (n)
staff room (n)
stairs (n)
university (n)

Word friends (schoolwork)
do exercises
do your homework
give presentations
make notes
write essays

Extra words
babysitter (n)
bike courier (n)
brilliant at (adj)
business (n)
communication skills (n)
crazy about (adj)
dog walker (n)
exam (n)
fond of (adj)
fruit picker (n)
future career (n)
good at (adj)
interests (n)
keen on (adj)
learn (v)
lesson (n)
lifeguard (n)
machine (n)
museum guide (n)
(not) bad at (adj)
personal qualities (n)
personal statement (n)
revision plan (n)
stressful (adj)
timetable (n)
workmate (n)

1 Use words from the wordlist to find these things.
1. five people you might find in a school *classmate, …*
2. three bad things that can happen in or after a test
3. two things you can get when you complete higher education
4. six jobs where you usually help people who have serious problems
5. five places in a school where pupils don't normally have lessons

2 In pairs, replace the words in bold to correct the sentences. Use words from the wordlist.
1. **Artists** often make plans for buildings. *Architects*
2. A **form tutor** is the most important person at school.
3. Teachers usually go to the **classroom** in their break.
4. **Secondary** school is for students who are five to eleven years old.
5. Gardeners usually work **indoors**.
6. Firefighters usually have to work **alone**.

3 In pairs, choose four words from the wordlist and write definitions for your partner to guess.

4 In pairs, use the wordlist to say which job you want to do and why.

5 Complete the text with one word in each gap.

> For me, schoolwork is OK. I think I'm quite good at revising ¹*for* tests and exams. I try to ²_____ notes and I often ³_____ exercises online too.
> I can't stand waiting to ⁴_____ the results though. Fortunately, I usually ⁵_____ my tests and exams. I don't always get very good ⁶_____ , but I never ⁷_____ in a test. I think that's wrong!

6 🔊 8.18 **PRONUNCIATION** Listen to the underlined letters in each word and decide which sound you hear. Write the word in the correct column.

> chair cheat chef ~~college~~ electrician engineer head teacher journalist manager politician receptionist

/dʒ/	/ʃ/	/tʃ/
college		

7 🔊 8.19 **PRONUNCIATION** Listen, check your answers to Exercise 6 and repeat.

Revision

Vocabulary

1 Choose the correct option.
1. My older sister's got a *full-time / part-time* job in our school! She works three hours every day.
2. In winter we play sports in the sports *room / hall*.
3. I want to be the *chef / boss* of my own business one day.
4. I started secondary school last September. My new *classmates / pupils* are all really nice.
5. I'd like to work *indoors / outdoors*, so I'll be a gardener.

2 In pairs, complete the texts with one word in each gap. Then match people 1–3 with jobs a–f. There are three extra jobs.

a accountant c pilot   e IT specialist
b care worker d gardener   f journalist

1 ☐ Zane
I want to have an interesting job where I can ¹*earn* good money. I'm interested in the world and I enjoy writing and meeting people. I want to travel, so I don't want to work ²_____ – I prefer to work part-time.

2 ☐ Gemma
I like to grow my own vegetables. I don't want to work ³_____ a large company. I want to work outside. I'm not going to work ⁴_____ an office, so I won't have to get to work ⁵_____ time!

3 ☐ Craig
I used to want to be a doctor, but I'm not keen on going to university to get a ⁷_____ . I'm good with people and I'm happy to work ⁸_____ a team. I don't mind working long hours.

3 Complete the questions with one word in each gap. Then answer the questions and compare your answers in pairs.
1. Do you usually get good *results* in tests?
2. Did you have to _____ tests again at your primary school when you _____ a test?
3. How do you feel when you _____ a test?
4. Do you prefer to study in the school _____ or at home?
5. Do you usually have more tests in a secondary school or a _____ school?
6. When you finish school, do you want to get a full-time _____ ?

I usually get good results in Maths tests, but not in Science tests.

Grammar

4 Complete the text with *will* or *won't* and the words in brackets.

There's a Careers Day at our school tomorrow. I think managers from a few local companies ¹*will talk* (talk) to us. I want to be an IT entrepreneur. ²_____ (IT companies/be) there? I hope so! I'm sure we ³_____ (not have) any lessons. The managers ⁴_____ (probably/give) presentations, and we ⁵_____ (make) some notes. After that, I think the pupils and teachers ⁶_____ (ask) the managers some questions. ⁷_____ (my friend Jackie/listen) carefully? I don't think so. She ⁸_____ (not listen), and our form tutor ⁹_____ (definitely/talk) a lot!

5 Complete the dialogue with the First Conditional form of the words in brackets.

Dad: How are you getting to your new job tomorrow?
Ivan: If it's OK with you, I ¹*'ll borrow* (borrow) your bike.
Dad: Sure. But what ²_____ (you/do) if the weather ³_____ (be) bad?
Ivan: It's OK. If it ⁴_____ (rain), I ⁵_____ (take) the bus.
Dad: But if the bus ⁶_____ (not come), how ⁷_____ (you/get) there?
Ivan: I ⁸_____ (phone) Mum for a lift if something ⁹_____ (go) wrong.
Dad: But if she ¹⁰_____ (not hear) her phone, you ¹¹_____ (not get) there.
Ivan: It'll be fine! Stop worrying.

Speaking

6 In pairs, take turns to say if these things will happen to you in the next ten years.
- go to university
- pass/fail your final school exam
- earn good money
- work for an international company
- travel across Europe
- get married

I will probably go to university.

Dictation

7 🔊 8.20 Listen. Then listen again and write down what you hear during each pause.

SET FOR LIFE

You've got a point!

Debating club

Tuesday
1 p.m. in Room 43

Are you nervous when you have to speak in class? Do you have lots of ideas, but you don't know how to share them? Or do you enjoy sharing opinions and asking questions?

- Discuss interesting topics.
- Meet interesting people.
- Win prizes.

Everyone's welcome! Join the debating club.

Here are the topics for this month:

1 Tests at school are unfair, and we shouldn't do them.

2 Social media is good for teenagers.

3 Parents should give teenagers some money once a week.

4 Learning online is better than learning in a classroom.

Come and share your opinions!

1 Look at the photo and read the notice. Is this a good idea for a club? Would you like to join it? Why?/Why not?

2 Read discussion topics 1–4 for the debating club. For each topic, tick (✓) your opinion.

	Topic 1	Topic 2	Topic 3	Topic 4
Strongly agree				
Agree				
Neutral				
Disagree				
Strongly disagree				

3 🔊 8.21 Listen to three students giving their opinion about the first topic on the list. Choose A if they agree with the topic or D if they disagree.

1 Lee A / D   2 Zoe A / D   3 Sasha A / D

4 🔊 8.21 Listen again. Match speakers 1–3 with statements a–c.

1 ☐   2 ☐   3 ☐

a He/She mentions a personal story from his/her life.
b He/She mentions a fact that he/she learned.
c He/She gives his/her opinion without any arguments.

Support your opinions with arguments

5 Read discussion topic 2 on the debating club's list. Tick (✓) the arguments you can use to agree with the topic. Cross (✗) the arguments you can use to disagree with it.
1. ☐ Social media can stop teenagers studying.
2. ☐ Teenagers can use social media to learn about technology.
3. ☐ You can communicate with people all over the world.
4. ☐ Some people present an image on social media that isn't real.

6 In pairs, take turns to give your opinion about discussion topic 2 from the debating club's list. Think of some arguments to support your opinion. Use the expressions from the Useful Phrases box and the ideas from Exercise 5 to help you.

A: In my personal opinion, social media IS good for teenagers! It helps you to be creative. I love taking photos for my social media accounts.
B: I feel that teenagers waste too much time on social media. I say this because …

7 Read the Useful Tips. In pairs, answer the questions about Exercise 6.
1. Did you give arguments to support your opinions?
2. Did you listen to your partner's opinions?

SET FOR LIFE

8 In groups, prepare to present your opinions on topic 3 or 4 from the debating club's list. Follow the instructions.

1 Choose a topic and form groups with people who share your opinion.

2 In your groups, make a list of arguments that support your opinion. Use the questions below to help you.
- Can you give any facts to support your opinion?
- Can you give examples from your life?
- Can you talk about something you see in the world?

3 Practise presenting your arguments as a group. Decide who can present which argument and in which order. Use the expressions from the Useful Phrases box.

4 Present all your opinions to the class. Who had the most arguments to support their opinion?

USEFUL TIPS

When you discuss a topic, it's important to support your opinions with logical arguments.

- Give facts (things that you know are true).
- Use examples from your own life.
- Talk about/Describe things you see in the world.
- Remember that people can have different opinions about the same topic.
- Listen to others, even if you don't agree with them.

USEFUL PHRASES

Giving your opinion
I think/don't think that …
I feel/don't feel that …
In my (personal) opinion, …
I agree/don't agree that …
I'm sorry, but I don't agree.

Giving arguments to support your opinion
I think/say this because …
Let me explain why I think like this.
I read a survey/report that said that …
For example, …

It's only natural

9

VOCABULARY
Geographical features | *In, on, by* |
Talking about countries | Phrasal verbs |
Outdoor activities | Sporting equipment

GRAMMAR
Present Perfect |
Present Perfect with *just, already* and *yet*

OUR AMAZING PLANET!
Kyle Peters takes us on a trip of fascinating facts about the world

A
B
C
D
E
F

High and Low
- The world's highest waterfall is the spectacular **Angel Falls** in Venezuela. It's 979 metres high.
- **The Kalaupapa Cliffs** on the island of Hawaii are high too. They stand more than 600 metres above the Pacific Ocean.
- **Mount Kilimanjaro** is the highest mountain in Tanzania, Africa. It's 5,895 metres high.
- The lowest lake is **the Dead Sea** in the Jordan Valley. It's 430 metres lower than the sea. It's full of salt, so it's easy to swim there.

Wet and Dry
- The wettest place on Earth is not in a jungle or a rainforest. It's **Mawsynram** in India. These villages get about 11,870 mm of rain every year! The fields and forests are very green.
- The driest desert is **the Atacama** in Chile. It only gets a few millimetres of rain every year.

Long and Short
- The longest beach in the world is **Praia do Cassino** on the coast of Brazil near the border with Uruguay. It's about 250 kilometres long.
- The shortest river is **Kuokanjoki** in Finland. It connects two lakes and is only 3.5 metres long.

Unit 9

9.1 Vocabulary

Landscapes

1 Look at photos A–F and try to match them with the countries below.
1. ☐ Brazil 3. ☐ Jordan 5. ☐ USA (Hawaii)
2. ☐ Chile 4. ☐ Tanzania 6. ☐ Venezuela

2 🔊 9.1 Read the text and check your answers to Exercise 1. Then label photos A–F with the names of the places from the text. Which place would you most like to visit? Why?
I'd like to visit Angel Falls. It looks spectacular.

3 🔊 9.2 Study Vocabulary box A. Work in pairs. Which of the geographical features can you see in photos A–F, and which of them can you see near you?

VOCABULARY A — Geographical features

beach cliff coast desert field forest hill
island jungle lake mountain ocean
rainforest river sea valley waterfall

4 🔊 9.3 In groups, do the quiz. Listen and check.

What do you know about our amazing planet? Try the quiz to find out.

1. **What's the longest river in Europe?**
   (It goes through Russia into the Caspian Sea.)
   a the Danube b the Volga

2. **What's the world's biggest ocean?**
   (It's between Asia and America.)
   a the Indian Ocean b the Pacific Ocean

3. **Where's Ben Nevis?**
   (It's the highest mountain in the British Isles.)
   a in Scotland b in Ireland

4. **What's the largest island in the world?**
   (It's a very cold place.)
   a Greenland b Australia

5. **How high is the highest hill in the Netherlands?**
   (The Netherlands is a very flat country.)
   a 323 metres b 434 metres

5 🔊 9.4 **WORD FRIENDS** Complete the phrases with the words below. Listen and check.

~~a forest~~ a hill a lake an island the mountains

in	a field ¹*a forest* a lake a valley
	² _____ the sea
on	a beach ³ _____ a mountain
	⁴ _____ the coast
by	⁵ _____ a river the sea

6 Complete the text with the correct prepositions.

We had a fantastic holiday. We stayed ¹*on* the south coast of France. We camped ² _____ a field ³ _____ a small river. In the mornings, we swam ⁴ _____ the sea, and Mum and Dad sunbathed ⁵ _____ the beach. On hot days, we spent our time ⁶ _____ the mountains.

7 Where is your favourite place in the countryside? Tell the class. Use the phrases from Exercise 5 to help you.
I love being in the mountains/by the sea.

8 🔊 9.5 Study Vocabulary box B. Complete the sentences about the UK with the words in the box.

VOCABULARY B — Talking about countries

border capital city flag official language population

1. The *official language* is English.
2. The _____ is red, white and blue.
3. The _____ is 67 million.
4. The _____ is London.
5. The _____ between England and Scotland is 154 kilometres long.

9 🔊 9.6 Listen and answer the questions about Miki's country. Where does she come from?
1. What is the country's population?
2. What colour is the national flag?
3. What is the country famous for?
4. How many countries does it share a land border with?
5. What is its capital city?
6. What is the official language? Are there any other languages?

VIDEO ▶ WIDER WORLD

10 ▶ 43 Watch five people talking about their countries. Write what is special about each country.

11 In groups, answer the questions in Exercise 9 for your country.
The population of my country is …

I can talk about landscapes and nature. 113 Unit 9

9.2 Grammar

Present Perfect

Ed Lynam is hoping to become one of the youngest people to visit every country in the world. The twenty-four-year-old Canadian has visited 150 of them and he hasn't finished (there are plenty more to see)! Planet Discovery talked to him.

PD: Tell us about your most exciting experience.

EL: Where to start? I've swum with dolphins off the coast of Ireland, I've played with bears in Romania and climbed Mount Kilimanjaro.

PD: Have you ever had any bad experiences?

EL: No, I haven't. Well, I've had some problems with visas. But I've never had any really bad experiences.

PD: Which countries have you enjoyed most?

EL: I think I've enjoyed Greece and Indonesia most – they're so beautiful. But in every country people have been nice to me. I've met a lot of very kind people, especially in some countries in Africa.

PD: Have you learned a lot from travelling?

EL: Yes, I have. I've learned that people everywhere are good and basically the same!

1 Do you think it is better to go on holiday abroad or to stay in your own country?

2 🔊 9.7 Read the text. How many countries has Ed Lynam visited? Which were his favourite places?

3 Study the Grammar box. Find more examples of the Present Perfect in the text.

GRAMMAR — Present Perfect

+	I've (have) swum with dolphins. He's (has) visited 150 countries. They've (have) learned a lot.
–	I haven't visited Africa. She hasn't finished the trip. They haven't had problems.
?	Have you learned a lot? / Yes, I have./No, I haven't. Has he enjoyed Thailand? / Yes, he has./No, he hasn't. Have they finished? / Yes, they have./No, they haven't. Which countries have you enjoyed most?

GRAMMAR TIME > PAGE 135

4 What are the Past Simple and Present Perfect forms of these verbs? Are they the same or different?

| ~~buy~~ | come | drink | eat | forget | have | look |
| meet | see | sleep | travel | visit | watch | write |

buy – bought, bought (the same)

5 Complete the sentences with the correct Present Perfect form of the verbs in brackets.
1 I *'ve met* (meet) people from all over the world.
2 My friend, Gio, _____ (write) a travel blog.
3 My parents _____ (not visit) the United States, but they _____ (be) to Canada.
4 My gran _____ never _____ (leave) her town!
5 Brett _____ (not eat) Indian food before.

6 Complete the questions with the correct Present Perfect form of the words in brackets. Then ask and answer in pairs. Write down your partner's answers.
1 *Have you ever been* (you/ever/be) to New York?
2 How many countries _____ (you/visit)?
3 _____ (you/ever/eat) something unusual?
4 How many times _____ (fly) in a plane?
5 _____ (you/ever/have) any problems when travelling?

A: *Have you ever been to New York?*   B: *No, I haven't.*

7 Use your notes in Exercise 6 to tell the class about your partner.

Kasia's never been to New York.

8 Tell the class about a surprising thing you have done in your life.

I've met/seen/won/lived in/been to/played …

YOUR WORLD

Unit 9   114   I can use the Present Perfect to talk about experiences.

9.3 Reading and Vocabulary

Exploring nature

1 Find the things below in the photo.

| backpack   ski boots   ski poles   skis   sled |
| waterproof jacket   waterproof trousers |

YOUNG HEROES: JADE HAMEISTER

Imagine this. You're fourteen years old. You've just **taken up** skiing. And now you're inside the Arctic Circle. You've skied over 100 kilometres pulling a fifty-kilogram sled behind you. You've climbed over high walls of frozen rocks. It's freezing: minus 30°C! You're scared. You haven't **come across** any polar bears yet, but the ice under your feet keeps moving. You're afraid you might fall into the ocean or get lost.

You come to a hole in the ice. It's like a river. It's too long to go around. You've crossed similar rivers by making a bridge with your sleds. But this one is too wide. What do you do? This is the problem that Australian Jade Hameister and her father, Paul, had to solve. It seemed impossible. But they didn't **give up** and **go back** home. Instead, they floated across the water on their sleds. Then they **carried on**. Finally, on 24 April 2016, after a journey of 150 kilometres that began on 13 April, they arrived at the North Pole.

Since then, Jade has crossed the Greenland ice cap and skied to the South Pole. (In 2017 she ate an Antarctic Christmas dinner at minus 50°C!) She's also written a book, been in a National Geographic documentary and given TED talks on climate change and women in society. Jade believes young women should try to live their dreams. She often tells them not to wait until they think they can do something perfectly. She says it's better to just get started.

2 🔊 9.8 Read the article and tick (✓) four problems Jade faced when she skied to the North Pole.
1. ☐ She got lost.
2. ☐ It was really cold.
3. ☐ She had to pull a heavy sled.
4. ☐ She had to cross walls of ice.
5. ☐ The ice changed position under her feet.
6. ☐ She didn't have the right equipment.

3 Read the article again and complete the notes with a word or a short phrase in each gap.

- Age when Jade went to the North Pole: ¹14 years old
- Lowest temperature during her journey to the North Pole: ² _____
- What they used to get across the hole in the ice: ³ _____
- Date Jade reached the North Pole: ⁴ _____
- Distance Jade skied to get to the North Pole: ⁵ _____
- Topics Jade has spoken about in public: women and ⁶ _____

FACT BOX
Jade Hameister
- From Melbourne, Australia
- Born 5 June 2001
- At twelve years old she hiked to Everest Base Camp (5,000 + metres high)
- At fourteen she became the youngest person ever to ski to the North Pole
- At fifteen she skied 550 km across the Greenland ice cap
- At sixteen she became the youngest person ever to ski to the South Pole

4 🔊 9.9 **WORD FRIENDS** Match the highlighted phrasal verbs in the article with the definitions. Listen and check.
1. Started doing a new activity. *taken up*
2. Return to a place.
3. Stop trying to do something.
4. Continued doing the same thing.
5. Find a thing or person without trying to.

5 Complete the text with the correct form of phrasal verbs from Exercise 4.

Jade tries to stay positive when she ¹*comes across* a problem. She didn't ² _____ skiing until she was a teenager. It wasn't easy at first, but she didn't ³ _____ . She ⁴ _____ practising until she was good at it.

VIDEO ▶ **WIDER WORLD**

6 ▶ 44 Watch two people talking about getting lost. Write down what happened to them and what they did.

7 Think of a true story when you got lost. In pairs, take turns to say what happened and how you felt.

I can understand an article about a teenage explorer.   **115** Unit 9

9.4 Grammar

Present Perfect with *just*, *already* and *yet*

VIDEO ▶ **THE HIKING TRIP**

Mia: Oh! Where is he? Have you texted him yet?
Mateo: Yes, I have. I've already sent two texts, but he hasn't replied yet.
Mia: Try again. I'm going to check the map.
Mateo: Mia! Noah's just sent a text. He'll be here soon.

Later

Noah: Hi guys.
Lena: Hi. Why haven't you brought your mountain jacket?
Noah: I lost it. I haven't bought a new one yet.
Mateo: Mia! He's just arrived.
Mia: Noah! Why haven't you brought your mountain jacket?
Noah: I've already told Lena. I lost it.
Mia: But I told you to bring a jacket!
Noah: I don't need one. I've just seen the weather forecast. It's going to be fine! I've brought a sun hat and I've already put on some sun cream.
Mia: OK, let's go! Where's your backpack? Why aren't you wearing boots?

1 ▶ 45 🔊 9.10 Describe the photo. What are the kids going to do? Watch or listen and check.

2 Study the Grammar box. Find more examples of the Present Perfect with *just*, *already* and *yet* in the dialogue.

GRAMMAR	**Present Perfect with *just*, *already* and *yet***
+	He's *just* sent a text. I've *already* sent two texts.
–	He hasn't replied *yet*.
?	Have you texted him *yet*?	Yes, I have./No, I haven't.

GRAMMAR TIME ▶ PAGE 136

3 Read the dialogue again. Use the words in brackets to write sentences about what the kids have or haven't done.
1 Noah/arrive (just)
  Noah has just arrived.
2 Noah/see the weather forecast (just)
3 Noah/buy a new mountain jacket (yet)
4 the kids/start walking (yet)

4 🔊 9.11 Choose the correct option. Listen and check.

Ewan: I've ¹*already / yet* done all my History revision and now I'm doing Maths. I've ²*just / yet* finished that unit on algebra. Have you started revising for your exams ³*already / yet*?
Joanna: No, I haven't opened my books ⁴*just / yet*. I've ⁵*already / just* come back from the park. I've ⁶*already / just* run thirty kilometres this week and it's only Tuesday.
Ewan: Have you played that new video game ⁷*just / yet*?
Joanna: No, I haven't had time ⁸*already / yet*.
Ewan: My brother has ⁹*just / yet* asked me to play, but I said no. I'm too busy.

YOUR WORLD

5 In pairs, talk about your news and recent activities. Use the Present Perfect with *just*, *already* and *yet*.
A: Have you done that History project yet?
B: No, I haven't finished it yet.

Unit 9 · 116 · I can use the Present Perfect to talk about recent events.

9.5 Listening and Vocabulary
Outdoor activities

A Kayaking
B Snowboarding
C Mountain biking
D Surfing

1 Look at the photos. Which activity would you like to do? Why?

2 🔊 9.12 Look at the photos and listen. Which activity A–D does each speaker think is the most exciting? What do you think?

Lucy ☐   Joel ☐   Katie ☐   Glenn ☐

3 🔊 9.13 Study Vocabulary box A. In pairs, add each activity to the correct category – water or land. Listen and check.

VOCABULARY A ▸ **Outdoor activities**

cycling   hiking   horse-riding   kayaking   mountain biking
rock climbing   sailing   scuba diving   skiing
snowboarding   surfing   swimming   windsurfing

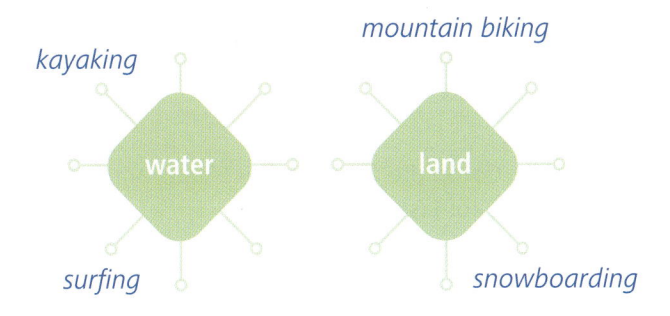

kayaking   *mountain biking*

    water   land

surfing   *snowboarding*

4 In groups, say which activities in Vocabulary box A you have/haven't tried and which are popular in your country.

5 🔊 9.14 Listen and match statements a–e with speakers 1–4. There is one extra statement.

1 ☐   2 ☐   3 ☐   4 ☐

a He/She says the activity can be dangerous.
b He/She is very good at the activity.
c He/She talks about the last time he/she did the activity.
d He/She talks about when he/she did the activity for the first time.
e He/She describes the good and bad sides of the activity.

6 🔊 9.15 Study Vocabulary box B. Which items of equipment can you find in photos A–D?

VOCABULARY B ▸ **Sporting equipment**

bike   boat   boots   compass   gloves   goggles
helmet   kayak   life jacket   map   paddle
saddle   snowboard   surfboard   wetsuit

7 🔊 9.16 Complete the notes with items of equipment from Vocabulary box B. Listen and check.

- **Hiking** – you need good walking [1]*boots*, a map and a [2]_____ so you don't get lost.
- **Windsurfing** – you need a [3]_____ to float in the water and a [4]_____ to keep you warm.
- **Skiing** – you need skis, ski poles, ski boots, a helmet, [5]_____ to protect your eyes, and [6]_____ for your hands.

8 🔊 9.17 Listen to four people talking about their activities. Mark the sentences T (true) or F (false).
1 ☐ Surfing started in islands in the Pacific Ocean.
2 ☐ It's easy to go the wrong way in a kayak.
3 ☐ A good mountain bike costs a minimum of €2,000.
4 ☐ Snowboarding started in the 1970s.

YOUR WORLD
9 In pairs, ask and answer the questions about the different activities in Vocabulary box A.
- Have you ever tried …?
- When was the last time you …?
- Did you enjoy it?

A: *Have you ever tried surfing?*
B: *Yes, I have.*

I can understand people talking about outdoor activities.

9.6 Speaking
Asking for, giving and refusing permission

VIDEO ▶ **CAN I SEE THE MAP?**

Lena: It's so hot! Do you mind if I borrow your sun cream, Noah?
Noah: I'm afraid not. I haven't got much. Just kidding. No problem. Here. Can I have a look at the map, Mia?
Mia: Sure.
Mateo: This is a great walk, Mia. Well done!
Lena: Yes, but is it OK to stop for a rest?
Mia: Yes, of course.

Later

Mia: Yes! We've reached the top of the path!
Lena: Thank goodness!
Mia: Where are Noah and Mateo?
Lena: I hope they haven't had an accident.
Mia: I've got no signal. Is it OK if I borrow your phone, Lena?
Lena: Sure, go ahead.
Mia: There's a signal, but they're not answering.
Lena: Can I see the map?
Mia: Sorry, but you can't. Noah's got it.
Lena: Is it all right to go back to look for them?
Mia: I'm afraid that's not a good idea. We should stay together.
Mateo: Hi!
Mia: Mateo! Noah! Where have you been?
Noah: We found an easier path. Can we eat now? I'm starving.
Mia: It's not cool to disappear like that, guys!
Noah: Sorry.
Mia: OK, let's eat.

SOUNDS GOOD! Thank goodness! • I'm starving! • It's not cool.

1 ▶ 46 ◀)) **9.18** In pairs, describe the photo and answer the questions. Watch or listen and check.
  1 What are the girls doing? How do they feel? Why?
  2 What happened to Noah and Mateo?

SET FOR LIFE

2 Which three skills are the most important for a good leader? Discuss in groups.
  • giving good advice
  • listening to everyone in the group
  • making everyone in the group feel good
  • preparing things well

3 Study the Speaking box. Find examples of the phrases in the dialogue.

SPEAKING — Asking for, giving and refusing permission

Asking for permission
Can I/we …?
Do you mind if I/we …?
Is it OK/all right (for me/us) to …?
Is it OK/all right if I/we …?

Giving permission
Yes, of course.   No problem.   Sure, go ahead.

Refusing permission
Sorry/I'm sorry, but you can't.
I'm afraid that's not possible.
I'm afraid that's not a good idea.

4 ◀)) **9.19** Complete the dialogues with one word in each gap. Listen and check.
  1 Jim: Is it OK *for* me to use your dictionary?
    Ella: Sure – go _____ .
  2 Ivy: _____ I have some juice?
    Max: _____ problem! There's a carton in the fridge.
  3 Ava: Is it all _____ if I use your phone?
    Lily: Yes, _____ course!
    Ava: Oh, and do you _____ if I borrow your charger?
    Lily: I'm afraid that's not _____ . We haven't got one!

YOUR WORLD

5 In pairs, ask for permission. Use the ideas below and the Speaking box to help you.
  • borrow a pen   • ask a favour
  • use a mobile   • look at the notes

I can ask for, give and refuse permission.

9.7 Writing
An informal email about a holiday

1 Read Natalie's email. Say what she has done so far and what she hasn't done yet.

2 Study the Writing box. Find examples of the phrases in Natalie's email.

WRITING An informal email about a holiday

Dear/Hi + person's name

Say where you are and what it's like
1 Here we are in …
   We're having a great/brilliant time in …
   It's a great/fantastic/beautiful place.
   It's the best place I've ever been.

Describe the weather
2 It hasn't rained yet!   It hasn't stopped raining.   It's been really sunny.
   The weather has been awful/amazing.
   The weather hasn't been great.

Say what you have done so far
3 So far, we've had some lovely walks.
   We've been to/visited/swum/sunbathed …
   We haven't gone kayaking yet.

Describe your plans
4 This afternoon/Tomorrow we're going to …
   We're coming home on Sunday.

End the email
5 See you soon!   Miss you!   (Lots of) love,

6 PS: You can add a PS (postscript) for extra news or information.

3 Study the Language box. Are the adjectives positive or negative? Which ones are in Natalie's email?

LANGUAGE Adjective synonyms to avoid repetition

Use synonyms to add variety to your writing.
good = amazing, brilliant, great, lovely
bad = awful, terrible
boring = dull
tired = exhausted, sleepy

4 Describe your last holiday. Use the ideas below and as many different adjectives from the Language box as you can.

buy souvenirs   eat ice cream   have a long walk   make friends
read a novel   swim in the sea   sunbathe   visit a museum/castle

I had an amazing time last summer. We went to Portugal. The weather was brilliant.

5 Imagine you are on holiday at the moment. Write some sentences about what you have done so far. Use the ideas in Exercise 4 and the Present Perfect.

I've swum in the sea, watched the sunset …

Hi Jamie!
I hope you're well.
1 We're having a brilliant time in Scotland. It's the best place I've ever been.
2 The weather hasn't been great. In fact, it's been awful, but it hasn't stopped us from having fun!
3 So far, we've had some lovely walks and we've visited a castle. We're hanging out with some of Margot's friends a lot of the time! I'm exhausted!
4 We haven't gone kayaking yet, but tomorrow we're going to try it. I've never done it before, so I hope I can do it!
5 See you soon!
   Natalie
6 PS: Have you heard the news about Margot's brother? He's won a big surfing competition!

WRITING TIME

6 Imagine you are on holiday at a popular tourist resort. Write an email to a friend.

1 **Find ideas**
   Make notes for your email.
   • Where are you? What's the weather like?
   • What have you done so far?
   • What are your plans?

2 **Plan**
   Organise your ideas into paragraphs. Use Natalie's email to help you.

3 **Write and share**
   • Write a draft email. Use the Language box and the Writing box to help you.
   • Share your email with another student for feedback.
   • Write the final version of your email.

4 **Check**
   • Check language: did you use a variety of interesting adjectives in your writing?
   • Check grammar: did you use the Present Perfect correctly?

I can write an informal email about a holiday.

Vocabulary Activator

WORDLIST 🔊 9.20

Geographical features
beach (n)
cliff (n)
coast (n)
desert (n)
field (n)
forest (n)
hill (n)
island (n)
jungle (n)
lake (n)
mountain (n)
ocean (n)
rainforest (n)
river (n)
sea (n)
valley (n)
waterfall (n)

Word friends
(*in, on, by*)
by a lake
by a river
by the sea
in a field
in a forest
in a lake
in a valley
in the mountains
in the sea
on a beach
on a hill
on a mountain
on an island
on the coast

Talking about countries
border (n)
capital city (n)
flag (n)
official language (n)
population (n)

Word friends
(phrasal verbs)
carry on (v)
come across (v)
give up (v)
go back (v)
take up (v)

Outdoor activities
cycling (n)
hiking (n)
horse-riding (n)
kayaking (n)
mountain biking (n)
rock climbing (n)
sailing (n)
scuba diving (n)
skiing (n)
snowboarding (n)
surfing (n)
swimming (n)
windsurfing (n)

Sporting equipment
bike (n)
boat (n)
boots (n)
compass (n)
gloves (n)
goggles (n)
helmet (n)
kayak (n)
life jacket (n)
map (n)
paddle (n)
saddle (n)
snowboard (n)
surfboard (n)
wetsuit (n)

Extra words
amazing (adj)
barbecue (n)
bridge (n)
camp (v)
climate change (n)
climb (v)
dry (adj)
dull (adj)
equipment (n)
exhausted (adj)
experience (n)
freezing (adj)
get lost
hang out with

heavy (adj)
high (adj)
holiday (n)
ice cap (n)
instructor (n)
irritating (adj)
kilometre (n)
land (n)
leader (n)
low (adj)
path (n)
reach the top
rest (n)
scared (adj)
share a border
ski (v)
ski boots (n)
ski poles (n)
skis (n)
sled (n)
souvenir (n)
spectacular (adj)
sun cream (n)
sunbathe (v)
sunset (n)
travel (v)
trip (n)
visa (n)
wet (adj)

---

1 Use words from the wordlist to find these things.
  1 four large areas of water *lake, …*
  2 two places which are higher than the land around them
  3 two bike sports
  4 two sports you can do in winter

2 In pairs, talk about the ideas below.
  • natural features that you haven't seen but would like to see
  • sporting activities that you enjoy and sports you'd like to try

3 Write the correct word for each definition. Then write two more definitions for your partner to guess.
  1 The activity of going for long walks in the countryside or mountains. *hiking*
  2 The number of people in a city or country.
  3 You sit on this when you ride a horse.
  4 You usually wear this when you go scuba diving.
  5 These stop your hands from getting cold.
  6 This keeps you safe when you go kayaking.

4 Complete the sentences with phrases from the wordlist. Are the sentences true for you?
  1 I often go hiking *in the fields* around my house.
  2 In the summer, my family often goes swimming _____ .
  3 I want to go rock climbing _____ .
  4 I really enjoy sunbathing _____ .
  5 I'd like to go cycling _____ .

5 🔊 9.21 **PRONUNCIATION** Listen to each phrasal verb in bold. Is the stress on the verb or the particle (*on, up*, etc.)? Listen again and repeat.
  1 Let's **carry on** up the hill.
  2 We **came across** a fox.
  3 Let's **go back** to the camp.
  4 Don't **give up** now!
  5 I want to **take up** skiing.

Revision

Vocabulary

1 Match the activities below with the groups of words. There are two extra activities. Say which activity you think is the most dangerous, tiring or exciting.

> hiking in the hills   kayaking   mountain biking
> rock climbing   skiing   ~~snowboarding~~   surfing

1 _snowboarding_ – gloves, goggles, snowboard
2 _____ – life jacket, paddle
3 _____ – helmet, bike
4 _____ – map, boots
5 _____ – wetsuit, surfboard

I think snowboarding is the most exciting activity, because you go fast.

2 Choose the correct option.

Cardiff is the ¹*capital / country / official* city of Wales in the UK. It's a university town ²*by / in / on* the south coast of Wales, about forty kilometres from the ³*city / border / mountain* with England. It has a ⁴*valley / flag / population* of about 477,000 people. The town has a famous sports stadium next to a bridge over the ⁵*ocean / river / water* Taff. There are some long sandy ⁶*beaches / cliffs / fields* nearby.

3 Complete the text with one word in each gap.

Last year, we were on holiday ¹_by_ the sea. I wanted to take ²_____ a new sport, and one day I saw an advert for scuba diving. I paid for a lesson, put on a wetsuit and waited ³_____ the beach for the instructor. We were ⁴_____ the sea for a long time! It was difficult at first, but I carried ⁵_____ and soon I was standing up on the board. I'm happy that I didn't give ⁶_____ because we ⁷_____ across some friendly dolphins! It was an amazing experience, and I plan to go ⁸_____ next year.

Grammar

4 Complete the text with the Present Perfect form of the verbs in brackets.

SUNDAY
Feeling nervous! We ¹*'ve just arrived* (just/arrive) at the summer sports camp. I ²_____ (never/be) on a holiday like this before. We ³_____ (not meet) any instructors yet, but everybody else is very friendly!

MONDAY
We ⁴_____ (already/get up) and we ⁵_____ (eat) a big breakfast. Our instructor ⁶_____ (just/tell) us we can go kayaking today. Yay!

THURSDAY
I ⁷_____ (never/feel) so tired, and the camp ⁸_____ (not finish/yet)! I ⁹_____ (not have) time to write my blog! It's brilliant though. ¹⁰_____ (you/ever/try) a sports camp?

5 Make questions in the Present Perfect. Then, in pairs, ask your questions and answer with *already*, *just* or *yet*.

1 you / ever / be / to a sports camp / ?
   Have you ever been to a sports camp?
2 you / ever / take / an English exam / ?
3 you / see / a waterfall / ?
4 you / climb / a mountain / in your country / ?
5 you / feel / exhausted / ?
6 your family / visit / capital city / of your country / ?

Speaking

6 In pairs, role play the situations. Student A, look below. Student B, go to page 144.

Student A

1 You want to go mountain biking tomorrow. Student B has got a better bike than yours. Ask for permission to use it. You haven't got a helmet. Try to borrow one from Student B.

2 Student B asks for permission to go hiking with you. Give permission. Ask if he/she has hiking boots. Refuse permission to lend your boots. You need them for the trip. Say trainers are OK.

Dictation

7 🔊 9.22 Listen. Then listen again and write down what you hear during each pause.

121   Unit 9

BBC CULTURE

Save our seas!

Oceans in danger

1 Fish is a popular meal for many people. It's healthy, tasty and often cheap because there are lots of fish in the sea. But are there? In the last thirty years the number of fish has fallen almost fifty percent because we've taken too many fish out of the sea. Humans have caused lots of problems to other sea animals too.

2 For example, there aren't many sea turtles left in the world. People kill them for food, and many also die in fishermen's nets. Plastic pollution is another problem for turtles – they sometimes eat plastic in the sea because it looks like their usual food. Turtles lay their eggs on beaches. That's dangerous for them too, because there are a lot of houses and hotels (and humans) on our coasts.

3 Another amazing animal in danger is the blue whale. It is the largest animal that has ever existed. But some countries still hunt and kill whales – about 1,000 a year. Climate change is a problem for whales too. As the oceans get warmer, the small animals that whales eat move to different areas. The whales have to travel large distances to follow them, which means that feeding is more difficult.

4 Luckily, lots of conservation groups around the world are working to solve these problems. In some places, people protect turtle eggs and help the baby turtles get back to the sea. There are legal limits on fishing to keep fish populations healthy. A lot of people have stopped throwing plastic away too. But there is still a lot more that we can do to help save our seas.

---

climate change (n) the change in the world's weather
conservation group (n) people who work to protect animals, plants, etc.
lay their eggs (phr) produce eggs
legal limits (n) the highest numbers that the law says you can have
net (n) something used for catching fish, insects or animals
pollution (n) making something dirty with dangerous chemicals or rubbish

---

1 ⟨VISIBLE THINKING⟩ In pairs, follow these steps.
SEE
1 Describe the photos. What sea animals can you see?
THINK
2 Why is the water full of plastic? What problems can it cause for the animals?
WONDER
3 Discuss one of the questions below.
   a Why are the things below dangerous for sea animals?

   ocean rubbish   fishing   temperatures

   b How can we help protect sea animals?

2 🔊 9.23 Read the article. In which paragraphs (1–4) can you find answers to questions a and b in the Wonder section?

3 Read the text again and answer the questions.
1 Why has the number of fish in our seas gone down?
2 Why do sea turtles sometimes eat plastic?
3 Why is it dangerous for turtles to lay eggs on beaches?
4 Why can it be difficult for whales to find food these days?
5 What stops people from catching too many fish?

4 In pairs, discuss the questions.
1 What other animals in the world are in danger?
2 How can we help with their conservation?
3 Why is the water full of plastic? What problems can it cause for the animals?

BBC ▶ Coral islands

5 Look at the photo from a TV programme about a coral reef. In pairs, discuss the questions.
1. Where in the world can you find one of the biggest areas of coral reef?
2. Is coral
   a. an animal?
   b. the product of an animal?
   c. a plant?
3. Is the coral in the photo dead or alive? How do you know?

6 ▶ 47 Watch the video and check your answers to Exercise 5.

7 ▶ 47 Watch again. Tick (✓) the facts that you hear in the video.
1. ☐ The Maldive Islands are in the Indian Ocean.
2. ☐ About 500,000 people live in the Maldive Islands.
3. ☐ The Baa Atoll is a nature reserve.
4. ☐ There are over 100 different types of coral.
5. ☐ The temperature of the sea affects the coral reefs.
6. ☐ Pollution and fishing are bad for the coral reefs.

8 In pairs, discuss the questions.
1. Do you think the climate is changing in your country?
2. Why do you say this? What do you notice?

PROJECT TIME

9 In groups of three, prepare a digital poster about another endangered animal. Follow these steps.

1 In groups, choose an animal. Decide who in your group can find the answers to these questions.
- How many of these animals are there? Where in the world does it live? What is its home? What does it eat?
- Why is it endangered? Are humans responsible? Is climate change responsible?
- How can people help to save this animal?

2 Individually, prepare your part of the poster.
- Find the answers to your questions and write a short text.
- Find photos to illustrate the information.

3 In your group, create your poster. You can use an online poster maker.
- Import everyone's text and photos.
- Decide on a layout.
- Think of a title for the poster.
- Check and edit the poster.

4 Share your poster with the class.
- Answer other students' questions.
- Look at the other posters. Ask questions.

Progress Check Units 1–9

Vocabulary and Grammar

1 Choose the correct option.

My brother, Jim, has ¹___ become a vegetarian and he doesn't go to the ²___ anymore to buy steaks. He now visits a health food shop in the shopping ³___ where he buys lots of interesting ingredients. Last Saturday he cooked me a lovely vegan meal. He made a no-meat burger. It was delicious. Anyway, our uncle works ⁴___ a chef, and we told him about the burgers. He ⁵___ these burgers on the menu at his restaurant last week, and everyone loves them! Now I think a vegetarian diet can be really good – I must ⁶___ the internet for some nice recipes!

1	a just	b yet	c not
2	a bakery	b butcher's	c newsagent's
3	a hall	b centre	c station
4	a at	b in	c as
5	a puts	b put	c used to put
6	a find	b switch	c check

2 Complete the text with one word in each gap.

Lots of teens love the outdoors in summer, especially those ¹*who* live in towns and cities. I'm really ²_____ nature. I love sunbathing and sitting on the grass ³_____ a lake. But this summer my parents have to work, so we won't leave the city. However, I believe there are lots of fun outdoor activities that teens can take ⁴_____ in parks. ⁵_____ you ever tried cycling or doing yoga? Parks are places ⁶_____ there are cycle paths and a lot of space for exercising. Or why not simply go for a walk, or have a picnic on the grass? Click ⁷_____ the link below to find out more in my vlog.

3 Complete the second sentence with the word in bold so that it means the same as the first one. Use no more than four words.

1. We need more nurses in the hospitals. **ENOUGH**
   We don't *have enough nurses* in the hospitals.
2. There are no fish in the sea here. **ANY**
   There _____ in the sea here.
3. My party is at my house on Saturday at 8 p.m. **HAVING**
   I _____ at my house on Saturday at 8 p.m.
4. I found an old map of the town in the cupboard. **ACROSS**
   I _____ an old map of the town in the cupboard.
5. All the films that I've seen were better than that one. **WORST**
   That's _____ that I've ever seen.
6. Train tickets are more expensive than bus tickets. **AS**
   Bus tickets are _____ train tickets.

Speaking

4 Match statements and questions 1–5 with responses a–f. There is one extra response.
1. ☐ Do you mind if I give John your phone number?
2. ☐ I'm studying hard.
3. ☐ I'm sorry I didn't call you.
4. ☐ Can I help you, sir?
5. ☐ I can't do this exercise. What should I do?

a Never mind.
b Sure, go ahead.
c I'll take this one.
d You'll probably pass the exam.
e Why don't you ask Mark to help you?
f Yes, please. I'm looking for the escalator.

5 In pairs, follow the instructions.
Student A: Go to page 139.
Student B: Go to page 144.

Listening

6 🔊 **PC1–9.1** Listen and complete the notes with a word or a short phrase in each gap.

> **Trip to the London Aquarium**
>
> Day and date: ¹*Monday* 10 March
> Leaving time: ² _____ a.m.
> Ticket price: £ ³ _____
> Free time afternoon break will last: ⁴ _____
> Parents must send a note: by email or ⁵ _____

7 What is your dream job? Why would you like to do it?

8 🔊 **PC1–9.2** Listen to four people talking about jobs. Match statements a–e with speakers 1–4. There is one extra statement.

1 ☐ 2 ☐ 3 ☐ 4 ☐

This speaker …
a describes the people he/she sees at work.
b would like to change his/her job in the future.
c doesn't want to work in another country.
d says how he/she will spend the money they earn.
e gives advice about how to choose a job.

Reading

9 Read the article *It's not fair!* Match people A–C with questions 1–5. Two people can match with more than one question.

Which person …
1 ☐ would like to spend time with family members in the afternoon?
2 ☐ doesn't get enough sleep because they have too many things to do?
3 ☐ gave up a hobby to do better at school?
4 ☐ does a lot for their parents?
5 ☐ has more lessons than other students?

It's not fair!

Are you fed up with schoolwork? Do you want more free time? You're not alone.

A Dan
I feel that we get so much homework that nobody can do all of it. I took up tennis, but I had to stop because I didn't have enough time. My goal is to do well in my exams, so I study hard. In the evening I don't even have an hour to read or watch TV as I go to bed early to get enough sleep. I'm getting better grades this year, and my parents are very pleased, but I think it isn't fair that I have to study all the time. Mum and Dad watch TV and relax in the garden on Saturday and Sunday. What about me?

B Betty
Music is my hobby and my biggest passion. I go to a special music school, so I have extra music lessons every afternoon. I get up early to get to school at 7.45, and we have normal lessons to 1 p.m. After lunch we have music for three hours. My sisters go to another school and they go home for lunch. And where am I? Still at school! I enjoy music and I'm a really good pianist now. However, I get annoyed about the long hours. I really want to go home for lunch and play with my sisters.

C Lee
I live on a farm. When I was younger I enjoyed feeding the chickens and brushing the horses, but I'm not so happy about doing all the work now. I feed the chickens at 6 a.m. and after school I help Dad with the cows. I do my homework in the evening and I go to bed late so I can finish. It's awful because I get up early and I sleep only five hours! That's not enough! The worst thing is that my parents want me to become a farmer one day, but I actually want to be a lawyer! How am I going to tell them?

Writing

10 Which of the after school activities below do you like?

> basketball   book club   chess   football   music lessons
> tennis   theatre club   volunteer work

11 Write an email to a friend about an after school activity you have taken up. Include the information below.
- what the activity is
- who does the activity with you
- what you have done so far
- what you like about it

125

Grammar Time

1.2

Present Simple: affirmative and negative | Adverbs of frequency

We use the Present Simple for habits and routines.

+	I/You/We/They He/She/It	watch animated films. studies photography.
−	I/You/We/They He/She/It	don't (do not) watch animated films. doesn't (does not) study photography.

Spelling rules

With *he/she/it* we add *-s*, *-es* or *-ies* to the verb.
- Most verbs, add *-s*: write – writes.
- Verbs ending in *-o*, *-ch*, *-sh*, *-ss* and *-x*, add *-es*:
  go – goes, catch – catches, wash – washes.
- Verbs ending in consonant + *-y*, cut *-y* and add *-ies*:
  fly – flies.

Adverbs of frequency

Adverbs of frequency *(always, usually, often, sometimes, never)* go before the verb, but after the verb *to be*.

always   usually   often   sometimes   never

I always listen to music on my phone.
I am usually busy after school.
We don't often watch documentaries at school.

1 Order the words to make sentences.
1. the guitar / at the weekend / a group / I / in / play
   I play the guitar in a group at the weekend.
2. science fiction / films / often / watch / we
3. busy / she / always / is
4. go out / don't / on Mondays / usually / I
5. comics / doesn't / my / read / sister

2 Complete the text with the Present Simple form of the verbs in brackets.

Sandi has a very unusual life

Sandi ¹*lives* (live) in the Arctic. She ² _____ (get) up at 4 a.m. every day. She ³ _____ (often/eat) pizza for breakfast. She ⁴ _____ (fly) to school in a helicopter every day. After school she ⁵ _____ (study) poetry. She ⁶ _____ (always/go) to bed at 7 p.m.

3 Compare your life to Sandi's from Exercise 2.
I don't live in the Arctic. I live in …

1.4

Present Simple: questions and answers

Yes/No questions and short answers

?	Do	I/you/ we/they	read novels?	Yes, I/you/we/they do. No, I/you/we/they don't.
	Does	he/she/ it	work in a bank?	Yes, he/she/it does. No, he/she/it doesn't.

Other questions and answers

How often do you go to the cinema?
Every Sunday./I go to the cinema every Sunday.
I never go to the cinema.
What time does the film start?
At 8 p.m./It starts at 8 p.m.
Where do they live?
In West Green./They live in West Green.

Time expressions

every day/week/month   at eight o'clock
in the morning/afternoon/evening   on Mondays
once/twice/three times a month   at the weekend

1 Make *Yes/No* questions in the Present Simple. Then ask and answer the questions in pairs.
1. you / like / taking photographs / ?
2. your favourite singer / write / songs / ?
3. your parents / watch / music videos / on TV / ?
4. you and your friends / like / dancing / ?
5. you / share photos / on social media / ?
6. you / often / read / novels / ?

A: *Do you like taking photographs?* B: *Yes, I do.*

2 Write questions for these answers. Sometimes there is more than one possible question.
1. *Where does your aunt live?*
   My aunt lives **in Italy**.
2. _____ ? Jon **walks** to school.
3. _____ ? The concert ends **at 11.30**.
4. _____ ? Sam has **pizza** for lunch.
5. _____ ? **No**, I don't.
6. _____ ? **Yes**, she does.

3 Imagine you are interviewing a favourite star/celebrity. Write seven questions about his/her life. Use the ideas below to help you.

How often …?   like …ing?   What kind of … like? When …?   Where …?   Who … with?

Do you like listening to music?

2.2

Present Continuous

We use the Present Continuous to talk about activities happening at the moment of speaking.

+	I	'm (am) wearing a hat.	
	You/We/They	're (are) playing a game.	
	He/She/It	's (is) sleeping.	
−	I	'm not (am not) wearing a hat.	
	You/We/They	aren't (are not) playing a game.	
	He/She/It	isn't (is not) sleeping.	
?	Am	I	wearing a hat?	Yes, I am. / No, I'm not.
	Are	you/we/they	playing a game?	Yes, you/we/they are. / No, you/we/they aren't.
	Is	he/she/it	sleeping?	Yes, he/she/it is. / No, he/she/it isn't.

Where are you going?
What is he doing?

Spelling rules
- Most verbs, add -ing: go – going, look – looking.
- Verbs ending in -e, cut -e and add -ing: live – living.
- Short verbs that end in consonant + vowel + consonant, double the last consonant: sit – sitting.

Time expressions
now right now at the moment today

1 Write a few sentences to describe the photo. Use the phrases below to help you.

> help her sister with homework   sit at the table
> talk on the phone   work on the computer

Mum and two sisters are sitting at the table.

2 Complete the dialogue with the Present Continuous form of the verbs in brackets.

Mum: Tom! Where are you?
Tom: Hi, Mum. I ¹*'m sitting* (sit) in the park.
Mum: What ² _____ (you/do)?
Tom: I ³ _____ (study) for an exam.
Mum: ⁴ _____ (Matt/study) too?
Tom: Yes, he is.
Mum: Really? We ⁵ _____ (drive) past the park now. You ⁶ _____ (not read)! You ⁷ _____ (play) football!
Tom: Yes, we ⁸ _____ (get) ready for our PE exam!

3 Imagine you are having a party. Use the Present Continuous to write ten sentences about what is happening.

I'm sitting on the sofa with my friend Joanna.

2.4

Present Simple and Present Continuous

- We use the **Present Simple** for facts, habits and routines.
  Rachel lives in South Street.
  Noah doesn't tidy his room.
  What time do you get up?

- We use the **Present Continuous** to talk about activities happening at the moment of speaking.
  What are you doing under the table?
  I'm looking for my earring!

- We also use the **Present Continuous** for something happening around now, but maybe not at the moment of speaking.

  Time expressions
  these days   at the moment   this week/month

  Is she taking part in the football game this month?
  He isn't talking to his best friend these days.

1 Complete the sentences with the Present Simple or the Present Continuous form of the words in brackets.
1 Oh no, it *'s raining* (rain) again!
2 I _____ (live) in Berlin, but I _____ (visit) London now.
3 He _____ (save) money at the moment to buy a leather jacket.
4 Gemma _____ (often/go) to Tenerife on holiday.
5 Jim _____ (know) a little Spanish.

Grammar Time **127**

Grammar Time

2 Complete the sentences to make them true for you. Then ask and answer in pairs.

Free time	I always _____ [activity] after school. Now I'm not _____ , I'm _____ .
Clothes	I often wear _____ [item of clothing]. I never wear _____ . At the moment I'm wearing _____ .
Music	I usually listen to _____ [type of music]. These days, I'm listening to _____ [group/artist/composer] a lot.

A: *What do you do after school?*
B: *I always run in the park after school.*

3 Use the Present Simple to write about your typical Sunday. Then use the Present Continuous to write about your unusual Sunday.

On a typical Sunday, I usually watch TV.
This Sunday, I'm not watching TV. I'm …

3.2

Past Simple: was/were

We use the Past Simple to talk about finished events and situations in the past. The Past Simple of *to be* is *was/were*.

+	I/He/She/It	was at school.
	You/We/They	were at home.
−	I/He/She/It	wasn't (was not) hungry.
	You/We/They	weren't (were not) late.
?	Was	I/he/she/it	hungry?	Yes, I/he/she/it was. No, I/he/she/it wasn't.
	Were	you/we/they	tired?	Yes, you/we/they were. No, you/we/they weren't.
	Where were you yesterday?			

The Past Simple of *there is/there are* is *there was/there were*.

+	There	was a bee on the flower.
	There	were two tigers.
−	There	wasn't (was not) a cow on the farm.
	There	weren't (were not) any people.
?	Was	there	a gift shop?	Yes, there was. No, there wasn't.
	Were	there	many people?	Yes, there were. No, there weren't.

Time expressions
yesterday
last Tuesday/week/month/year
two days/a week ago
this morning
at one o'clock
in June/2020

1 Complete the questions with *was/were*. Then ask and answer in pairs.
1 How <u>was</u> your last English test?
2 _____ it cold yesterday?
3 Where _____ you last summer?
4 _____ you at a party last weekend?
5 Where _____ you five hours ago?
6 How old _____ you in 2015?
7 _____ you late for school this morning?

A: *How was your last English test?*
B: *It was easy!*

2 Rewrite the sentences in the Past Simple.
1 'Are you bored?' 'Yes, I am.'
'Were you bored?' 'Yes, I was.'
2 'Is it cold?' 'Yes, it is.'
3 'Are you at home?' 'No, I'm not.'
4 There is an annoying noise coming from downstairs.
5 'Is there a letter for me?' 'No, there isn't.'
6 We aren't very hungry.
7 There aren't any tickets for the aquarium.

3 Write ten sentences about a recent day out (concert or sports game).
Last Saturday I was at a Coldplay concert.
I was with … It was at … There were …

3.4

Past Simple: regular and irregular verbs

+	Tony	watched TV.
−	Penny	didn't (did not) read.
?	Did	they	sleep long?	Yes, they did. No, they didn't.
	What did Paolo watch? Where did Rena study?			

+	She	took my camera.
−	He	didn't (did not) take my camera.
?	Did	you	take my camera?	Yes, I did. No, I didn't.

Spelling rules
- Most regular verbs, add -*ed*: watch – watch*ed*.
- Verbs ending in -*e*, add -*d*: live – live*d*.
- Verbs ending in consonant + *y*, cut -*y* and add -*ied*: try – tr*ied*.
- One-syllable verbs ending in vowel + consonant, double the consonant and add -*ed*: stop – stop*ped*.

128 Grammar Time

1 Write the Past Simple form of these verbs.
1. cook – *cooked*
2. carry – _____
3. play – _____
4. marry – _____
5. leave – _____
6. make – _____
7. meet – _____
8. read – _____

2 Complete the sentences with the Past Simple form of the words in brackets.
1. Mel *tidied* (tidy) her room.
2. '_____ (they/get) a pet?' 'No, they _____.'
3. I _____ (not watch) TV last night.
4. '_____ (you/finish) writing your blog?' 'Yes, I _____.'
5. We _____ (not talk) to her yesterday.
6. He _____ (drop) his phone, and it _____ (stop) working.

3 Write questions about the sentences below.
1. She listened to music all day.
   Did she listen to music all day?
2. James got a new pet.
3. She watched a film last night.
4. They studied English yesterday.
5. I took my cat to the vet last week.

4 Complete Lena's story with the Past Simple form of the verbs below.

| fall | feel | get | ~~have~~ | hit | hurt | sit |

I was sitting by the pool under an umbrella. I ¹*had* my smartphone with me. As I got up to take a photo, I ² _____ my head on the umbrella's arm. It really ³ _____. I ⁴ _____ bad, so I ⁵ _____ down, and my smartphone ⁶ _____ in the pool! I couldn't get up, but my dad ⁷ _____ the phone out of the pool for me. Now I need a new phone!

5 Write five things you did last weekend and five things you didn't do. Use the sentences in Exercise 3 to help you.

I wrote a blog post, I …
I didn't cook a meal, I …

4.2
Used to

We can talk about past habits or states with *used to*.

+	Jenny **used to have** long hair. We **used to swim** in the lake.	
–	We **didn't use to have** phones.	
?	**Did** you **use to skate** in the park?	Yes, we **did**. No, we **didn't**.
	How **did** you **use to travel** to work?	

1 Complete the sentences with *used to* and the correct form of the verbs in brackets.
1. Lena *used to sing* (sing) in the school concert.
2. Paolo _____ (not run) fast when he was young.
3. The children _____ (eat) ice cream twice a week.
4. _____ (people/have) mobile phones in 1970?
5. Harry _____ (not study) hard last year.
6. We _____ (write) letters to our grandparents every month.
7. How often _____ (Greg/go) to the gym?
8. Dad _____ (drive) to work, but now he rides his bike.

2 Rewrite the sentences with *used to*.
1. Dave had a digital camera when he was seventeen.
   Dave used to have a digital camera when he was seventeen.
2. Did Mum go to the bank every week?
3. My sister didn't eat vegetables when she was younger.
4. Did you wear a uniform in the 1950s?
5. I never sent text messages to my dad.

3 Think about your life two years ago. What did you use to do? What didn't you use to do? Write five sentences.

I didn't use to play the guitar.

Grammar Time 129

Grammar Time

4.4

Verb patterns

- We use **to + the infinitive** after these verbs:
  agree, decide, forget, learn, need, remember, try, want, would/'d like
  We agreed to switch off our phones.
- We use **verb + -ing** after these verbs:
  can't stand, don't mind, enjoy, finish, hate, keep, like, love, prefer, stop
  I prefer texting to writing emails.

1 Complete the sentences with the correct form of the verbs in brackets.
  1 I'm learning _to type_ (type) without looking.
  2 When did you finish _____ (do) your homework?
  3 Denise never forgets _____ (do) her homework.
  4 Sue keeps _____ (send) me videos of cats.
  5 My dad can't stand _____ (talk) on the phone.
  6 We tried _____ (spend) a day without our phones.

2 Choose the correct option.
  1 My little sister is learning *to swim / swimming*.
  2 I would like *buying / to buy* a new laptop.
  3 I hate *to get up / getting up* early.
  4 Mark is learning *to play / playing* the piano.
  5 Did she decide *to go / going* to the exhibition?
  6 Louise enjoys *to surf / surfing* the internet.

3 Think of a person you know very well. Use the verbs from the Grammar box to write six sentences about him/her.

  My best friend always tries to help other people. She enjoys …

5.2

Defining relative clauses

We use relative clauses to refer to a person, thing or place we are talking about.
- We use **who** or **that** for people.
  Paola is the girl who won the competition.
  I sit next to a boy that is a football champion.
- We use **which** or **that** for things or animals.
  There are some books which I want to buy this week.
  This is the cat that lives next door.
- We use **where** for places.
  This is the house where I used to live.

1 Choose the correct option.
  1 I like the flowers *who / which* are on the table.
  2 This is the place *which / where* we meet every Sunday.
  3 The thing *that / who* I can't stand is doing the washing up.
  4 Do you know the woman *who / where* is standing over there?
  5 Let's see the new film *that / who* everyone is talking about.
  6 He bought the vacuum cleaner *where / that* was on sale.

2 Complete the sentences with *who*, *where* or *which*.
  1 The school _where_ she goes is in the centre of the town.
  2 Mary is the girl _____ is my best friend.
  3 I don't like the buildings _____ are in my neighbourhood.
  4 Can you tell me about the girls _____ live next door?
  5 This is the restaurant _____ famous people eat.
  6 Do you like the game _____ I bought you?

3 Write six sentences about your home, school and family. Use relative clauses.

  I love the cakes which my mum makes on special occasions.

5.4

Modal verbs: *can*, *have to* and *must*

Can
We use *can* to talk about rules that other people make for us.
I *can* go online when I want. (It's OK/allowed.)
I *can't* watch TV after 10 p.m. (It isn't OK.)
Can you invite friends to stay? (Is it OK?)

Have to
We use *have to* to say that something is necessary and *don't have to* to say that something isn't necessary.
You *have to* come home before nine. (It's necessary.)
You *don't have to* come home before nine. (It isn't necessary.)
Do I *have to* come home before nine? (Is it necessary?)

+	I/You/We/They	have to help.
	He/She/It	has to clean.
−	I/You/We/They	don't (do not) have to help.
	He/She/It	doesn't (does not) have to clean.
?	Do	I/you/we/they	have to help?	Yes, I/you/we/they do. No, I/you/we/they don't.
	Does	he/she/it	have to clean?	Yes, he/she/it does. No, he/she/it doesn't.

Must

- *Must* has a similar meaning to *have to*, but *have to* is more common.
  I *have to/must* cook dinner.
- We use *mustn't (must not)* to talk about what you're not allowed to do.
  You *mustn't* stay up late. (Don't!)
- *Don't have to* and *mustn't* have different meanings.
  You *don't have to* go there. (You can, but it's not necessary.)
  You *mustn't* go there. (Don't!)

1 In pairs, say where you can find these signs. Then make sentences with *you have to* or *you mustn't* for each sign.

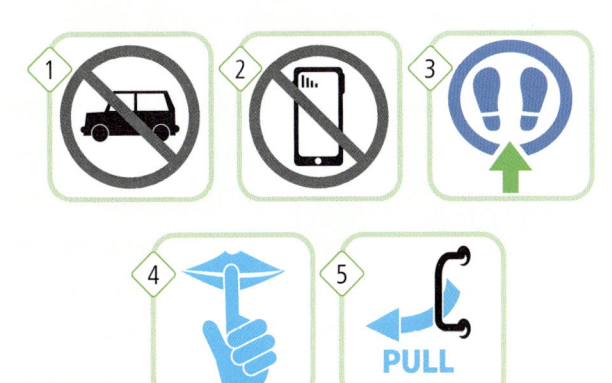

1 You mustn't park here.

2 In pairs, choose the verb which makes the sentence true for your school.

At our school:
1 You *can / mustn't* borrow books from the library.
2 You *can / mustn't* run in the corridor.
3 You *have / don't have* to learn a foreign language.
4 You *have to / mustn't* use a mobile phone in class.
5 You *can / can't* wear jewellery.

3 Choose one situation below and write six sentences with rules about what you can, can't, have to and mustn't do.
- Someone wants to visit your country.
- Someone wants to play your favourite video game.
- Someone is going on holiday with your family.

You don't have to have a visa.

6.2

Countable and uncountable nouns | Quantifiers

Countable	Uncountable
How many bottles of water have we got?	How much water is in that bottle?
I haven't got many hobbies.	I haven't got much time.
There are too many olives on my pizza.	There's too much ice in my drink.
I bought some bananas. We eat a lot of oranges. We don't eat many crisps.	She bought some popcorn. We eat a lot of cheese. We don't eat much bread.
Have you got any biscuits? There aren't any eggs in the fridge. There aren't enough pizzas for everyone.	Have you got any juice? There isn't any milk in the fridge. There isn't enough water in the bottle.

1 Choose the correct option. Then discuss in pairs.
1 How *many / much* meals do you eat every day?
2 Do you think you eat too *many / much* unhealthy food?
3 Have you got *any / some* food in your school bag?
4 There isn't *too / enough* time for lunch on schooldays.
5 *A lot of / Much* students eat sandwiches for lunch. What about you?

Grammar Time **131**

Grammar Time

2 Complete the restaurant review with *a lot of, any, many, much* or *some*.

Stewie's Steakhouse ★☆☆☆☆

Stewie's Steakhouse looks nice, but it's very small and there are too ¹*many* tables, so there isn't ² _____ space! There aren't ³ _____ things on the menu, and they all have meat in them. There aren't ⁴ _____ dishes for vegetarians – there's no salad! The food wasn't great. I had a steak and ⁵ _____ cold chips. There was too ⁶ _____ meat on my plate, but it wasn't very good. Finally, they didn't have ⁷ _____ juice or cola, only water from the tap!

3 Write ten sentences about your family's eating habits.

There's a lot of yoghurt in our fridge.
My dad doesn't eat much chocolate.

6.4

Past Continuous and Past Simple

We use the Past Continuous to say something was in progress at a precise moment in the past.

+	I/He/She/It You/We/They	was watching TV. were sleeping at 9 p.m.	
–	I/He/She/It You/We/They	wasn't (was not) watching TV. weren't (were not) sleeping at 9 p.m.	
?	Was	I/he/ she/it	watching TV?	Yes, I/he/she/it was. No, I/he/she/it wasn't.
	Were	you/ we/ they	sleeping at 9 p.m.?	Yes, you/we/they were. No, you/we/they weren't.
	Where was he going? What were you doing?			

Time expressions
at three o'clock this morning   forty minutes ago
at 5.15 last Tuesday   while

Past Continuous and Past Simple

We often use the Past Continuous with the Past Simple. We use the Past Simple for a short/complete action (e.g. *I broke my leg*) and the Past Continuous for a longer activity in progress at the same time (e.g. *I was playing football*).

- Before the Past Continuous we use **while** or **when**.
  While/When I was playing football, I broke my leg.
  I broke my leg while/when I was playing football.
- Before the Past Simple we normally use **when**.
  What were you doing when the accident happened?
  When the accident happened, what were you doing?

1 Complete the sentences with the Past Continuous form of the verbs in brackets.

1. The phone rang while they *were sleeping* (sleep).
2. Anna _____ (not dance) at one o'clock in the morning.
3. Where _____ (Sue/go) when she fell?
4. We _____ (play) football when it began to rain.
5. I _____ (not listen) when the doctor told me his name.
6. What _____ (you/do) when you cut your finger?

2 Complete the story with the Past Simple or the Past Continuous form of the verbs in brackets. In pairs, compare your answers.

Last Sunday at four o'clock, I ¹*was riding* (ride) my bike home. It ² _____ (rain) a lot, so I ³ _____ (put) on my waterproof jacket. While I ⁴ _____ (go) past the station, I ⁵ _____ (see) Jennifer Aniston! She ⁶ _____ (get) into a taxi. I ⁷ _____ (not look) where I ⁸ _____ (go), so I ⁹ _____ (ride) my bike into the back of a car! I ¹⁰ _____ (fall) and ¹¹ _____ (hit) my head. I was lucky I ¹² _____ (not break) my neck.

3 Use the Past Simple and the Past Continuous to describe a) something surprising that happened to you, or b) a dream you had.

One day last year I was walking in the town centre with a friend when we saw an elephant. It was standing on two legs and …

7.2

Comparatives and superlatives of adjectives

- We use the comparative form of adjectives with *than* to compare two people or things.
  He's *taller than* me.
- We use the superlative form of adjectives to compare one thing in a group with all the others in that group.
  She's *the nicest* person I know.

Adjectives		Comparative	Superlative
with one syllable	near	near**er**	the near**est**
with one syllable ending in *-e*	wide	wid**er**	the wid**est**
with one syllable ending in vowel + consonant	hot	hot**ter**	the hot**test**
ending in consonant + *-y*	lazy	laz**ier**	the laz**iest**
with two or more syllables	intelligent	**more** intelligent	the **most** intelligent
irregular	good bad	**better worse**	the **best** the **worst**

We usually use *the* before superlative adjectives. But we don't use *the* after *my/your/his/her/its/our/their*.
He's *their youngest* son. NOT ~~He's their the youngest son.~~

We can also compare things using *(not) as … as*.
This book isn't *as interesting as* the first one.

1 Write the comparative and superlative forms of these adjectives.
  1 fat – *fatter, the fattest*   4 expensive – _____
  2 easy – _____   5 young – _____
  3 late – _____   6 happy – _____

2 How much can you remember about last year? Complete the questions with the superlative form of the adjectives in brackets. Then ask and answer the questions in pairs.
  1 What was *the most beautiful* (beautiful) place you visited?
  2 What was _____ (happy) day for you?
  3 What was _____ (long) journey you made?
  4 What was _____ (tasty) meal you ate?
  5 What was _____ (bad) film you saw?

3 Do you prefer shopping in a shopping centre or small shops? Use the ideas below and write five sentences to answer the question.

Price	low/high
Shop assistants	friendly/unfriendly
Service	quick/slow
Other	busy/quiet cold/hot/warm/wet good/poor choice relaxing/stressful

I prefer shopping in a shopping centre because the prices aren't as high as in small shops …

7.4

Going to and Present Continuous for the future

We use *going to* or the Present Continuous to talk about intentions, plans and arrangements in the future.

Going to
We use *going to* to talk about intentions and plans which will perhaps change in the future.
I'*m going to get* there early.
We'*re not going to invite* them.
Are you *going to watch* the football?

+	I	'm (am) going to buy a new car.
	You/We/They	're (are) going to go shopping.
	He/She/It	's (is) going to come home.
–	I	'm not (am not) going to buy a new car.
	You/We/They	aren't (are not) going to go shopping.
	He/She/It	isn't (is not) going to come home.
?	Am	I	going to buy a bike?	Yes, I am. No, I'm not.
	Are	you/we/they	going to go to a party?	Yes, you/we/they are. No, you/we/they aren't.
	Is	he/she/it	going to stay?	Yes, he/she/it is. No, he/she/it isn't.
	When are they going to visit Gran?			

Present Continuous
We use the Present Continuous to talk about arrangements. We often mention a time and/or place to show that something is more than just an intention.
The game *is starting* at two o'clock.
My mum *isn't working* tomorrow.
Are you *going* to the party on Friday?

Time expressions
tonight   next Monday/weekend
tomorrow   on Thursday morning/afternoon

Grammar Time

1 Finish these New Year's resolutions with *going to* and the ideas below (or your own).

> buy   ~~get up~~   revise   spend less/more time
> study   take up

1. I missed the school bus again. This year, I*'m going to get up earlier every morning*.
2. I'm not fit. This year, I _____ .
3. I was so horrible to my sister last year. This year, I _____ .
4. I feel so unfashionable. This year, I _____ .
5. My marks for Maths are terrible. This year, I _____ .
6. English is such a useful language. This year, I _____ .

2 Complete the questions with the Present Continuous form of the words in brackets. Then use Noah's note to ask and answer in pairs.

> TRIP TO LONDON – Saturday
> • train from West Green to Liverpool Street Station, London, leave 8.30 a.m. and arrive 9.45 a.m.
> • meet Aunty Hannah for lunch, National Gallery café, 12.30 p.m.
> • train to West Green from Liverpool Street Station, 6.35 p.m.

1. What station *is Noah leaving* (Noah/leave) from?
   He's leaving from West Green.
2. What time _____ (he/arrive) in London?
3. What time _____ (he/catch) the train home?
4. Who _____ (Noah/meet) in London?
5. What time _____ (he/meet) her?
6. Where _____ (they/have) lunch?

3 Use *going to* to write three intentions you have for the next summer holidays. Then use the Present Continuous to write three plans for this evening.

Next summer I'm going to help my mum decorate the kitchen.
This evening I'm watching the football match at 8 p.m.

8.2

Will for future predictions

We use *will* to make predictions about the future.

+	I/You/He/She/It/We/They	'll (will) win the match.	
–	I/You/He/She/It/We/They	won't (will not) lose.	
?	Will	I/you/he/she/it/we/they	win?	Yes, I/you/he/she/it/we/they will. No, I/you/he/she/it/we/they won't.
	What time will the game start? How will you get there?		

I think/I don't think + will

When we want to express uncertainty, we add *not* to the verb *think*, not to the clause which follows.
I think we will win the match.
I don't think we will win the match.
NOT ~~I think we won't win the match.~~

Time expressions
tomorrow   next week/month/year
in 2035/twenty years' time/the next five years/the future
by (= before) 2035/New Year/my twentieth birthday/this time tomorrow/the end of the week

1 Complete the sentences with *will* or *won't*. Then look at your sentences with *won't* and write what will happen.
1. My country *won't* win the next football World Cup. *Germany will win it.*
2. It _____ be bright and sunny tomorrow.
3. I _____ become famous in fifteen years.
4. The world _____ end in 2040.
5. I _____ find a new job by New Year.

2 Use *I think* and *I don't think* to transform your sentences from Exercise 1. In pairs, compare your sentences.

I don't think my country will win the next football World Cup. I think Germany will win it.

3 Use your imagination to write a few sentences about life on Earth in 3000. Use the questions below to help you.
- How long will people live?
- What technology will they use?
- How will they travel?
- Will people live on other planets?

Life on Earth will be very different in 3000. People will probably live to 150 years.

8.4

First Conditional

We use the First Conditional for things that will possibly or probably happen in the future if something happens.

Present Simple	will + verb
If she studies hard,	she'll pass the test.
If you don't pass,	I'll be disappointed.
If he doesn't pass,	his mum won't be happy.

We can change the order of the parts of the sentences without changing the meaning. We don't use a comma if we put will/won't in the first part of the sentence.

will + verb	Present Simple
She'll pass the test	if she studies hard.
I'll be disappointed	if you don't pass.
His mum won't be happy	if he doesn't pass.

In questions it's more usual to begin with will.

will + verb	Present Simple
Will you be angry	if you don't pass the test?
What will you do	if you get the best mark?

1 Complete the First Conditional sentences with the correct form of the words in brackets.
1. If I _become_ (become) famous, I _won't forget_ (not forget) my friends.
2. I _____ (tell) Mum if you _____ (do) that again.
3. If my dad _____ (not get) a new job, we _____ (not move) house.
4. You _____ (not pass) if you _____ (not do) any homework.
5. If Patrick _____ (help) me, I _____ (help) him.
6. How _____ (you/feel) if you _____ (not pass) the test?
7. _____ (she/help) me if I _____ (ask) her?

2 In pairs, use the ideas below to make First Conditional sentences.

1. pass all my exams → have a party → we make a lot of noise → my parents tell us to be quiet → play a board game

2. have my Maths exam → stay home to study → invite a friend to study with me → get tired of studying → play a computer game

1 *If I pass all my exams, I'll have a party. If I have a party, we'll …*

3 Write five First Conditional sentences about what you will do if you don't have homework.

1 *If I don't have homework, I'll go to a café and have an ice cream with my friends.*

9.2

Present Perfect

We use the Present Perfect to talk about completed actions in the past, but we don't say or know when they happened.

+	I/You/We/They	've (have) seen dolphins.	
	He/She/It	's (has) visited Ireland.	
–	I/You/We/They	haven't (have not) seen dolphins.	
	He/She/It	hasn't (has not) visited Ireland.	
?	Have	I/you/ we/they	enjoyed it?	Yes, I/you/we/they have. No, I/you/we/they haven't.
	Has	he/she/it	learned a lot?	Yes, he/she/it has. No, he/she/it hasn't.
	Where have you been?		

To form the Present Perfect, we use *have/has* and the Past Participle. For regular verbs, the Past Participle is the same as the Past Simple.

I have finished.   She hasn't tried.   We've stopped.

Many Past Participles are irregular (see verb list on page 137).
They have eaten.   He's gone.   Have you slept?

Present Perfect with *ever/never*

We often use the Present Perfect with *ever* in questions. It means 'at any time before now'.
Have you ever been to Spain?

We also use the Present Perfect with *never*. It means 'at no time before now'.
No, I've never been to Spain.

Grammar Time 135

Grammar Time

1 Complete the text with the Present Perfect form of the verbs in brackets.

ASK TODD!
Gemma ¹*has written* (write) to ask me if it's better to travel alone or with other people. Well, it depends. Some of my nicest travel experiences ² _____ (be) with my friends. My best friend Scott ³ _____ (travel) with me to a lot of countries, and we ⁴ _____ (have) a lot of fun and we ⁵ _____ (not fall) out! But my sister ⁶ _____ (never/be) abroad with me because we always argue when we're travelling!

2 Make questions with *ever* and the Present Perfect. Use the phrases below or your own ideas. Then ask and answer the questions in pairs.
- go on a school trip abroad
- go to a restaurant with friends
- meet someone from another continent
- travel alone
- write a poem

A: Have you ever travelled alone?
B: No, I've never travelled alone./Yes, I have.

3 Write five sentences about things you have never done but hope to do in the future.

I've never been to New York – I hope to go there in the future.

9.4
Present Perfect with *just*, *already* and *yet*

- We use *just* and *already* in affirmative sentences with the Present Perfect. *Just* and *already* usually come immediately before the main verb.
  He's *just* phoned. (= recently/a short time ago)
  I've *already* checked the timetable. (= earlier than expected)
- We use *yet* in negative sentences and questions with the Present Perfect. *Yet* usually comes at the end of the negative statements or questions.
  We haven't bought all the food *yet*. (It hasn't happened, but will probably happen soon.)
  Have you bought the tickets *yet*?

1 Complete the sentences with *just* and the Present Perfect form of the verbs below.

~~do~~ fix go make miss tidy

1 There's a lot of food in the fridge. I*'ve just done* the shopping.
2 I _____ my computer. It's working again!
3 Mark _____ breakfast. It's on the table.
4 Rona _____ her bedroom. It's looking better now!
5 I'm afraid you can't speak to Mum now. She _____ to work.
6 We _____ the bus – we'll be late now!

2 Rewrite the sentences in bold using *yet* or *already*.
1 Jason has arrived at the campsite. He's putting up his tent.
   Jason has already arrived at the campsite.
2 I'm not hungry, thanks. **I've had breakfast.**
3 Hurry up! **Have you finished?**
4 Wow – you're slow! **We've finished.**
5 She can't come. **She hasn't done her homework.**
6 **Have they got their exam results?**

3 Make questions with *yet* about the things below. Then ask and answer the questions in pairs.

eat lunch   decide what to do at the weekend plan your holiday   see [name of film] at the cinema start learning for the next test

A: Have you eaten lunch yet?
B: No, I haven't./Yes, I've already eaten lunch.

4 Write five sentences with news about your favourite stars or other people you know well. Use *just*, *already* or *yet*.

Messi has already scored more than 700 goals in his career.
My sister has just started university.

Irregular Verbs

🔊 10.1

Infinitive	Past Simple	Past Participle
be	was/were	been
become	became	become
begin	began	begun
break	broke	broken
bring	brought	brought
build	built	built
burn	burned/burnt	burned/burnt
buy	bought	bought
can	could	been able to
catch	caught	caught
choose	chose	chosen
come	came	come
cost	cost	cost
cut	cut	cut
do	did	done
draw	drew	drawn
dream	dreamed/dreamt	dreamed/dreamt
drink	drank	drunk
drive	drove	driven
eat	ate	eaten
fall	fell	fallen
feed	fed	fed
feel	felt	felt
fight	fought	fought
find	found	found
fly	flew	flown
forget	forgot	forgotten
forgive	forgave	forgiven
get	got	got
give	gave	given
go	went	gone
grow	grew	grown
hang	hung	hung
have	had	had
hear	heard	heard
hit	hit	hit
hold	held	held
hurt	hurt	hurt
keep	kept	kept
know	knew	known
learn	learned/learnt	learned/learnt
leave	left	left

Infinitive	Past Simple	Past Participle
lend	lent	lent
let	let	let
lie	lay	lain
lose	lost	lost
make	made	made
meet	met	met
pay	paid	paid
put	put	put
read	read	read
ride	rode	ridden
ring	rang	rung
run	ran	run
say	said	said
see	saw	seen
sell	sold	sold
send	sent	sent
set	set	set
show	showed	shown
sing	sang	sung
sit	sat	sat
sleep	slept	slept
speak	spoke	spoken
spend	spent	spent
stand	stood	stood
steal	stole	stolen
sweep	swept	swept
swim	swam	swum
take	took	taken
teach	taught	taught
tell	told	told
think	thought	thought
understand	understood	understood
wake	woke	woken
wear	wore	worn
win	won	won
write	wrote	written

Student Activities

Unit 1 Revision Speaking Exercise 7

Student B
- Think of a film you want to watch. Tell Student A your idea. Ask for his/her opinion.
- Ask Student A what he/she wants to watch.
- Give your opinion of Student A's film.
- Decide together on a film to watch.

Unit 2 Lesson 2.1 Exercise 7

WHAT'S IN THE PHOTO?
Can you name these clothes and accessories?

1.
2.
3.
4.
5.
6.

Unit 2 Revision Speaking Exercise 7

Student B
- Think of some interesting news to tell Student A. Use the ideas below to help you.

  can't find phone   go on a shopping trip   visit a friend

- Say hello to Student A.
- Respond to Student A's question and tell him/her what's new in your life.
- Ask what's new in Student A's life.
- Listen and respond to Student A's news.

Unit 3 Lesson 3.1 Exercise 8

RIGHT or WRONG?
What do you know about animals?

1 ✗ Penguins have fur, not feathers.
2 ✓ Polar bears have white fur but black skin.
3 ✗ Tigers have stripes on their fur and on their skin.
4 ✓ Cats' front paws have five toes, but their back paws have four toes.
5 ✓ Bees can beat their wings 200 times a second.
6 ✓ A brown bear's claws can grow to over fifteen centimetres.
7 ✗ Butterflies have two wings.
8 ✓ The tail of a giraffe can grow to over 2.5 metres.

1, 3 and 7 are wrong.
1 Penguins are birds, so they have feathers – but very fluffy ones.
3 Tigers don't have stripes on their skin.
7 Butterflies have four wings.

Unit 3 Revision Speaking Exercise 6

Student B
- You took Student's A seat at the cinema. Apologise.
- Student A is late to meet you. Respond to his/her apology.
- You dropped Student A's new guitar. Apologise.
- Student A forgot to feed your pet. Respond to his/her apology.

Progress Check Units 1–3 Exercise 5

Student A

Describe the photo. Use the questions below to help you.
1 What can you see in the photo?
2 What is the girl doing?
3 What is she wearing?
4 How is she feeling?

Unit 4 Lesson 4.6 Exercise 6

Student A

First, tell Student B about these problems with your computer. Ask for help.
- *My computer's really slow.*
- *I can't connect my phone to my computer.*

Then listen to Student B's computer problems and use these prompts to help him/her.

> good anti-virus   switch it off and on again

Unit 5 Revision Speaking Exercise 7

Student B
- Give Student A advice on how to change the decoration in his/her bedroom. If he/she rejects your ideas, give him/her different advice.
- You want to organise a surprise party for a friend. Ask Student A for advice. Then accept or reject the advice.

Unit 6 Revision Speaking Exercise 6

Student B
- Say hello to Student A.
- Say you had an accident and broke a leg/ankle/arm/bone.
- Tell Student A what happened.
- Listen and react to Student A's advice. Thank Student A and ask how he/she is.
- Listen to Student A's symptoms and give him/her some advice.
- Say goodbye.

Progress Check Units 1–9 Exercise 5

Student A

You're at home and you feel ill. Your friend calls and asks why you didn't come to school.
- Tell your friend that you are ill.
- Tell your friend what symptoms you have.
- Tell your friend when you will probably go back to school.
- Ask to borrow the lesson notes.

Progress Check Units 1–6 Exercise 5

1 Look at the photos that show different ways of spending free time. Do you like these ways of spending free time? Why?/Why not?

2 In pairs, ask and answer the questions. Give reasons to explain your answers.

Do you think …
- shopping is fun?
- playing sports is healthy?
- reading is boring?
- playing games is a waste of time?
- meeting friends in a café is nice?

3 In pairs, take turns to ask and answer the questions.
   1 Do you prefer spending free time alone or with other people? Why?
   2 Do you prefer spending time at home or outside? Why?

LITERATURE

CLIL 1

Animals in Fiction

There are a lot of books about animals. Many of these are books for children, but some aren't. Can you think of any famous books for adults about animals?

One very famous book with animal characters is *Animal Farm* by the English author, George Orwell, published in 1945. It's quite short – only ten chapters – but it's an important classic. The story is about a group of animals who live on a farm. A pig, Old Major, dreams about a life on the farm without humans. He tells the animals that they can work on the farm and make their own decisions. There is a fight, and the animals chase Mr Jones, the unkind farmer, off the farm. Then they run the farm themselves. They make some rules. An important one is: 'All animals are equal'.

There are many wonderful animal characters in the book. Boxer is the big horse who is strong and works hard. There are three very clever pigs, Snowball, Squealer and Napoleon. For a while the animals work well together, but then the pigs start to become powerful. Napoleon wants to be the leader and he chases Snowball away. The meetings stop, and the pigs make all the decisions. They also begin to wear human clothes and behave like humans. They live in the warm farmhouse and eat and drink well. The other animals have difficult lives. They work hard, but they are often cold and hungry. Now the important rule says: 'All animals are equal, but some are more equal than others.' Other farmers come to the farmhouse and eat and drink with the pigs. When the animals look through the window, it's impossible to know which are animals and which are humans.

Animal Farm seems quite a simple story, but George Orwell used it to give his opinions about important events at that time. It's a very clever book. It makes us think a lot about our lives and society.

---

1 🔊 10.2 Look at the characters in the picture. Who do you think they are? Read the article and check.

2 Read the article again and complete the factfile.

> Title: [1] *Animal Farm*
> Author: [2] _____
> Nationality: [3] _____
> Published in: [4] _____
> Number of chapters: [5] _____
> Main characters: [6] _____

3 In pairs, answer the questions.
1 What rule do the animals have on the farm at first?
2 How does this rule later change? Why?
3 Would you like to read the story? Why?/Why not?

4 Look at the book titles and animals below. Do you know any of the books? Match titles 1–5 with animals a–e that appear in them. Go to page 144 to check your answers.
1 ☐ *Watership Down*   a a horse
2 ☐ *Charlotte's Web*   b a bear and a panther
3 ☐ *Black Beauty*   c rabbits
4 ☐ *The Jungle Book*   d a wolf
5 ☐ *White Fang*   e a spider and a pig

5 **GO ONLINE** Use the internet to research one of the books in Exercise 4. Make notes about:
- the author and when he/she wrote the book.
- the story.
- the characters.
- where it takes place.

6 **SHARE IT** Write a short paragraph about the book and present it to the class. Use your notes from Exercise 5 and the phrases below.

> … wrote *Watership Down* in …
> The story is about …
> One of the characters is …
> The story takes place in …

HISTORY

CLIL 2

The changing palace

The Winter Palace in St Petersburg, Russia, is one of the largest palaces in the world. It was the official home of the Russian kings (called tsars) and queens from 1732 to 1917. They used to have many dinner parties in a dining room for 1,000 guests. The beautiful green and white palace is around 200 metres long and about twenty-two metres high.

In 1763, Empress Catherine II (also known as Catherine the Great) lived at the palace. At that time, Russia fought a lot of wars and became a larger and more powerful country. The last tsar to live in the palace was Alexander II, who was killed in 1881.

After Alexander's death, the palace was still used for official events and parties, and in 1903 there was a final great Imperial party – it was a fancy-dress ball. After this time, many Russians were unhappy with their lives and with the tsars. So, in 1905 there were violent protests outside the palace, and many people died – this was called Bloody Sunday. Then in 1917 there was a revolution which ended the monarchy and the royal history of the palace.

Today the palace is a museum – the State Hermitage Museum, where you can see many paintings and sculptures from around the world. Every year 3.5 million people visit it, and as well as looking at the art, they can meet the Hermitage cats who live there. The cats used to walk around the galleries, but now they live in the basement and outside the palace.

1 In pairs, look at the photos and discuss the questions.
1 What do you know about the Winter Palace?
2 Do you know any famous people who lived there?

2 🔊 10.3 Read the article and check your answers to Exercise 1.

3 Read the article again and answer the questions.
1 Who was the palace for?
2 Who was the last tsar to live in the palace?
3 What was the reason for protests in 1905?
4 What can you see at the palace now?
5 Who lives there now?

4 Read the article again and complete the missing dates in the palace timeline.

The Winter Palace – A timeline	
1708	Peter the Great builds the palace
1731–1735	Anna of Russia builds a larger palace
1 _____	Catherine the Great lives at the palace
1837	There is a fire
2 _____	Alexander II is killed
3 _____	The last big ball
4 _____	Bloody Sunday
1915	The palace becomes a hospital
5 _____	Revolution and the palace becomes a museum

5 Would you like to visit the Winter Palace? Why?/Why not? Discuss in pairs.

6 (GO ONLINE) Use the internet to research a historic building in your country. Make notes about:
• where it is.
• who built it and when.
• what historic events took place there.
• how people use it today.

7 (SHARE IT) Present your research to the class. Use your notes from Exercise 6 and the phrases below.

> The palace/castle is in …   It was built in …
> In … there was …   … used to live there, but now it's a …

141 CLIL

SCIENCE

CLIL 3

Antibiotics

1 🔊 10.4 Read the article and match headings A–D with paragraphs 1–4.
   A How antibiotics work
   B A problem for scientists
   C Antibiotics and bacteria
   D The first antibiotics

2 Read the article again and answer the questions.
   1 Who discovered the first antibiotic?
   2 When did he discover it?
   3 What was it called?
   4 What are antibiotics?
   5 Name two types of bacteria.
   6 Name two types of antibiotics.
   7 What is the problem today?
   8 Give two causes of that problem.

3 Do you think we sometimes use antibiotics when we don't need to? Why?/Why not? Discuss in pairs.

4 Work in pairs. Look at the list of things a–f which scientists do to develop a new antibiotic drug. Put the stages in the order in which you think they happen.
   a ☐ Test the drug on people who have the illness.
   b ☐ Test the new drug using a computer model.
   c ☐ Test the drug on human cells in a laboratory.
   d [1] Find a new source for an antibiotic.
   e ☐ Stop testing if the drug damages the cells.
   f ☐ Test the drug on healthy humans.

5 Compare your ideas from Exercise 4 with another pair. Do you agree on the order? Go to page 144 to check your answers.

6 Now cover the list and take turns with your partner to give the correct stages.

1 ☐ Antibiotics are very important medicines in our lives. Doctors use them to fight many different kinds of infections. However, before 1928 scientists didn't know about them! At that time people could die from, for example, cuts on the skin. Alexander Fleming, a Scottish scientist, discovered an antibiotic called penicillin – just by mistake! Now, we use antibiotics all the time.

2 ☐ Antibiotics are chemicals that kill bacteria and stop infections. There are many different types of antibiotics because there are different types of bacteria and infections. One type of bacterium is called Gram-positive. These bacteria have very thin cell walls, and antibiotics can go through the walls easily. The second is called Gram-negative, and these have very thick cell walls.

3 ☐ The antibiotics kill the bacteria and stop them from making new cells. They make the cell walls weak and they break. There are 'broad spectrum' antibiotics that can fight all types of bacteria, and doctors use them for lots of different infections. There are also 'narrow spectrum' antibiotics which are good for attacking special problems.

4 ☐ Today doctors are worried. Many bacteria are getting resistant – that means they get stronger, and a lot of antibiotics don't kill them. This is because we use them too often. Also, we should finish all our tablets, but sometimes we don't do this because we feel better. Then, the bacteria which are still in our bodies get stronger. In the past, doctors had a lot of different antibiotics to give us, but now many of them don't work. Scientists need to find new antibiotics, but it isn't easy. If they don't find new antibiotics, people may die from minor illnesses again.

7 **GO ONLINE** Use the internet to find information about one of the famous scientists below. Make notes about:
   • what nationality they were.
   • what they discovered and when.
   • how their discovery helped people.

   Louis Pasteur   Wilhelm Conrad Röntgen   Joseph Lister

8 **SHARE IT** Present your research to the class. Use your notes from Exercise 7 and the phrases below.

   (Louis Pasteur) was …   … discovered … in …
   His discovery helped people because …

CLIL 142

GEOGRAPHY

CLIL 4

YELLOWSTONE'S HOTSPOT

Yellowstone National Park in the USA was probably the first national park in the world. Yellowstone is very popular and very big (8,983 km²). It's a wonderful place to see wildlife and different natural features such as mountains, forests, canyons, rivers, lakes and waterfalls. But many people don't realise that this amazing park is sitting on top of something that is very dangerous – one of the biggest supervolcanoes in the world!

Deep under Yellowstone National Park is a volcanic 'hotspot'. Heat from inside the Earth melts the rocks above it, and this makes a big pool of magma. Sometimes this magma erupts and sends out huge amounts of lava, rock and ash. A really big eruption throws out nearly all the magma, and then the land above the magma pool falls in. This creates a huge hole called a caldera. The Yellowstone Caldera is fifty-five kilometres wide and eighty kilometres long! Another natural feature of Yellowstone National Park is its many geysers: rainwater goes down through the rocks, the magma heats it, and then very hot water rises back up to the surface. The water rises fast into the air with clouds of steam. The most famous geyser at Yellowstone is called 'Old Faithful' and it erupts nearly every hour.

The Yellowstone Supervolcano has erupted several times in the last two million years (the last time about 640,000 years ago) and it's still active. It will erupt again! The ash will cover the whole of North America and cause some climate changes for a long time. But scientists don't think that this will happen soon – maybe in one or two million years. They study the area very carefully with special equipment. They are always checking for movements in the crust (the hard outer layer of the Earth) that might cause earthquakes. They hope that they will be able to tell people a long time before an eruption happens.

1 Have you ever heard of Yellowstone National Park? What do you know about it?

2 🔊 10.5 Read the article. What natural features can you find in Yellowstone National Park?

3 Read the article again and answer the questions.
   1 How big is Yellowstone National Park?
   2 What do many people NOT know about Yellowstone National Park?
   3 How big is the Yellowstone Caldera?
   4 If there is another eruption, what will happen?
   5 When do scientists think this might happen?

4 Choose a diagram (A or B) below. Study the diagram. Find the part of the article that explains your diagram and read it again.

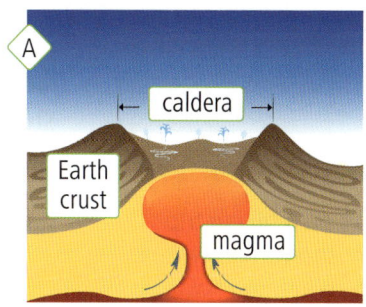

5 Work in pairs. Cover the article. Use your diagram to explain to your partner how a volcano or a geyser works.

6 (GO ONLINE) Use the internet to find information about another supervolcano. Make notes about:
   • where it is.
   • the landscape around it.
   • how dangerous it is.

7 (SHARE IT) Write a factfile about the supervolcano you have chosen. Add pictures. Present your factfile to the class.

143 CLIL

Student Activities

Unit 7 Lesson 7.5 Exercise 2

BETEEN MAGAZINE

TO SAVE OR TO SPEND?

Give yourself 2 points for every a) answer and 1 point for every b) answer.

4 points
For you, money is like water. When you're thirsty, you have to drink. When you have money, you have to spend it. You don't know how to save money.

5–6 points
For you, money is useful and important, but you don't worry about it all the time. You are generous but intelligent with your money. You don't spend more than you have, but you don't try to save every penny.

7–8 points
For you, money is a wonderful thing. It is so wonderful that you don't want to spend it. Maybe you need to learn how to enjoy spending money.

Unit 9 Revision Speaking Exercise 6

Student B

1 Student A wants to go mountain biking tomorrow and asks for permission to use your bike. Refuse permission. You want to use the bike yourself tomorrow. Then Student A asks for permission to borrow a helmet. Give permission.
2 You hear that Student A is going on a hiking trip with some friends. Ask for permission to go with him/her. If Student A agrees, say you don't have boots and ask for permission to borrow a pair of Student A's boots.

Progress Check Units 1–3 Exercise 5

Student B

Describe the photo. Use the questions below to help you.
1 What can you see in the photo?
2 What are the people doing?
3 What are the people wearing?
4 How are the people feeling?

Unit 4 Lesson 4.6 Exercise 6

Student B

First listen to Student A's computer problems and use these prompts to help him/her.

> delete old files/games   new USB cable

Then tell Student A about these problems with your computer. Ask for help.
- *My computer crashed. The screen's frozen.*
- *My internet connection is really slow.*

Progress Check Units 1–9 Exercise 5

Student B

You are Student A's friend. Your friend didn't come to school. Call him/her and ask what happened. Use the phrases below to help you.
- *Hello. How are you?*
- *What's the matter?*
- *When can you go back to school?*
- *Of course! No problem.*

CLIL 1 Literature Exercise 4

1c   2e   3a   4b   5d

CLIL 3 Science Exercise 5

1d   2b   3c   4e   5f   6a

Pearson Education Limited
KAO Two
KAO Park
Hockham Way
Harlow, Essex
CM17 9SR
England
and Associated Companies throughout the world.

pearsonenglish.com/widerworld2e

© Pearson Education Limited 2022

All rights reserved; no part of this publication may be reproduced, stored in a retrieval system, or transmitted in any form or by any means, electronic, mechanical, photocopying, recording, or otherwise without the prior written permission of the Publishers

First published 2022

ISBN: 978-1-292-34244-3

Set in Frutiger Next Pro
Printed in Mexico

Acknowledgements
The Publishers would like to thank all the teachers and students around the world who contributed to the development of Wider World Second Edition: Milena Aleksić, Tuğba Arslantaş, Gülşah Aslan, Mahgol Baboorian, Katarzyna Beliniak, Burcu Candan, Seri Diri, Hanna Dudich, Sema Karapinar, Nadiia Kasianchuk, Duygu Kayhan, Iryna Kharchenko, Ana Krstić, Ilknur Manav, Fulya Mertoğlu, Ivana Nikolov, Banu Oflas, Duygu Özer, Jagoda Popović, Marija Šanjević, Karmen Irizar Segurola, Elif Sevinç, Ludmila Shengel, Ayşe Sönmez, Anna Standish, Natalia Tkachenko, Pamela Van Bers, Jelena Vračar, Agnieszka Woźnicka, Münevver Yanık.

The Publishers would like to thank the following people who commented on the Wider World Second Edition content: Milena Aleksi, Mahgol Baboorian, Hanna Dudich, Izabela Kołando, Karmen Irizar Segurola, Joanna Srokosz, Anna Zając.

We would also like to thank the authors of the first edition of Wider World whose work has been the basis for creating this adaptation: Kathryn Alevizos, Carolyn Barraclough, Catherine Bright, Sheila Dignen, Lynda Edwards, Rod Fricker, Suzanne Gaynor, Bob Hastings, Jennifer Heath, Liz Kilbey, Stuart McKinlay, Sarah Thorpe, Tasia Vassilatou, Damian Williams, Sandy Zervas.

Photo Acknowledgements
123RF.com: Andriy Popov 75, David Tiberio 107, evaletova 25, 138, gstockstudio 57, Jacek Chabraszewski 139, Kobby Dagan 39, marctran 101, Maria Sbytova 75, mihtiander 117, milkos 101, Monika Wisniewska 75, Moose Henderson 39, NejroN 139, Panoramic Images 1, Rodrigo Mello Nunes 39, Stephen Mcsweeny 37, stokkete 100, Tatsiana Yatsevich 7, Viacheslav Iakobchuk 13, vitcom 11, Vladislav Gajic 141, zakaz 91; **Alamy Stock Photo**: agefotostock 65, Antonio Guillem 34, Clarence Holmes Photography 88, Cofiant Images 121, Grant Rooney Premium 72, imageBROKER 46, John Birdsall 84, Joshua Rainey 60, Lisandro Trarbach 112, Mark Phillips 45, Paulo Oliveira 122, rvisoft 124, Tetra Images, LLC 139, Tom Craig 98, ZUMA Press, Inc 12; **BBC Studios**: 23, 47, 73, 99, 123; **Getty Images**: Alex Hibbert/The Image Bank 115, Ambre Haller/Moment Open 41, anandaBGD/E+ 100, Andersen Ross/DigitalVision 34, Areasur/DigitalVision Vectors 10, blackCAT/E+ 69, Brighton Dog Photography/Moment 41, Brooks Kraft/Corbis Historical 88, By Eve Livesey/Moment 60, By Neil Donovan. Visit www.neildonovan.net for more/Moment 112, Carol Yepes/Moment 36, coberschneider/RooM 117, ColorBlind/Photodisc 46, Cyndi Monaghan/Moment 64, DAJ 31, Dave G Kelly/Moment 19, DavidGoh/DigitalVision Vectors 87, denkcreative/DigitalVision Vectors 71, dmphoto/E+ 87, Drazen_/E+ 14, 14, Emilija Manevska/Moment 75, Eugene Gologursky/Getty Images Entertainment 103, filo/DigitalVision Vectors 59, franckreporter/E+ 124, Gerard Ruiters/Moment 143, Ghislain & Marie David de Lossy/The Image Bank 87, Hello World/Stone 11, Hillary Kladke/Moment 41, Ilan Shacham/Moment Open 112, Image Source 91, Imagno/Hulton Fine Art Collection 141, Jasmin Merdan/Moment 50, 95, Juanmonino/E+ 95, Justin Lambert/DigitalVision 139, Justin Paget/DigitalVision 127, kali9/E+ 110, Lane Oatey/Blue Jean Images 100, Louise Heusinkveld 67, Lu ShaoJi/Moment 125, Luis Alvarez/DigitalVision 100, Maciej Frolow/Photographer's Choice RF 63, Manoj Shah/Photodisc 43, Marco Bottigelli/Moment 11, Marko Geber/DigitalVision 144, Maskot 34, 51, Megan Evans/Moment 119, mixetto/E+ 15, Nastasic/E+ 50, PepeLaguarda/E+ 91, Peter Cade/Stone 77, 117, Piero Damiani/Moment 112, pixelfit/E+ 50, Pongnathee Kluaythong/EyeEm 11, portishead1/E+ 15, Ray Bobrownicki/EyeEm 28, recep-bg/E+ 17, Reimar Gaertner/UIG 112, Rick Gomez 7, saemilee/DigitalVision Vectors 37, SDI Productions/E+ 34, 81, selimaksan/E+ 91, SolStock/E+ 34, Stephen Simpson/DigitalVision 105, stevegeer/E+ 143, Stigur Már Karlsson/Heimsmyndir 19, THEPALMER/E+ 37, 138, Thomas Wierzbicki/EyeEm 87, TravelCouples/Moment 139, urbazon/E+ 60, Vladimir Razgulâev 90, Westend61 7, 34, 100, YinYang/E+ 19, zonadearte/DigitalVision Vectors 55; **Mateusz Mach**: 103; **Pearson Education Ltd**: 140, Jon Barlow 6, 7, 8, 9, 10, 16, 18, 26, 30, 40, 42, 52, 56, 66, 68, 76, 80, 92, 94, 104, 106, 116, 118, Jules Selmes 19; **Shutterstock.com**: 29, Agil Leonardo 143, Aksenova Natalya 37, Alexander Lysenko 128, Alexia Khruscheva 37, Anton Gvozdikov 12, anton_novik 140, Batshevs 33, BigMouse 128, Boris Medevedev 25, 138, Bradley Blackburn 45, Corona Borealis Studio 53, Designua 143, Dmitry Kalinovsky 48, durantelallera 12, ESB Professional 25, fizkes 50, Fotosoroka 25, 138, Gemma Ellen 33, Gorodenkoff 100, Heinz-Peter Schwerin 112, hvoya 25, 138, Iakov Filimonov 37, Ian Duffield 67, ic36006 78, Ipatov 117, Jim Cumming 37, Jurga Jot 75, Kamira 37, Kamomeen 140, Kateryna Kon 142, Kaya 25, 138, Ljupco Smokovski 21, Look Studio 24, Maria Francesca Moccia 91, marpan 51, Masyle 140, mimagephotography 114, mphot 11, MyPro 33, Natali Ximich 91, Oksvmin 128, Pavel Kruglov 25, 138, Pavlo S 2, 3, PetlinDmitry 40, Petr Ya 141, Phase4Studios 86, Phovoir 7, pickingpok 102, Pixel-Shot 24, 24, Roman Samborskyi 24, Romariolcn 41, Roompoctliar 140, sima 12, Skalapendra 140, Studio 72 29, Syda Productions 27, synto 91, Tatsiana Tsyhanova 129, Tim Rooke 115, TonelloPhotography 88, UfaBizPhoto 22, vetkit 25, Viktoriia Hnatiuk 60, Vlad Klok 140, WAYHOME studio 49, yuris 138, Zekka 33

Illustrated by Amber Day (IllustrationX) 20; Rohan Eason (IllustrationX) 34; Adam Larkum (IllustrationX) 36, 50, 91; Maguma AKA Marcos Guardiola Martin (IllustrationX) 35, 61, 85, 111; May Van Millingen (IllustrationX) 68; Maxim Usik (IllustrationX) 72; Roger Stewart (Beehive) 60; Rupert Van Wyk (Beehive) 77, 87.
All other images © Pearson Education

Cover photo © *Front:* **Alamy Stock Photo**: Panoramic Images